THE BEDFORD SERIES IN HISTORY AND CULTURE

Women's Rights Emerges within the Antislavery Movement, 1830–1870

A Brief History with Documents

Second Edition

THE BEDFORD SERIES IN HISTORY AND CULTURE

Women's Rights Emerges within the Antislavery Movement, 1830–1870

A Brief History with Documents

SECOND EDITION

Kathryn Kish Sklar

State University of New York, Binghamton

 bedford/st.martin's
Macmillan Learning
Boston | New York

For Bedford/St. Martin's

Vice President, Editorial, Macmillan Learning Humanities: Edwin Hill
Senior Program Director for History: Michael Rosenberg
Senior Program Manager for History: William J. Lombardo
History Marketing Manager: Melissa Rodriguez
Developmental Editor: Mollie Chandler
Content Project Manager: Lidia MacDonald-Carr
Senior Workflow Project Manager: Lisa McDowell
Production Supervisor: Robert Cherry
Senior Media Project Manager: Michelle Camisa
Media Editor: Mary P. Starowicz
Manager of Publishing Services: Andrea Cava
Project Management: Lumina Datamatics, Inc.
Composition: Lumina Datamatics, Inc.
Text Permissions Manager: Kalina Ingham
Permissions Associate: Allison Ziebka
Director of Rights and Permissions: Hilary Newman
Director of Design, Content Management: Diana Blume
Cover Design: William Boardman
Cover Image: Anti-Slavery Coins and Medal (metal) (reverse) (for obverse see 187696)/American School/Michael Graham-Stewart/Private Collection/ Bridgeman Images
Printing and Binding: LSC Communications

Manufactured in the United States of America.

1 2 3 4 5 6   23 22 21 20 19 18

For information, write: Bedford/St. Martin's, 75 Arlington Street, Boston, MA 02116

ISBN 978-1-319-11312-4

Acknowledgments
Acknowledgments and copyrights appear on the same page as the text and art selections they cover; these acknowledgments and copyrights constitute an extension of the copyright page.

To Susan and Leonard and Amy and their progeny,
Nevona, Nadav and Cedar

Builders for a better tomorrow

Foreword

The Bedford Series in History and Culture is designed so that readers can study the past as historians do.

The historian's first task is finding the evidence. Documents, letters, memoirs, interviews, pictures, movies, novels, or poems can provide facts and clues. Then the historian questions and compares the sources. There is more to do than in a courtroom, for hearsay evidence is welcome, and the historian is usually looking for answers beyond act and motive. Different views of an event may be as important as a single verdict. How a story is told may yield as much information as what it says.

Along the way the historian seeks help from other historians and perhaps from specialists in other disciplines. Finally, it is time to write, to decide on an interpretation and how to arrange the evidence for readers.

Each book in this series contains an important historical document or group of documents, each document a witness from the past and open to interpretation in different ways. The documents are combined with some element of historical narrative — an introduction or a biographical essay, for example — that provides students with an analysis of the primary source material and important background information about the world in which it was produced.

Each book in the series focuses on a specific topic within a specific historical period. Each provides a basis for lively thought and discussion about several aspects of the topic and the historian's role. Each is short enough (and inexpensive enough) to be a reasonable one-week assignment in a college course. Whether as classroom or personal reading, each book in the series provides firsthand experience of the challenge — and fun — of discovering, recreating, and interpreting the past.

Lynn Hunt
David W. Blight
Bonnie G. Smith

"I am persuaded that woman is not to be as she has been,

a mere second-hand agent in the regeneration of a fallen world,

but the acknowledged equal and co-worker with man in this glorious work."

— Angelina Grimké, in a letter written from
Groton, Massachusetts, August 10, 1837

Preface

The first women's rights movement in the United States emerged in the early years of the struggle to abolish slavery in the 1830s. As such, it involved African American as well as white women, who mobilized their communities, created local organizations, and provided crucial financial support for the antislavery cause. This book focuses on women who supported the radical vision of the American Anti-Slavery Society (AASS), founded in 1833 by William Lloyd Garrison and others with the dual aim of abolishing slavery and ending racial prejudice. By the late 1830s white women's efforts within this mixed-race but predominately white organization were so successful that women became unwilling to abide by the rules that limited their participation in public life. In defending themselves against critics who deplored their departure from "woman's assigned sphere," antislavery women launched a women's rights agenda that resonates to the present day.

The chief actors in this dramatic story were two sisters—Angelina and Sarah Grimké, daughters of a prominent slaveholding family in Charleston, South Carolina. Their migration out of the South and recruitment into the AASS set the stage for their innovations on behalf of women's rights.

To tell their story I have chosen documents that reveal their subjective experience. They and other women's rights advocates were responding to their immediate experience, both public and private. This subjectivity was an important basis for the Grimkés' rights claims and became a major force behind the movement's rapid growth after 1840.

Documents in this collection show how women's gendered identity drew them together across race and class differences. "Woman" was a powerful category of life and thought, invoked by antislavery activists on behalf of enslaved women, by free black women who were constructing their own liberation from the oppression of racial prejudice as well as opposing slavery, and by white women shocked by slavery's brutality.

This revised edition highlights the larger context of the struggle against slavery and racial prejudice, especially as seen through the eyes of free black women. As slavery spread in the South, many northern states rescinded the civil rights of free blacks, leaving them in a middle ground between slavery and freedom. This edition includes the new voices of free black women Sarah Mapps Douglass and Lucy Stanton. And it newly features the voice of Frances Ellen Watkins in the 1850s. The revised Introduction draws on recent scholarship to reinterpret the effects of slavery's expansion on American society and the importance of campaigns against race prejudice by women in the antislavery movement from the 1830s through the 1850s.

This collection of sources illuminates the separate paths taken by different groups of women in the 1850s after the explosion of women's rights activism ended the prohibition against women speaking in public forums. The women's rights convention movement provided a platform for discussions of women's hopes and needs, which white women dominated. Meanwhile free black women became prominent antislavery speakers in many venues, especially as speakers for the AASS, putting into practice the rights that white and free black women had sought in the 1830s. Thus, a generation after women claimed the right to address public meetings within the antislavery movement, black as well as white women occupied prominent positions in American public culture.

African American women and white women brought diverse strengths to the women's rights movement after the Civil War. In their endorsement of post-war amendments to the U.S. Constitution, black women supported the enfranchisement of black men even if women would not be enfranchised, while white women were divided on the question of postponing women's enfranchisement.

This new edition invites us to witness how history has been shaped by the contingent, the unexpected, and the unlikely. No general laws could have forecast the events depicted in these pages. There is a love story here—but even it has an unpredictable outcome.

A NOTE ABOUT THE TEXT

Some spelling, punctuation, and capitalization in the documents have been modernized for ease of comprehension. In some cases, where a word was part of an original document's title (for example, Maria Stewart's *Address before the Afric-American Female Intelligence Society of Boston,* Document 3), the older spelling has been retained.

ACKNOWLEDGMENTS

All historians, especially those who edit primary sources, are indebted to archivists who aid in their quest for the perfect document. I am particularly grateful to William Faucon in the Rare Books and Manuscripts Department of the Boston Public Library, and Arlene Shy and Cheney J. Schopieray and Jayne Ptolemy at the William L. Clements Library in Early American History at the University of Michigan. Thanks also to Sam Sfirri of Special Collections at the Addlestone Library of the College of Charleston for assistance with Grimké family wills.

Erica Ball and Carla Peterson generously shared their rich knowledge of free black women in the 1830s and 1850s. Rifa'at Abou el-Haj pointed out the crucial significance of Angelina Grimké's moratorium in the early 1830s. John McClymer drew on his documentary work with the Worcester Woman's Rights Convention of 1850 to help me locate pertinent documents.

I thank Madison Williams for consistently helpful assistance with the preparation of this second edition. Thanks also to the folks at Bedford/St. Martin's for their author-friendly approach to publishing. Senior Program Director Michael Rosenberg, Senior Executive Program Manager William Lombardo, Senior Editor and series editorial adviser Heidi Hood, History Marketing Manager Melissa Rodriguez, Content Project Manager Lidia MacDonald-Carr, Cover Designer William Boardman, and Development Editor Mollie Chandler provided just the right level of guidance and advice for this second edition.

Readers of the manuscript—Robert Abzug, Nancy Hewitt, Julie Roy Jeffrey, and John McClymer—improved the book with helpful suggestions. Tom Dublin read the manuscript in its many incarnations, always offering valuable insights and timely encouragements.

Kathryn Kish Sklar

Contents

☐ = Scan & compare if...

The New Movement Debates Questions of
Race and Sex, 1866–1869   **191**

APPENDIXES

Illustrations

Illustrations

THE BEDFORD SERIES IN HISTORY AND CULTURE

Women's Rights Emerges within the Antislavery Movement, 1830–1870

A Brief History with Documents

Second Edition

PART ONE

Introduction:
"Our Rights as Moral Beings"

In the summer of 1837, two sisters from South Carolina, Angelina and Sarah Grimké (age 32 and 45, respectively) began a speaking tour of Massachusetts that permanently altered American perceptions of the rights of women. What began as a set of lectures promoting the abolition of slavery precipitated a struggle to defend women's right to speak to political gatherings—and ended by introducing the new concept of women's rights into American public life.[1] Between May and September the Grimkés ignited a debate about the equality of the sexes that first enveloped the abolitionist movement and then extended into the lives of other women, some of whom were already active in other reforms, precipitating dramatic changes in consciousness and in women's access to public life in a relatively short period of time. Black women as well as white women participated in these changes—their shared abhorrence for slavery meant that their stories were interwoven. By the 1850s, when Frances Ellen Watkins, a free African American, became one of the most popular antislavery lecturers sponsored by the American Anti-Slavery Society, she spoke publicly without needing to defend her right to do so.

Changes that made Watkins's 1850s lectures possible took root in the 1830s and 1840s in the fertile soil of a society in crisis over the expansion of slavery. A heightened awareness of human rights evolved alongside the dilemma of how to end the increasingly profitable slave labor system. Having developed within the antislavery movement in the 1830s and 1840s, women's rights emerged in 1848 at a Women's Rights Convention at Seneca Falls, New York, as an autonomous social movement. A cascade of women's rights conventions in the 1850s carried the movement into towns and villages throughout the Northeast and Midwest. After the Civil War, the movement consolidated around women's right to vote, forming two national organizations in 1869—the National Woman Suffrage Association in New York and the American Woman Suffrage Association in Boston. Scores of local organizations conducted hundreds of campaigns at the state level for women's voting rights during the next fifty years, generating enormous vitality and energy within American civil society. In 1920 the ratification of the Nineteenth Amendment to the U.S. Constitution granted voting rights to women in states where rights had not yet been won—mostly in the South. Approaching the centennial of that amendment, voting rights are once again a highly contested aspect of American politics and once again involve racial and gendered aspects of American citizenship.

Rights-seeking activity is a fundamental feature of American politics, and women's struggle for the right to speak publicly in the antislavery movement is one of the best examples of how new rights are created to meet new needs. It was also one of the most transformative moments of rights history in the United States. Before 1840 women were culturally prohibited from speaking at political gatherings, especially those that included men as well as women. The main exceptions were at religious venues, especially among Quakers. Itinerant women preachers—black as well as white—unauthorized by any established church, spoke in public but were relegated to the margins of respectability, often speaking in the open air. These women claimed spiritual, not social, authority. One historian has called them "Biblical Feminists" because they asserted the spiritual equality of women. Yet their otherworldly powers did not translate into political personhood.[2]

The exclusion of women speakers from political gatherings was part of the culture of British common law that William Blackstone described in *Commentaries on the Laws of England* (1765–1769). There he noted that the principle of "femme couvert" meant that a woman's legal identity became absorbed within her husband's identity upon marriage. Inheritance patterns among white families in British North America passed land and houses to sons, giving daughters the less valuable "moveables" of clothes and household effects. Single women could own property, but they lost those rights upon marriage.[3] Thus the prohibition against women's public speaking was part of the white male monopoly of legal personhood in pre-industrial Anglo-American society.

The changes that brought women's voices into public life helped build a more democratic and more racially-mixed civil society in the

1840s and 1850s. Yet these changes were extremely difficult to achieve and far from inevitable. Their origins lay with the magnitude of the struggle to end slavery in the United States.[4] Women were also active in the British antislavery movement, which abolished slavery in the West Indies in 1833 through an act of Parliament, but their activism did not generate an equivalent British women's rights movement.[5] In the United States slavery finally ended a generation later through one of the costliest wars in human history. The power of slavery in American society required the antislavery movement to innovate and step outside the boundaries of respectability in ways that did not occur in England. Other forces also contributed to the emergence of a strong women's rights movement in antebellum America, including new views of sexuality championed by women in the Female Moral Reform Society, which sought to end men's control of women's bodies.[6] Yet the movement toward an independent women's rights movement began with the unique position of the Grimké sisters within the campaign to abolish slavery immediately and unconditionally.

PRELUDE: BREAKING AWAY FROM SLAVE SOCIETY

Angelina and Sarah Grimké held a special place in the antislavery movement between 1835 and 1839 because they were the daughters of an elite southern slaveholding family who left the South and joined the antislavery movement. Their compelling public lectures about the horrors of slavery attracted audiences that otherwise might have remained indifferent to antislavery appeals. Livelihoods in the North were intertwined with the economic success of slavery in the South. Northern merchants profited by selling southern cotton to English manufacturers; New England textile workers depended on southern cotton for their earnings. And almost all northern clergymen supported the status quo.[7]

Before 1830 the Grimké sisters seemed an unlikely pair to launch a revolution. Born to a prominent slaveowning family of Huguenot (French Protestant) descent in Charleston, South Carolina, Sarah was the sixth and Angelina the last of fourteen children. Their father was chief justice of the state's highest court; their mother's brother served as governor of North Carolina. The family's wealth derived from a plantation that they never visited, two hundred miles away in the Carolina "up-country," run by a hired overseer. Their mansion in Charleston required the labor of many enslaved servants, most of whom had relatives on the plantation.[8]

The seeds for the sisters' loathing of slavery were sown in its embrace; during their privileged childhood they sympathized with the sufferings of enslaved children, witnessing the forced separation of enslaved children and parents. Sometimes the children of house servants were sent to the plantation; sometimes children were brought from the countryside to work in the house. In either case, children's bonds with their parents were ignored; they were treated like property rather than human beings.

A girlhood friend of Angelina's who lived near the place where enslaved people were sent to be punished, "often heard the screams of the slaves under their torture." At about age thirteen Angelina attended a school where "nearly all the aristocracy" sent their daughters. One day a young enslaved boy about her age was called into the classroom to open a window. He had been so "dreadfully whipped that he could hardly walk." His "heartbroken countenance" awed her as much as his bloodied back.[9]

Sarah and Angelina's mother, Mary Grimké, supervised her household with callous disregard for the well-being of the people who served her. Bondspeople slept on the floor without bed or bedding, ate from tin plates without a table, and had no lighting in their quarters. Seamstresses were required to work after dark in winter by staircase lamps, which were so dim that they had to stand to see their work. "Mother," Angelina wrote in her diary in 1828, "rules slaves and children with a rod of fear."[10] After their father died in 1819, and brother Henry became the head of household, punishments of household servants became even more severe. One of Henry's blows to the head of the family butler left him with epileptic fits. Disorder was a close companion of violence in the Grimké household. When her sisters blamed the family's enslaved servants for the household's lack of order and discipline, Angelina replied that "the servants were just what the family was . . . not at all more rude and selfish and disobliging . . . and how could they expect the servants to behave, when they had such examples continually before them?"[11]

Cruelty inside slaveowning households was, of course, part of a system in which enslaved persons worked and were held in bondage against their will. Vast profits were extracted from enslaved people through the imposition of violence and terror. Charleston's twenty thousand whites in 1820 were far outnumbered by the city's sixty thousand enslaved blacks, a ratio that bred fears of slave revolts and elicited brutal reprisals against potential uprisings. In Charleston in the summer of 1822 a free black carpenter, Denmark Vesey, secretly organized an extensive revolt that was discovered before it erupted. Vesey and thirty-six other black men were hanged.[12]

During the Grimké sisters' childhood and young adulthood, the slave labor system grew stronger and no effective opposition emerged to challenge it. Slave owners' economic and political power increased, accelerated by the invention of the cotton gin in 1793 and the territorial expansion of the Louisiana Purchase of 1803. By 1820 enormous profits based on cotton flowed into the Anglo-American economies, and southern slaveholding elites began to imagine an empire that extended into Texas, Cuba, Mexico, and Nicaragua. Political compromise between North and South became increasingly difficult; the Missouri Compromise of 1820 was essentially revoked by the Compromise of 1850, which opened the way for slavery's expansion into the western territories of the United States.[13]

Yet, like most southern critics of slavery, Angelina and Sarah Grimké would probably have accepted their circumstances as beyond their ability to alter had they not embarked on a search for a more meaningful religious faith than the comfortable Episcopalianism of their mother. Each in her own way came to reject slavery by first rejecting the religious alternatives available in Charleston, then migrating to join the Quaker community in Philadelphia, where each came to accept the Quaker view of slavery as sinful and joined the movement for immediate abolition.[14]

THE SECOND GREAT AWAKENING EMPOWERS WOMEN TO SPEAK OUT AGAINST SLAVERY

The Grimké sisters were part of a sea change in American Protestantism called the Second Great Awakening—a diverse religious movement between 1800 and 1860 that transformed and revitalized American Protestantism and also reshaped civil society. Affecting vast numbers in mainstream Protestant denominations, the Awakening emphasized the sacred power of the individual will. Named for the "Great Awakening" of the 1730s and 1740s, which located religion in subjective feelings rather than theological arguments, the Second Great Awakening overturned secular Enlightenment attitudes of the Revolutionary era. Congregationalists (the New England denomination begun by the Puritans), Presbyterians, Baptists, and Methodists were all profoundly altered by the evangelical "good news" that individuals could will their own conversion from sin and achieve salvation. The liberating message of the Awakening released an explosion of energy in the 1830s and 1840s, as average people believed themselves able to construct better lives for their families and communities. In its most extreme form, this doctrine became perfectionism—belief that humans could become free of sin.

Also called "ultraists," perfectionists often viewed secular and religious authority as corrupt and unnecessary.

The Second Great Awakening's power was fueled significantly by an emerging middle class, which consolidated its hegemonic position in society by embracing the Awakening's moral authority. The power of middle-class laity was enhanced by the separation of church and state that occurred throughout the new nation at this time. When ministers ceased to be supported by taxation, they had to rely on voluntary contributions. Many thereafter preached a gospel that exalted the voluntary efforts of their members, especially women, who often shaped their family's choice of churches.[15] This empowerment of the laity challenged the traditional authority of ministers and opened space for new ideas. Antislavery activists were part of that sea change in American religious life and sought to shape it at the same time that they were shaped by it.[16]

Sarah, thirteen years older than Angelina, was the first to be touched by the powerful forces of the Second Great Awakening, experiencing religious conversion in Charleston under the guidance of a visiting Presbyterian minister in 1813.[17] He preached that her soul would never be saved while she enjoyed fashionable Charleston society—dances, teas, house parties, and other frivolities. Her conversion did not lead her to church membership in Charleston, but it did instill long-lasting guilt over her privileged life and alienated her from self-satisfied Episcopalianism. In 1819, when Sarah traveled with her ailing father to consult Quaker physicians in Philadelphia and he died at a seaside resort they had recommended, she was befriended by Quakers. After his death she lingered two months under their calming influence, absorbing their spirituality, their belief in the unmediated relationship between God and the individual conscience, their plain style of dress, few servants, orderly habits, and condemnation of slavery as ungodly.[18] After two years back in Charleston, where she found nothing that could match the appeal of the Philadelphia Quaker community, Sarah returned to Philadelphia and soon thereafter converted to Orthodox Quakerism.

Sarah's ties with her family were stretched but not broken. Far from demonizing the North, her family, like many wealthy southerners, drew on its resources. Her older brother, Thomas, to whom she had been closely attached as a child, graduated from Yale University in Connecticut. Sarah returned home several times, including a stay of six months during the winter of 1827, when she revived the close relationship she had forged with Angelina since the younger sister's birth in 1805. Sarah was Angelina's godmother and in many ways became a more meaningful parent than their mother. Angelina's letters to Sarah in Philadelphia addressed her as "dearest Mother" and Sarah called her "my precious child."[19]

In 1827 Sarah returned to find Angelina at the center of a vibrant religious circle created by a young, northern-born Presbyterian minister and his congregation. Attracted by his successful community organizing, Angelina had formed an intensely personal relationship with him. At the church she led a "colored Sunday school," organized prayer meetings, participated in religious societies, did charity work among the poor, and attended a "female prayer meeting" where Baptists, Methodists, Congregationalists, and Presbyterians met monthly to discuss their responsibilities as women.[20] At home Angelina had organized daily prayer meetings that were attended by her mother and sisters, the enslaved family servants, and slaves from other households. Influenced by the Second Great Awakening, many southern families and churches participated in such interracial efforts before 1830.[21]

A struggle for Angelina's soul ensued, with her "beloved" Presbyterian minister on one side and Sarah's Quakerism on the other. At issue was the question of whether Quakers or Presbyterians offered the more reliable route to religious salvation. Sarah won, but only after an intense battle. The older sister's victory was sealed when Angelina cut up her Walter Scott novels and stuffed a cushion cover with laces, veils, and trimmings that had adorned her clothing. Three months after Sarah returned to Philadelphia, Angelina joined her there in July 1828.

ANGELINA GRIMKÉ'S GROWING ALIENATION FROM CONSERVATIVE QUAKERS

Years of uncertainty followed. The sisters' escape from Charleston had religious rather than antislavery motives.[22] They joined the conservative Quaker community that had consoled Sarah when their father died. That community, more interested in maintaining its internal hierarchy than in critiquing social injustice, was the antithesis of the one Angelina had recently relinquished. Her Charleston flock had been gregarious, stylish, and hospitable. Her new congregation valued silence, was deliberately dour, and prohibited mingling with outsiders. Participation in "popular" causes—that is, those not exclusively Quaker—was strongly discouraged. The sisters lived comfortably in the home of a Quaker woman who had befriended Sarah in 1819; their small inheritance from their father made it unnecessary for them to earn money, but both sought greater meaning and usefulness. They decided to become Quaker ministers.[23]

Figure 1. *Angelina Grimké at about age 39, c. 1845.*
Her piercing eyes and firm countenance conveyed conviction to those in her
1830s audiences.
Fotosearch/Getty Images

Quakers did not support a "settled ministry." Instead their ministers
were unpaid itinerants for whom the "inner light" of their calling sufficed
to qualify them as clergy. Unlike other Protestants, Quakers sanctioned
women ministers, though they expected women to minister primarily
to the needs of their own sex. Separate women's meetings gave the
Grimkés and other women the opportunity to gain speaking and leadership skills. Quaker religious meetings consisted of silence broken only
by those (women as well as men) who were inspired, however briefly, to
share their thoughts.[24]
    Sarah took both her religious quest and her ministerial calling
quite seriously. Her speaking style was halting and tentative, but she

regularly expressed her thoughts in Sunday meeting, and traveled to visit and speak at other Quaker gatherings, especially groups of women. Angelina, by contrast, was less interested in the theological than the social practice of religion, never spoke in meeting, and grew increasingly alienated from the austere services. Searching for other avenues of usefulness, she explored the possibility of becoming a teacher, and visited Catharine Beecher's renowned female seminary in Hartford, Connecticut. Beecher, the daughter of prominent evangelical Congregational minister Lyman Beecher, was promoting the feminization of the teaching profession as an opportunity for women to become self-supporting and to exercise greater public authority. But Angelina's Quaker mentors disapproved of such a move because it would take her out of the community. Permitted by the congregation to return to Charleston to care for her mother in 1829, Angelina spent nine anguished months viewing slavery for the first time through eyes that judged it a sin.

Returning to Philadelphia, Angelina found no outlet for her growing antislavery passion. In 1827 a schism had split American Quakers into two groups. One, called "Hicksite" (after their leader Elias Hicks, a Long Island farmer), continued the traditional Quaker belief in the power of individual conscience over all other sources of authority, sacred or secular. The other group called themselves "Orthodox" but actually were innovators who were adopting a creed that took precedence over individual conscience.[25] For example, they began to require members to profess a belief in the divinity of Jesus. In the great social issues of the day, including slavery, Hicksite Quakers tended to promote radical reform and Orthodox Quakers tried to avoid controversy. Angelina and Sarah's friends were affiliated with the Arch Street Meeting House, a seat of Orthodox Quaker conservatism. "We mingle almost entirely with a Society which appears to know but little of what is going on outside of its own immediate precincts," Angelina wrote upon her return to Philadelphia in 1829. By 1836 she put it more strongly, "My spirit is oppressed and heavy laden, and shut up in prison."[26]

Cut off from the city around her, Angelina Grimké withdrew into a five-year moratorium between late 1829 and early 1835, during which she never spoke in meeting. Outwardly manifesting no opinions about herself or her society, she drifted in a protective cloud removed from her origins and from any need to declare her views. When she emerged from this retreat she was reborn as a person who sought not to adapt herself to southern or northern opinion, but to change both regions to conform to her view of right and wrong.[27]

SEEKING A VOICE: ANTISLAVERY WOMEN JOIN GARRISON'S MOVEMENT, 1831–1833

The Grimké sisters' isolation and their initial pursuit of religious rather than antislavery goals in the early 1830s account for their failure to ally with Lucretia Mott (1793–1880), a Hicksite Quaker minister and a leading abolitionist in Philadelphia. In 1831 Mott befriended William Lloyd Garrison, a white journalist who had lived in Baltimore and witnessed the brutality of slavery, and who earlier that year had founded the nation's first newspaper to call for the immediate and unconditional emancipation of enslaved people—*The Liberator.*[28] In 1833 Mott participated in the founding of Garrison's new militant organization, the American Anti-Slavery Society (AASS), which sought the dual goals of the abolition of slavery and the end of racial prejudice.[29] (See Document 9.) The founding meeting of the AASS was not publicly announced because organizers feared the mobs that plagued Garrison's public appearances.

Although women could join the AASS and its local branches, women also formed separate female organizations. In 1833 Mott helped create the Philadelphia Female Anti-Slavery Society, which included both white and African American women among its founders, and also sought the dual goal of ending slavery and combatting racial prejudice. Such public action was new for women of all races. In the 1820s white women began to create maternal societies where they discussed the new meaning of motherhood in their culture, but before 1835 these groups usually met under religious auspices with ministerial leadership. Though a frequent speaker in Quaker meetings, Lucretia Mott did not feel capable of chairing the founding meeting of the Philadelphia Female Anti-Slavery Society. Motivated perhaps by her desire to recruit African American women members, she asked an African American man to preside.[30] (See Document 9.)

Garrison and Mott were part of a surge of militant white activism in the 1830s that joined the militant free black activism generated in the 1820s. Both groups were responding to the rising power of the American Colonization Society (ACS), founded in 1816, which sought to create an all-white society by sending free blacks and emancipated slaves to Liberia, a colony created for that purpose in Africa.[31] Those early decades of the nineteenth century witnessed the emergence of many social movements in education, religion, and family life; in Hartford, Connecticut, a school for the deaf was founded in 1817 and a retreat for mentally disturbed in 1824. Yet white support for free people of color was decisively repressed. When Simeon Jocelyn, a New Haven,

Connecticut, engraver, sought to create a school for "people of color" in 1831, citizens voted against the measure 700 to 4; when he continued his campaign, a mob assaulted his home in 1836 "in a brutal and cowardly manner."[32] Thus racial prejudice, foundational to racial slavery, also limited the rights of free people of color in the North. The gradual abolition of slavery in the North from 1780 to 1840 did not necessarily confer citizenship on free blacks. By 1840 more than 90 percent of northern free blacks lived in states that denied them the right to vote; some states amended their constitutions in the 1830s to end the voting rights of free blacks.[33] This statistic reflects the insistent identification, legally and culturally, of free blacks with racial slavery. They occupied a middle ground of unfreedom between slavery and freedom that was highly contested in the antebellum decades, and they were finally judged in the 1857 Dred Scott decision of the U.S. Supreme Court to have "no rights which the white man was bound to respect."[34] Garrison's antislavery movement, already vilified for its goal of immediate abolition, expanded to include a parallel movement for the rights of free people of color—the only such movement for whites, and for free African Americans a bulwark for their own rights-seeking institutions.[35]

William J. Watkins, a free black abolitionist educator in Baltimore, exemplified the overlap between rights-seeking institutions created by African Americans and the antislavery movement. The nation's first African American newspaper, *Freedom's Journal*, founded in New York City in 1827, printed a letter from Watkins that year in which he vigorously insisted that African Americans "are as truly Americans as the President of the United States, and as much entitled to the protection, rights, and privileges of the country" as the founders of the American Colonization Society.[36] Baltimore was home to the nation's largest free black community, where free and enslaved persons lived side by side. In 1828 William Watkins brought his orphaned three-year-old niece, Frances Ellen Watkins, into his home. She grew up in a household that revered William Lloyd Garrison and opposed racial prejudice as well as slavery. When she was twelve, her uncle served as a founding Vice President of the American Moral Reform Society, which conducted a study of "the progress and present state of the coloured population," sending observers into northern cities, where they collected data on the size of the "colored population," the value of their real estate, the number of reform organizations, literary societies, churches, schools, mechanics, paupers, and criminals.[37]

The 1830s was a transformative decade for free black women as well as free black men. Their public activism was encouraged by cultural

forces that endorsed women's solidarity and by antislavery politics
that confronted the injustice of racial stereotypes. African American
women led the way in creating female antislavery societies as part of
the Garrisonian movement. In Massachusetts, the Salem Female Anti-
Slavery Society, founded by African American women in 1832, was the
first women's antislavery society; in 1834 it expanded its membership to
include white women.[38]

In even greater numbers than those who joined antislavery societies,
free black women in northern cities created women's literary societies
with the explicit purpose of challenging racial prejudice and promoting racial equality. In addition to supporting the antislavery movement,
these groups developed members' skills in public discourse and trained
leaders. They included the Afric-American Female Intelligence Society, founded in Boston in 1832; the Ladies Literary Society and the
Female Literary Society, each founded in New York City around 1834;
the Minerva Literary Association, founded in Philadelphia in 1834; the
Young Ladies Literary Society, founded in Buffalo around 1835; and the
Ladies Literary and Dorcas Society, founded in Rochester in 1833.[39]

The Female Literary Association of Philadelphia, founded in September 1831, launched this movement and served as a model. In November
1831, Sarah Mapps Douglass, one of the group's founders and a teacher
at her mother's school for free black children, sent the society's constitution to Garrison along with money she had collected for *The Liberator*.[40]
Garrison immediately published the constitution and its preamble, which
praised "the cultivation of the intellectual powers, bestowed upon us by
the God of nature." The preamble defined members' duty "as women, as
daughters of a despised race, to use our utmost endeavors to . . . break
down the strong barrier of prejudice." (See Document 1.) Following up
on Douglass's initiative, Garrison launched a "Ladies' Department" in
The Liberator in January 1832, which became an important venue for
African American women's voices, including that of Maria Stewart, one
of the first women to address a public meeting of men and women. (See
Documents 2 and 3.)

Under the pen name Zillah, Sarah Douglass's writings appeared eight
times in *The Liberator* in 1832, twice in the "Ladies' Department." In
July 1832, the "Ladies' Department" included her speech before the
Female Literary Association—"Mental Feasts"—published under her
own name. There Douglass described how her attitude toward slavery
changed when a slave kidnapper appeared "on the border of my own
peaceful home."[41] (See Document 4.)

Garrison credited the idea for the "Mental Feasts" to Simeon Jocelyn; male sponsorship and patronage were skills that Garrison practiced to bring women's voices into public venues on political questions. But Douglass's eloquence shows that the idea could have just as well have come from her. The column included a description of the evening's events by a visitor, probably white, which offered glimpses of the group's actions and feelings. First, Douglass read her essay. Then the "fifty-fourth beautiful and encouraging chapter of Isaiah" was read, which many Liberator readers would have known to include the scriptural passage: "no weapon that is fashioned against you shall prosper." The visitor felt that the group created a "precious covering" which "bespoke that divine goodness was near," and that this "greatly injured people" would serve God well, whether "separately by themselves, or collectively with white people." (See Document 4.)

Sarah Douglass was a third-generation Quaker and her leadership in this group might account for its spiritual depth and clarity. The evening carried participants through the terror of Douglass's description of the kidnapper, the healing of familiar scripture, multiple voices "forcibly" depicting slavery, and another healing interval of singing. This process built individual strength as well as new forms of identity and community. Meetings like this in other literary societies forged new forms of social consciousness, shaping African American women's struggle with racial prejudice and the looming disaster of racial slavery.[42]

Yet to step outside the women's group and speak publicly about social issues, as men did, to groups that included men and women, was a step too far for most women—African American or white. The hazards of such a step were dramatically depicted in the experience of a young African American widow in Boston, who in 1832 became one of the first women to speak publicly on social issues to an assembly of men and women, but who was then shunned and left the city in 1833. Thereafter Maria W. Stewart supported herself in New York City, Baltimore, and Washington, D.C. as a teacher and, after the Civil War, an administrator of aid to freed people, but she did not resume her career as a public speaker. A closer look at her place in the surge of antislavery activism in the early 1830s helps us understand her turbulent experience in Boston.

Almost the same age as Sarah Douglass, but a generation older than Frances Watkins, Maria Stewart tested gender, class, race, and social structures when she burst into public life in Boston during the 1830s surge of activism against the American Colonization Society.[43] Stewart's recently deceased husband, James Stewart, had been a ship outfitter and an ally of David Walker. Walker lived in Charleston during the 1822 Vesey uprising, and in 1829 he authored *Appeal to the Colored Citizens of the World,* a pamphlet that predicted and urged armed rebellion in the South, causing an uproar in North and South alike. James Stewart and David Walker were members of the Massachusetts General Colored Association (founded 1826), which challenged racial prejudice and promoted "the welfare of the race by working for the destruction of slavery."[44] In 1833 that organization became an auxiliary of Garrison's New England Anti-Slavery Society.

Deeply affected by the Second Great Awakening, Maria Stewart drew on her confident use of religious discourse to write about her vision of a way forward for Boston's African American community. In 1831 she brought her writings to Garrison. When he later reminisced about their meeting, he was impressed with her "intelligence and excellence of character," she "in the flush and promise of a ripening womanhood, with a graceful form and a pleasing countenance." He described their interaction:

> [Y]ou made yourself known to me by coming into my office and putting into my hands, for criticism and friendly advice, a manuscript embodying your devotional thoughts and aspirations, and also various essays pertaining to the condition of that class with which you were complexionally identified. . . . You will recollect, if not the surprise, at least the satisfaction I expressed on examining what you had written — far more remarkable in those early days than it would be now, when there are so many educated persons of color who are able to write with ability. I not only gave you words of encouragement, but in my printing office put your manuscript into type, an edition of which was struck off in tract form.[45]

Adopting Stewart as a protégé, Garrison published her writings as a pamphlet, excerpting one essay in *The Liberator*'s first "Ladies' Department" column in January 1832. There Stewart urged black women to imitate the rights-seeking activities of "Americans." She probably astonished many readers by challenging the authority of black men, writing: "How far shall a mean set of men flatter us with their smiles, and enrich themselves with our hard earnings, — heir wives' fingers sparkling with rings, and they themselves laughing at our folly?" (See Document 2).

Garrison encouraged Stewart to become a public speaker and in April 1832 she addressed the Afric-American Female Intelligence Society. Yet her reputation seems to have preceded her and she noted that "a lady of high distinction among us observed to me, that I might never expect your homage." In an editorial note on another page in *The Liberator,* Garrison explained that Stewart's talk was "published at her own request, and not by desire of the Society before whom it was delivered." (See Document 3.)

The high point of Stewart's activism in Boston occurred in September 1832, when she addressed a mixed audience of men and women in the hall where the New England Anti-Slavery Society held its meetings. There she urged organized improvements in the lives of young wage-earning free black women, and sought white women's sympathy. (See Document 5.) Stewart bade farewell to Boston a year later, describing herself as inspired by "the spirit of God" and willing to defy St. Paul's belief "that it was a shame for a woman to speak in public." (See Document 6.)

How to explain Boston's rejection of this talented activist? Many causes seem to have contributed: her racial radicalism, especially her association with David Walker; her youth — still in her twenties; her gendered radicalism in her call for black women to be independent of black men; and, of course, the culture's prohibitions against women speaking in public. Stewart's inability to find a supportive platform for her activism seems crucial. The Afric-American Female Intelligence Society's unwillingness to sponsor the publication of her address was a turning point in that regard. And Garrison's provision of the Franklin Hall venue could not sustain her as a public speaker. Prominent black Bostonian, William Cooper Nell, who became the first historian of African Americans, in an 1852 letter to Garrison recalled the editor's "early and constant advocacy of woman's equality." Nell remembered that in "the perilous years" of the early 1830s, Stewart, "fired with a holy zeal to speak her sentiments on the improvement of colored Americans, encountered an opposition even from her Boston circle of friends that would have damped the ardor of most women. But your words of encouragement cheered her onwards and her public lectures awakened an interest acknowledged and felt to this day."[46] After her departure, Garrison arranged the publication of Stewart's collected writings, which probably helped establish her later reputation in New York City's Female Literary Society. There one observer listened "on more than a few occasions, to some of her compositions and declamations."[47]

Responding to Garrison's call for the immediate, unconditional abolition of slavery, northern women of both races joined organizations that increased in numbers and militancy during the 1830s. Their mobilization was boosted in 1833, when the British Parliament voted to abolish slavery in the British West Indies.[48] The Slavery Abolition Act

of 1833 provided compensation for slaveholders and funded appren-
ticeship programs that kept many workers in place, yet British inves-
tors soon sought new sources of cheap labor in India, and in North
America the Abolition Act destabilized the future of profits derived from
slave-produced American cotton. When Garrison sponsored British
antislavery leader George Thompson on a celebratory lecture tour, a
mob assaulted a meeting of the Boston Female Anti-Slavery Society
and dragged Garrison through the streets with a rope around his waist.
He was saved from lynching by a posse organized by the mayor.
A member of the women's antislavery group described in a letter published in *The Liberator* the "gentlemen of standing and influence" who
led the mob.[49]

Garrison and Garrisonian antislavery societies were reviled not
only because they advocated immediate emancipation but also because
they promoted racial equality. In his 1832 book, *Thoughts on African
Colonization,* Garrison scornfully asked those who believed that blacks
and whites could never live together harmoniously: "Are we pagans, are
we savages, are we devils?" Quoting scripture, he insisted: "In Christ
Jesus, all are one: there is neither Jew nor Greek, there is neither bond
nor free, there is neither male nor female."[50]

The Grimké sisters soon tested the gendered depth and breadth of
that vision of human equality.

WOMEN CLAIM THE RIGHT TO ACT: ANGELINA GRIMKÉ LEADS THE WAY

Angelina Grimké was jarred out of her moratorium in 1834, when she
responded to Garrison's efforts to carry a new, militant antislavery message into the South as well as the North. Despite the disapproval of her
Orthodox Quaker community, she heard George Thompson, a prominent British abolitionist, speak in Philadelphia in March 1835. That year
she also attended meetings of the Philadelphia Female Anti-Slavery
Society, which had cosponsored Thompson's talk. She began to read
The Liberator, where she found thrilling accounts of the heroism and
martyrdom of abolitionists threatened by angry mobs, and she read
about antislavery appeals by free black women. (See Documents 1–4.)

In a step that unofficially severed her ties with her respectable Quaker
community in the summer of 1835, Angelina Grimké publicly joined the
vilified abolitionist movement. She did so just after Garrisonians carried
their message to Charleston. The AASS launched a "postal campaign"

that sent vast amounts of abolitionist literature through the mails that summer—175,000 pieces through the New York City post office in July alone.[51] Mobs reacted by destroying these "inflammatory appeals" and attacking abolitionist meetings. In Charleston a mob broke into the post office, seized the AASS literature, and burned it beneath a hanged effigy of Garrison. With the bonfires in Charleston on her mind, in August Angelina sent a letter to Garrison that emphasized her profoundly personal commitment, saying, "it is my deep, solemn, deliberate conviction, that *this is a cause worth dying for.*" She explained,

O,! how earnestly have I desired, *not* that we may escape suffering, but that we may be willing to endure unto the end. If we call upon the slaveholder to suffer the loss of what he calls property, then let us show him we make this demand from a deep sense of duty, by being ourselves willing to suffer the loss of character, property—yes, and life itself, in what we believe to be the cause of bleeding humanity.[52]

Angelina Grimké had found her voice. And, at the age of thirty, she had found a platform for her leadership.

Three other Americans who later played major parts in the national drama over slavery were relatively oblivious to its importance in 1835. Abraham Lincoln, twenty-six years old, was a freshman state legislator and law student in New Salem, Illinois. Jefferson Davis, twenty-six years old and later President of the Confederate States of America, had just moved with his bride and eleven slaves to establish a cotton plantation on rich Mississippi delta land. Harriet Beecher, twenty-four years old and future author of *Uncle Tom's Cabin* in 1852, was not yet married and was teaching school in Cincinnati. When Lincoln, Davis, and Harriet Beecher Stowe later became large public figures, they joined a discourse that had been shaped by the Grimké sisters and other Garrisonians.

At first Sarah strongly disapproved of her sister's actions, writing in her diary: "The suffering which my precious sister has brought upon herself by her connection with the antislavery cause, which has been a sorrow of heart to me, is another proof how dangerous it is to slight the clear convictions of truth." Truth, for Sarah, lay in the Quaker admonition to be still and avoid conflict. Angelina wrote to her: "I feel as though my character had sustained a deep injury in the opinion of those I love and value most—how justly, they will best know at a future day."[53]

Angelina moved ahead, independently of her sister. She took refuge with a sympathetic friend in Shrewsbury, New Jersey, and spent the winter of 1836 writing *Appeal to the Christian Women of the South.*

(See Document 11.) Writing as a southerner and a woman, she created a gendered and regional place for herself within the new Garrisonian movement. Promptly published and widely distributed by the AASS, her *Appeal* urged southern women to follow the example of northern women and mobilize against slavery. Rather than limit their influence to their domestic circles, Angelina argued, women should speak out and take public action. "Where *woman's* heart is bleeding," she wrote, "Shall *woman's* heart be hushed?" She called on readers, in one of the nation's first expressions of civil disobedience, to follow higher laws if championing the cause of the enslaved required them to break local laws. She especially urged readers to petition the national government to end slavery. The recent abolition of slavery in the British West Indies, she argued, was due to women's petitions. Sixty female antislavery societies in the North had already followed the British women's example, and she urged southern women to do the same.

By endorsing the petition movement Angelina Grimké promoted the most political aspect of women's abolitionist activism before 1837. Women's antislavery petitions affirmed the potential power of the national government to redress grievances and restore "rights unjustly wrested from the innocent and defenseless." (See Document 10.) Viewing petitions as a political expression to which they were entitled, women became the main participants in petition campaigns to abolish slavery in Washington, D.C. Petitions enlarged the public space that women occupied and brought them into direct contact with the national government at a time when that government was a distant and somewhat vague concept in the lives of most Americans.

Disfranchised individuals, like women and enslaved persons, had petitioned the U.S. Congress since the 1790s, drawing on the First Amendment to the Constitution, which guaranteed the right of "the people . . . to petition the government for a redress of grievances." What was new in the 1830s was the increase in group petitions with many signatures. The first of these was a sabbatarian campaign led by Lyman Beecher to stop the movement of U.S. mail on Sunday. A distinct women's campaign emerged in the early 1830s, when northern women, including Catharine Beecher, petitioned against President Andrew Jackson's forced removal of Cherokee people from their ancestral lands in Georgia.[54] The AASS's campaign to end slavery in the District of Columbia carried this new form of political expression into the most explosive issue in American politics.

Recognizing the growing numbers of women's antislavery societies, and the dedication of their members, the AASS printed a petition form especially designed for women. (See Document 10.) The new women's societies dedicated themselves to gathering signatures, walking door to door, and driving wagons or carriages through their communities. The first such petition, signed by "eight hundred ladies," was presented by a New York Congressman to the U.S. House of Representatives in February 1835.[55] Historians estimate that women contributed 70 percent of the signatures on antislavery petitions.[56] They collected three times as many signatures as those previously obtained by paid male AASS agents. By 1836 the petition campaign so disrupted the proceedings of the U.S. House of Representatives that a "gag rule" was passed to prevent congressmen from reading or otherwise presenting antislavery petitions to the House. Passed with each Congress between 1836 and 1844, gag rules expanded support for the antislavery cause by linking it to free speech.

The AASS sent piles of Angelina Grimké's *Appeal* to Charleston. There, postmasters publicly burned the pamphlets. The city's mayor told Mrs. Grimké that her daughter would be arrested if she tried to enter the city; if she visited, Angelina's friends wrote her, "she could not escape personal violence at the hands of the mob."[57] Justifying her actions to Sarah, Angelina acknowledged that her pamphlet was "a pretty bold step . . . of which my friends will highly disapprove, but this is a day in which I feel I must act independently of consequences to myself." The South must be reached, she felt, and "an address to men will not reach women, but an address to women will reach the whole community."[58]

Even before Angelina submitted her *Appeal* to the American Anti-Slavery Society, Elizur Wright, its secretary, invited her to come to New York and, under the sponsorship of the AASS, meet with women in their homes and speak with them about slavery. Preceded by the reputation of her brother, Thomas, whom Garrison and other AASS members knew as a member of the American Peace Society, as well as by the eminence of her deceased father, Angelina was enthusiastically welcomed into the AASS fold. She was like a distinguished visitor from a hostile nation, who for reasons of her own had changed allegiance and now moved confidently among them.

Sarah, meanwhile, was rebuked in the Arch Street Meeting House in a way that led her to leave Philadelphia. Although her speaking skills remained unimpressive, and her southern accent reminded her listeners of her outsider status, Sarah often spoke in meeting. In July 1836, a presiding elder, probably expressing a consensus reached with others, rose and cut her off, saying: "I hope the Friend will now be satisfied." Silenced, Sarah sat down. This breach of Quaker discipline seemed designed to silence her permanently in the meeting. For nine years she had struggled to develop ministerial speaking gifts, keenly aware of the cold indifference with which the elders viewed her efforts. That day she decided "that my dear Saviour designs to bring me out of this place." On learning the news, Angelina rejoiced: "I will break your bonds and set you free."[59] Within a few weeks Angelina had convinced Sarah of the righteousness of her Garrisonian views, and Sarah acknowledged the younger sister's leadership in setting their future course.

Renouncing the respectable comforts of northern as well as southern society, the sisters traveled to New York City in the autumn of 1836. There during most of November 1836, they joined a training workshop of about thirty men who were serving as the paid agents of the AASS. With this group of men they forged new identities as antislavery agitators. "We sit," Angelina wrote to a friend, "from 9 to 1, 3 to 5, and 7 to 9, and never feel weary at all," discussing biblical arguments against slavery and answering questions like "What is slavery?"[60]

Although they declined to accept pay from the AASS, the sisters launched their new identities as the first women agents of the AASS on December 16, 1836, when they spoke in a Baptist meeting room in New York, no home being large enough to hold the three hundred women who wanted to hear them. Antislavery women had heretofore spoken to small groups of women, mostly neighbors, in their homes or churches, but to speak in a forum of this scale they had to be willing to break the custom that prohibited women from addressing public gatherings and to openly oppose the scriptural authority of Paul's admonition to the early Christians in I Corinthians 14:34: "Let your women keep silence in the churches; for it is not permitted unto them to speak." Angelina initially lost her nerve, fearing it would be "unnatural" for her to proceed, but charismatic Theodore Weld, a leader in their training group, whom Angelina would later marry, revived the sisters' courage by disparaging social norms that "bound up the energies of woman" and reminding them of the high importance of their message. (See Document 12.)

By the mid-1830s with the expansion of universal white male suffrage, public speaking had become a form of performance that was strongly associated with the explicitly masculine virtues of virility, forcefulness, and endurance. Much of the vitality of the new nation's public life emanated from styles of popular oratory that emerged, first in the pulpit, then in politics. These new styles were part of the democratic process by which the authority of the clergy and of landed elites was gradually replaced in public life by the power of other groups, especially the broad middle class that embraced artisans as well as professionals. The rise in public oratory placed great demands on both speaker and audience. Speakers were expected to engage their audiences' emotions in ways that entertained as well as enlightened, and they were not expected to be brief. Literacy was universal in the North, but the spoken word still had the authority that came in part from its identification with religious authority, as in (John 1:1): "In the beginning was the Word, and the Word was with God, and the Word was God."

Women were permitted to enter this arena of competitive oratory as consumers, not producers, of eloquence. Even the term used to describe a mixed audience of men and women—*promiscuous*—conveyed the era's distrust of women moving freely in public spaces. Addressing a new audience each week, Angelina's confidence in her public performances grew as she learned to trust her feelings. In January 1837 she wrote her Philadelphia friend, Jane Smith, "I love the work." (See Document 13.) By February she described her animated speaking style as yielding to "impulses of feeling." She was also beginning to defend women's "rights & duties" to speak and act on the topic of slavery. (See Document 14.)

In addition to propelling women into public activism and creating greater awareness of the brutality of slavery, the Grimkés' speaking tour of 1836 brought them into interaction with large numbers of African Americans, and gave them the opportunity to act on Garrisonian principles and to oppose racial prejudice. "The more I mingle with your people, the more I feel for their oppressions & desire to sympathize in their sorrows," Angelina wrote Sarah Mapps Douglass. (See Document 15.) In Poughkeepsie, New York, in March 1837, the sisters spoke to a group that included men as well as women. "For the first time in my life I spoke in a promiscuous assembly," Angelina wrote. (See Document 17.)

The sisters' contact with northern racism began with their Philadelphia Quaker community. Even wealthy African Americans who belonged to the Arch Street Meeting sat in a segregated pew. Angelina wrote Sarah Douglass that such customs now made her "feel ashamed for my country, ashamed for the church," though she thought "the time is coming when such 'respect of persons' will no more be known in our land." (See Document 17.)

The Grimkés challenged the racial prejudice of their New York sisters by meeting with the board of the New York Female Anti-Slavery Society. "I believed it right to throw before them our views on the state of things among them, particularly on prejudice," Angelina wrote Jane Smith. "No colored Sister has ever been in the board, & they have hardly any colored members." The meeting was emotional. "What we said to them was from a sense of duty in love & tears, but it was hard work, & I believe as much as they could possibly hear from us." Angelina gave up her plan to create a national organization of antislavery women when she realized that racial prejudice among New York abolitionist women would banish "our colored sisters from an equal & full participation in its deliberations & labors." (See Document 16.) When Angelina asked Sarah Forten, daughter of an elite African American Philadelphia abolitionist and a member of the Philadelphia Female Anti-Slavery Society, to educate her about the effects of racial prejudice, Forten eloquently described the "weight of this evil."[61] (See Document 18.) Thus the Grimkés' perception of the human rights of their "colored sisters" evolved alongside their perception of "the rights and duties of women," and they sought to merge those two sets of rights.

The rapid growth of women's antislavery associations, and the stir that the Grimkés created in its ranks, led to an unprecedented event in May 1837—a national convention of antislavery women. Organized by Angelina Grimké and other women abolitionist leaders, including Maria Weston Chapman of the Boston Female Anti-Slavery Society and Lucretia Mott and others in the Philadelphia Female Anti-Slavery Society, the convention was scheduled to meet in conjunction with the annual meeting of the American Anti-Slavery Society. Planning the convention, Angelina urged Sarah Douglass to attend despite the prejudice she could expect to encounter there—from women abolitionists as well as the public at large. Accompanied by her mother, Douglass did attend. The three-day event attracted about two hundred women from nine states; about one in ten was African American.[62] (See Document 18.)

The women's antislavery convention marked a new stage in the emergence of women's rights within the abolitionist movement. There Angelina presented her *Appeal to the Women of the Nominally Free States,* a lengthy pamphlet that defiantly defended women's right to speak and act. "The denial of our duty to act, is a bold denial of our right to act; and if we have no right to act, then may *we* well be termed 'the white slaves of the North'—for, like our brethren in bonds, we must seal our lips in silence and despair." Grimké's *Appeal* also contained a Garrisonian assault on racial prejudice. (See Document 19.)

At the convention women adopted resolutions that urged women to circulate petitions annually, that decried the indifference of U.S. churches to the sin of slavery, that censured northern women and men who married southern slaveholders, and that called for white women to associate with African American women "as though the color of the skin was of no more consequence than that of the hair, or the eyes."[63]

Just as radically, the convention approved a resolution supporting women's rights. It declared that "certain rights and duties are common to all moral beings," and that it was the duty of woman "to do all that she can by her voice, and her pen, and her purse, and the influence of her example, to overthrow the horrible system of American slavery." Although most of the convention's resolutions were adopted without discussion, this one "called forth an animated and interesting debate." Twelve delegates opposed the resolution so strongly that they had their names recorded in the minutes "as disapproving." (See Document 20.) Many women thought that their mere attendance at the convention was sufficiently daring. "To attend a Female convention!" one exclaimed. "Once I should have blushed at the thought."[64]

Angelina thought that the convention debate was healthy, since it "very soon broke down all stiffness & reserve, threw open our hearts to each others' view, and produced a degree of confidence in ourselves & each other which was very essential & delightful." She predicted that their resolutions would "frighten the weak and startle the slumbering, particularly those on Southern intermarriages, the province of women, the right of Petition."[65]

Although two other conventions of antislavery women were subsequently held in Philadelphia, in 1838 and in 1839, no resolutions on women's rights and duties were offered there, perhaps because they were perceived as too divisive. Nevertheless, by 1837 women's rights ideas had taken root within the antislavery movement. Critics of women's public activism kept the topic in the public spotlight and escalated the debate's scope and intensity.

The first critic was Catharine Beecher, whose 1837 book, *An Essay on Slavery and Abolitionism, with Reference to the Duty of American Females,* appeared just before the May convention as a reply to Angelina Grimké's *Appeal to the Christian Women of the South.* (See Document 21.) Beecher had moved with her father and siblings to the urban frontier of Cincinnati, Ohio, seeking to claim the West for New England Congregationalism. Like most of her family at that time, Beecher viewed Garrisonian abolitionism as a disruptive force in American society that imperiled their efforts to transplant New England culture in the Northwest Territory and shape a nation that included the South. Her *Essay* argued that the abolitionist emphasis on immediate emancipation shut off communication between North and South, and invited the creation of a separate "Southern republic" with slaveholding preserved in perpetuity.[66] Not so much a defender of traditional male privilege as a centrist competitor with the radical Grimkés for the loyalty of middle-class churchgoing women, Beecher promoted women's power in family life and opposed women's participation in the abolitionist movement because "the attitude of a combatant" threw women out of their appropriate sphere—the "domestic and social circle." This enabled her to make her own goals—particularly the feminization of the teaching profession—appear conservative and respectable.

Both Beecher and the Grimkés were trying to construct new notions of female citizenship that permitted women to assume new public responsibilities within the larger male-dominated social projects with which they were affiliated in the new Republic—Beecher with middle-class Evangelicalism and the Grimkés with Garrisonian abolitionism. Both efforts were aspirational because the larger project of the American Republic was also aspirational.

REDEFINING THE RIGHTS OF WOMEN: ANGELINA AND SARAH GRIMKÉ SPEAK IN MASSACHUSETTS, SUMMER 1837

Following the inaugural meeting of the Anti-Slavery Convention of American Women, the Grimkés launched their historic speaking tour of Massachusetts in the summer of 1837. Beginning in Boston, they felt that they pleaded "not the cause of the slave only" but "the cause of woman as a responsible moral being." In parlor meetings where they strategized with their supporters, men as well as women were glad that their "fetters were broken." Many allies believed "that women could not perform their duties as moral beings, under the existing state of public sentiment," and thought "that a new order of things is very desirable in this respect." Angelina was stunned by this turn of events. "What an untrodden path we have entered upon!" she wrote Jane Smith. "Sometimes I feel almost bewildered, amazed, confounded & wonder by what strange concatenation of events I came to be where I am & what I am." (See Document 22.)

Reinforced by this support, Angelina described to Jane Smith her speech to three hundred members of the Female Moral Reform Society in Boston. There she urged her audience to see women's rights as a personal issue: "that this reform was to begin in *ourselves.*" Emphasizing the personal impact of gender inequalities, she said that women were "polluted" by men's attitudes toward them, and declared: "My heart is pained, my womanhood is insulted, my moral being is outraged continually." (See Document 22.)

The sisters found support for this critique of male dominance when they left Boston to lecture in the Massachusetts countryside. Maria Weston Chapman, an elite leader of the Boston Female Anti-Slavery Society, sent a letter "to Female Anti-Slavery Societies throughout New England" to support the Grimkés' discussion of "the condition of woman; her duties and her consequent rights." Disdaining those "who were grinding in the narrow mill of a corrupt publick opinion on this point," Chapman urged antislavery women to show the sisters "hospitality of the heart."[67] (See Document 23.)

People came to hear the sisters because they were curious about the phenomenon they now represented — southern women speaking in public about their firsthand encounters with the horrors of slavery and about their right to speak publicly about those horrors. Their reception varied. "Great apathy" sometimes reigned in small towns; but before large audiences in Boston and Lynn, Angelina found it "very easy to speak because there was great openness to hear." Men became an increasing part of their audiences. In and around Boston they could "fill a house containing 1000 persons with ease." (See Document 24.) Seven months after their first speaking engagement they had successfully overturned the custom that prohibited women from speaking publicly to mixed audiences of men and women.

The Grimkés maintained a grueling pace between June and November. Speaking every other day, sometimes twice a day, often for two hours at a time, they reached thousands. Angelina's record in her letters to Jane Smith shows that in June she spoke seventeen times in ten towns, to more than eight thousand people. In July she gave nineteen lectures in fourteen towns, reaching nearly twelve thousand. In August, even though Angelina was ill for half the month, she gave eleven lectures in nine towns with six thousand present. In September, she spoke seventeen times in sixteen towns with more than seven thousand persons attending. In October she spoke fifteen times in fifteen towns, with twelve thousand in her audiences. During these five months she lectured seventy-nine times to audiences that totaled more than forty thousand people.[68]

Since Sarah kept no equivalent record, we do not know if she ever spoke independently of Angelina, but it seems she did not. Angelina was the one people came to hear. Her inspired oratory offered audiences the 1830s equivalent of an award-winning movie about slavery. "Never before or since have I seen an audience so held and so moved by any public speaker, man or woman," said a Massachusetts minister in whose pulpit she lectured.[69] Wendell Phillips, a prominent Boston abolitionist, said that she "swept the cords of the human heart with a power that has never been surpassed, and rarely equalled." Phillips was impressed by "her serene indifference to the judgment of those about her. Self-poised, she seemed morally sufficient to herself." He thought her power derived from "the profound religious experience of one who had broken out of the charmed circle, and whose intense earnestness melted all opposition." Audiences felt that "she was opening some secret record of her own experience;" their "painful silence and breathless interest told the deep effect and lasting impression her words were making."[70]

Angelina's impact on her audiences came in part from her mastery of an oratorical style that infused the religious discourse of her time with a needed purpose. "Cast out first the spirit of slavery from your own hearts," she said. "The great men of this country" and the "church" have become "worldly-wise, and therefore God, in his wisdom, employs them not to carry on his plans of reformation and salvation." Instead, he has chosen "the weak to overcome the mighty." This use of familiar metaphors to convey new ideas had deep roots in Judeo-Christian traditions. Angelina stood in a long line of prophets who used traditional metaphors to introduce new concepts to their cultures. Like them, she was denounced by established religious authorities, who saw her as a defiant challenge to their leadership. Her ally Lydia Maria Child equated her to Isaiah and the Massachusetts clergy to Old-Testament Jewish priests. (See Document 39.)

Yet despite Angelina's greater oratorical gifts, the sisters' success was achieved jointly; neither could have done alone what they were able to accomplish together. Traveling among strangers, some of whom were friendly, some hostile, they could rely on one another. Neither bore the burdens of their grueling schedule alone. Sarah was becoming a capable speaker on women's rights, and Angelina relied on her to elaborate that aspect of their message. "Sister Sarah does preach up woman's rights most nobly & fearlessly," Angelina wrote in July. When Sarah's voice failed due to a cold, Angelina complained that she "had to bear the brunt of the meeting" for two days. (See Document 25.)

One measure of the sisters' success was the exponential growth in membership of the American Anti-Slavery Society immediately after their speaking tour. Each meeting harvested new "subscribers" to the AASS. In 1837 the AASS claimed 1,000 auxiliaries and 100,000 members. A year later their membership had more than doubled to 250,000, and the number of affiliated antislavery societies had increased by a third.[71]

Many of these new members were women who responded enthusiastically to the Grimkés' "breach in the wall of public opinion." Angelina wrote Jane Smith, "we find that many of our New England sisters are ready to receive these strange doctrines, feeling as they do, that our whole sex needs an emancipation from the thraldom of public opinion." In villages as well as cities, "the whole land seem[ed] roused to discussion on the *province of woman*" (See Document 25). While the South Carolina sisters led the way, others willingly followed. Disciples attracted to their side—like Abby Kelley (1810–1887), a Quaker teacher in Lynn, Massachusetts—now embraced women's rights as well as Garrisonian abolition.[72]

In June the Grimkés' campaign created a constituency for women's rights; in July their opponents emerged. Their most powerful adversaries were the Congregational clergy, who issued a Pastoral Letter condemning "those who encourage females to bear an obtrusive and ostentatious part in measures of reform, and countenance any of that sex who so far forget themselves as to itinerate in the character of public lecturers and teachers." The letter especially censured the naming of "things which ought not to be named," meaning the sisters' testimonials about the sexual exploitation of enslaved women. Indirectly the letter forbade clergymen to permit the Grimkés to speak in their churches. (See Document 26.)

In contrast to most British churchmen, who led public opinion in the campaign for Parliament to abolish slavery in the British West Indies, most northern clergymen in the United States did not support abolition before the Civil War. Even after most Protestant denominations split into southern and northern branches (Presbyterians in 1837), northern clerical opinion opposed Garrisonian radicalism more than they opposed slavery.[73] Exceptions to this rule included ministers who invited the sisters to speak in their churches, as well as clergymen like Henry Clarke Wright, some of whom were AASS agents.

Clerical opposition to the Grimkés was fueled in part by this general unwillingness to endorse abolition, but also by ministers' desire to contain the power of the female laity in their own congregations. Historically excluded from leadership positions, except among Quakers, in the late 1830s women began to express views on a wide range of issues in their communities, including temperance and moral reform as well as abolition. The temperance movement strove to limit the consumption of alcohol. The moral reform movement sought to end men's control of women's bodies and attacked the sexual double standard.[74] The growing autonomy of women's voices on these and other issues threatened to undercut ministers' moral leadership, especially after 1834, when the Congregational Church ceased to be financed by state taxation.[75]

By August, Angelina felt that "a storm was gathering all around against our *womanhood*," and feared that most ministers would close church doors against them. (See Document 27.) She and Sarah tried to identify their allies among antislavery men. Their strongest supporter was Henry Clarke Wright, who had trained with them in New York in November 1836. When they arrived in Boston in June 1837, the sisters had stayed in the Wright home, where, Angelina said, "we enjoyed the green pastures of christian intercourse & the still waters of *peace* in his lovely family." Angelina praised him to Jane Smith as "one of the best men I ever met with" and "one of the holyest men I ever saw."[76] Wright arranged most of the details of the sisters' speaking tour that summer, and in *The Liberator* he defended the sisters' discussion of women's rights.

Because Wright was in close daily contact with the Grimkés and because he supported other reforms in addition to antislavery, Theodore Weld and others blamed him for the sisters' diversion into women's rights. Weld was now secretly in love with Angelina and jealously resented Wright's influence with her. At the end of July, probably at Weld's insistence, the AASS Executive Committee transferred Wright to Pennsylvania. "I would gladly stay & avert every arrow of scorn & obloquy from their devoted heads," Wright noted in his diary. But the sisters had to proceed without him, even though his replacement did not fully approve of them and therefore could not be relied upon to book their meetings.[77] "*This burden we did not expect to have to bear, and it is often perplexing*," Angelina complained to Weld.[78]

In ways that probably expressed her desire to know Weld more intimately, Angelina's letters in August invited him to answer questions about his views of equality in marriage. The first of these asked him to join her struggle against the opponents of women's rights. (See Document 28.) Angelina noted that the personal, subjective nature of women's rights touched "every man's interests at home, in the tenderest relation of life." She and Sarah had not sought this controversy, she emphasized. "We are placed very unexpectedly in a very trying situation, in the forefront of an entirely new contest—a contest for the *rights of woman* as a moral, intelligent & responsible being." Crossing her letter in the mail, a letter from Weld must have greatly disappointed her because it urged her to give up the women's rights campaign. (See Document 29.)

While Angelina was writing a response to Catharine Beecher's *Essay* in July and August, Sarah began to publish a series of essays in defense of women's rights. Weld entreated them both to cease such publications and stay focused on slavery. As "*southerners*," he argued, they could "do more at convincing the North than twenty *northern* females," an advantage that they lost by pursuing *"another* subject . . . hence your testimony; testimony TESTIMONY is the great desideratum."[79] John Greenleaf Whittier, a Quaker poet and abolitionist writer, seconded Weld's view, supporting the sisters' public speaking on women's rights, but urging them not "to enter the lists as controversial writers on this question." (See Document 30.)

Standing her ground, Angelina explained to both men why she and Sarah felt they now had to defend women's rights in their speaking and writing. "If we surrender the right to *speak* to the public this year, we must surrender the right to petition next year," she wrote, "What *then* can *woman* do for the slave, when she herself is under the feet of man & shamed into *silence?*" (See Document 31).

Many women's antislavery societies joined the Grimkés' fight for women's rights. At their October 1837 meeting, the Ladies Anti-Slavery Society in Providence, Rhode Island, resolved "that we act as moral agents" and "that our rights are sacred and immutable, and founded on the liberty of the gospel, that great emancipation act for women." (See Document 34.) A majority of the members of the nation's largest and most powerful women's abolitionist group, the Philadelphia Female Anti-Slavery Society, also voted their approval. The sisters had a practical reason for insisting that they needed to continue to write about women's rights. At this early moment in the debate, people did not know how to "sustain their ground by argument." (See Document 31.) In a burst of writings in 1837 and 1838, Angelina and Sarah Grimké sought to provide such arguments.

In October 1837, the sisters settled into the home of friends in Brookline, Massachusetts. "Oh how delightful it was to stretch my weary limbs on a bed of ease, and roll off from my mind all the heavy responsibilities which had so long pressed upon it," Angelina wrote Jane Smith.[80] She and Sarah each wrote essays in the form of letters to their opponents that were later published as books: Sarah's as *Letters on the Equality of the Sexes and the Condition of Woman, Addressed to Mary S. Parker, President of the Boston Female Anti-Slavery Society* (1838); Angelina's as *Letters to Catherine E. Beecher, in Reply to An Essay on Slavery and Abolitionism* (1838).[81] Glowing with a white-hot radiance on the "woman question," their writings became the standard for women's rights thinking until a decade later, when the Women's Rights Convention of Seneca Falls, New York, sparked another outpouring of commentary.

The sisters' writings on women's rights relied primarily on religious arguments. Yet because they buttressed these arguments with Enlightenment notions about human equality and natural rights contained in the Declaration of Independence and the Bill of Rights, their vision of female equality extended further than the "Biblical Feminism" of itinerant female preachers. In these "letters" they explored the implications of the ideas they had developed during their speaking tour. Their arguments had three major dimensions. First, they insisted that all rights were grounded in "moral nature." Second, they explored the personal aspects of moral identity and of rights. Third, they analyzed the social and political meaning of women's rights.

Angelina's twelfth letter to Catharine Beecher was in many ways the most eloquent of the sisters' writings on women's rights. (See Document 32.) She began with a tribute to the abolition movement as a school that taught her about women's rights:

> Since I engaged in the investigation of the rights of the slave, I have necessarily been led to a better understanding of my own; for I have found the Anti-Slavery cause to be the high school of morals in our land—the school in which human rights are more fully investigated, and better understood and taught, than in any other benevolent enterprise.

That "investigation" led Angelina to understand the parallels between enslaved persons' lack of liberty and her own unfreedom as a white woman. She offered "one great fundamental principle" capable of sustaining equal rights for women and men, enslaved and masters—"the rights of all men, from the king to the slave, are built upon their moral nature: and as all men have this moral nature, so all men have essentially the same rights." These rights might be "plundered," she said, "but they cannot be alienated." If rights were "founded in moral being," she insisted, "then the circumstances of sex could not give to man higher rights and responsibilities, than to woman." Those who argued that it did, she thought, denied "the self-evident truth, 'that the physical constitution is the mere instrument of the moral nature.'"

Angelina's argument was based on her interpretation of the equality of men and women at the moment of their creation, which naturalized women's equality and denaturalized male superiority, thereby stepping around the difficulties of constructing feminist interpretations of scripture.[82] Since women and men were created equal, she argued, women should have equal rights in the secular, social, and political world as well as in spiritual realms. She supported woman's "right to be consulted in all the laws and regulations by which she is to be governed, whether in Church or State." With words that must have thrilled some readers and shocked others, she further insisted "that woman has just as much right to sit in solemn counsel in Conventions, Conferences, Associations, and General Assemblies, as man—just as much right to sit upon the throne of England, or in the Presidential chair of the United States, as man." "The fundamental principle of moral being" was a flexible concept that allowed Angelina to see two dimensions in women's equality with men: in some ways they were the same as men, and in some ways different. Urging the similarity between women and men, her twelfth letter denounced "the anti-christian doctrine of masculine and feminine virtues." But this did not prevent her from arguing, as she did throughout her public years, that women's social circumstances created moral duties particular to women: "Where *woman's* heart is bleeding, shall *woman's* heart be hushed?" (See Document 11.) In her last public speech in 1838 she mentioned her special duties as a southerner; so, too, women had special duties. Since women had no right to vote, she thought it "peculiarly your duty to petition." (See Document 36.) Thus "moral being" is a concept that offers much to current debates in feminist theory. Recognizing women's circumstances as historically and socially constructed, it could support arguments on behalf of affirmative action (a collective treatment of women that tries to promote women's equality with men by recognizing their socially constructed differences from men) as well as arguments for women's equal rights as human beings.[83]

In her *Letters on the Equality of the Sexes,* Sarah Grimké also based her arguments on the equality of men's and women's "immortal being." She offered scathing social criticisms on a topic of compelling interest to all women—the institution of marriage. In her twelfth letter—"Legal Disabilities of Women"—Sarah drew parallels between the legal status of married women and that of enslaved people. Woman was deprived of "responsibility . . . as a moral being, or a free-agent" by laws that submerged her "very being" into that of her husband. (See Document 33.) Sarah Grimké's focus on legal issues might have been reinforced by her father's will. Although she was with him when he died, having traveled with him to seek medical treatment in Philadelphia, she and his other daughters were treated as second-class citizens in his will, which left all his many properties to his sons and left his daughters small cash amounts of $1,000 and $2,000. Might she have protested this traditional inheritance pattern to her mother? Interestingly, Sarah was the only living child not named in her mother's will.[84]

In addition to the legal system, personal relations between husband and wife were shaped by scriptural authority that required wives to submit to their husbands. For nineteenth-century women this often meant submitting to unwanted sexual intercourse, and, since intercourse often led to pregnancy, submitting to unwanted pregnancy. Indirectly addressing this vital issue, Sarah's thirteenth letter offered a new interpretation of the biblical admonition, "Wives, submit yourselves unto your own husbands."[85] The Bible also required husbands to honor their wives, she said. Moreover, "submit" and "subjection" were terms that recommended a Christian spirit of humility, not a literal rule of husbands over wives.

After writing the last of their essays in the winter of 1838, Angelina and Sarah ended their careers as public speakers with a series of spectacular events. In January they participated in a debate at the Boston Lyceum on the question, "Would the condition of woman and of society be improved by placing the two sexes on an equality in respect to civil rights and duties?" In February Angelina became the first woman to address the Massachusetts state legislature, speaking in Representatives' Hall on the slave trade in the District of Columbia and on the interstate slave trade. "We Abolition Women are turning the world upside down," Angelina wrote Sarah Douglass.[86] In March and April, under the auspices of the Boston Female Anti-Slavery Society, they offered a series of lectures, the first of which was attended by 2,800 people.

In early February 1838, Theodore Weld declared his love and proposed marriage to Angelina Grimké. To gain her consent he told her that her 1835 letter to Garrison "formed an era in my feelings and a crisis in my history that drew my spirit toward yours." Her response revealed how deeply she felt about that 1835 turning point in her life; she attributed insights to Weld that he may not have had:

> You speak of my letter to W. L. G. Ah! you felt then that it was written under tremendous pressure of feelings bursting up with volcanic violence from the bottom of my soul—you felt that it was the first long breath of *liberty* which my imprisoned spirit dared to respire whilst it pined in hopeless bondage, panting after freedom to *think aloud.*[87]

She agreed to marry Weld, saying that she loved him as "a kindred mind, a congenial soul" with whom she "longed to hold communion."[88] They set a wedding date for May.

The "volcanic violence" of Angelina Grimké's commitment to Garrisonian abolitionism helped her break customary limits on women's participation in public life. By thinking aloud—fearlessly—she and her sister brought new words and new concepts into public life. Yet, reflecting the burdens and unsustainability of their three pathbreaking years, Angelina retired from public life after her marriage to Theodore Weld, and Sarah joined the couple in their rural New Jersey retreat. Theodore, the most charismatic male speaker employed by the AASS, had lost his voice after an exhausting lecture tour in 1836, and never fully regained it. He supported the growing family by running a school, while also writing for the antislavery movement. His 1839 book, *American Slavery as It Is,* documented the horrors of slavery, drawn from personal narratives (including those written by Angelina and Sarah) and from southern newspapers published between 1837 and 1839.[89]

THE ANTISLAVERY MOVEMENT SPLITS OVER THE QUESTION OF WOMEN'S RIGHTS, 1837–1840

Just after her wedding in May 1838, Angelina Grimké spoke in public for the last time at the second annual convention of antislavery women in Philadelphia. Her lecture, the only time she was recorded by a stenographer, highlights how she stood up to the pressure of a mob estimated at about 10,000 men, some of whom threw rocks that broke windows of the hall as she spoke. (See Document 36.) The convention had gathered in newly completed Pennsylvania Hall, a building constructed by Garrisonian abolitionists and other radical groups who were often denied access to the city's other public buildings, especially its churches. The mob was especially enraged by the interracial character of the women's convention. While some black men attended AASS meetings, the women's conventions included a higher proportion of black participants. In the midst of the din, the mayor asked the women to adjourn. They filed out, arm in arm, two and three abreast, black women protected on each side by white women, into the multitude of "fellows of the baser sort" who parted to make a narrow path. After breaking into the building and smashing its furnishings, the next night the mob burned Pennsylvania Hall to the ground.[90] (See Document 37.)

Angelina's antislavery career ended as it had begun three years earlier—amid the turbulence of mob violence. That violence symbolized the intractability of slavery as an issue in American society, and highlighted the degree to which Garrisonians challenged the racist assumptions on which slavery rested. Nevertheless, this violent rejection of their message led many abolitionists to conclude that Garrisonian tactics were not working, and that electoral, political strategies might be more effective.

The Garrisonian movement itself was changing. In addition to women's rights, other reforms—most notably perfectionist views of pacificism and opposition to government—were emerging within it.

Garrison began to express perfectionist views in *The Liberator* in 1837, adding "Universal Emancipation" to the paper's motto, "Our Country is the world—our countrymen are all mankind." Henceforth, he said, the paper would support "emancipation of our whole race from the dominion of man, from the thraldom of self, from the government of brute force, from the bondage of sin." Garrison's new views on government were especially radical:

> As to the governments of this world . . . we shall endeavor to prove, that, in their essential elements, and as presently administered, they are all Anti-Christ; that they can never, by human wisdom, be brought into conformity to the will of God; that they cannot be maintained except by naval and military power.[91]

These ideas became the basis of the New England Non-Resistant Society, founded by Garrison and others in 1838. Springing from a religious quest for perfect holiness to which Garrison and many of his supporters rededicated themselves, their perspective on government was consistent with their view of slavery as a system based on coercion and of official and clerical authority as tolerant of that coercion. But it also radically rejected human institutions as a means of achieving human freedom.

Angelina approved of Garrison's move, writing Henry Clarke Wright in August 1837: "What wouldst thou think of *The Liberator* abandoning Abolition as a primary object and becoming the vehicle for all these grand principles? Is not the time rapidly coming for such a change. . . . O how lamentably superficial we are, to suppose that one truth can hurt another; as well might we suppose that to teach one branch of science is to undermine another."[92] Angelina also wrote approvingly to Jane Smith about Wright's perfectionism: "I am truly glad to find that Brother Wright has been with you long enough to explain his ultra peace views. . . . How terrible must be the shaking which will shake down the vast structures which man has built up to fetter the mind & body of his fellow man."[93]

Between 1838 and 1840 these changes within Garrisonian abolitionism generated internal conflicts that split the antislavery movement. Many abolitionists—men and women—feared that Garrison's promotion of perfectionist views brought disrepute to the movement. Certainly they made it difficult for his associates to use political institutions to combat slavery. In 1839–1840 the movement split into three branches. Garrison's supporters maintained control of the AASS; and after 1839, women exercised even greater power within the society. Garrison's opponents formed two new groups. Some created the American and

Foreign Anti-Slavery Society (A&FASS) in 1839, excluding women from membership and relegating them to auxiliary groups. (Both its supporters and opponents called this "the new organization.") Others put their energies into politics and in 1840 formed the Liberty Party, to which women, as nonvoters, contributed chiefly as fundraisers.[94]

Garrison's critics justified their separation from the AASS on the grounds that the society deviated unacceptably from the goal of ending slavery by encouraging women's leadership within the organization. The precipitating cause was the appointment of Abby Kelley to the AASS business committee in 1840. Kelley first spoke publicly at the Second Women's Anti-Slavery Convention. She joined Garrison in founding the New England Non-Resistant Society in 1838, and in 1839 she became an AASS lecturer and the first woman appointed to a governing committee of the AASS.

Officers of the new organization blamed AASS members for the split, since they brought "females into the business meetings to vote and speak, and also that they should be appointed officers of the Society." If the word "person" in the AASS Constitution was meant to include women, they argued, "then, it must, of course, include, not only women, but children also." The AASS Executive Committee decried the new organization's limitation of membership rights to men. They insisted that the AASS did not require members to believe in the equality of the sexes, nor adopt ultraist views of government. However, the AASS did refuse "to dictate to abolitionists" on these topics or repress unpopular views. This, they said, was what the new organization wanted.[95]

Angelina and Sarah Grimké viewed the fracturing of the abolitionist movement from their domestic retreat. In a world in which unmarried women were almost never able to maintain their own homes, Sarah lived with Angelina and Theodore for the rest of her life. All three were determined to show that Angelina and Sarah's advocacy of women's rights had not made them unfit for family life. "Now I verily believe that we are *thus* doing *as much* for the cause of woman as we did by public speaking," Angelina wrote Anne Weston in the summer of 1838. "For it is absolutely necessary that we should show that we are *not* ruined as domestic characters." (See Document 38.) In the next six years Angelina gave birth to three children. Yet she was confident that women's rights could "no more be driven back . . . than the doctrine of Human rights, of which it is a part, & a very important part"; she thought that women's rights should become a part of "*every* reform." (See Document 38.)

Supporters of women's rights within the antislavery movement included Lydia Maria Child, who, in September 1839, offered her own account of why the movement was splitting into pro- and anti-Garrison factions. Married but without children, Child had sacrificed a comfortable career as a writer for young people when she joined the abolitionist movement in 1833 by writing *An Appeal in Favor of That Class of Americans Called Africans.*[96] Child explained that she and others had not pushed women's rights: "Instead of forcing this 'foreign topic' into antislavery meetings or papers, we have sedulously avoided it." But when Garrison's critics asked women to withdraw from the AASS, she refused. She thought that clergymen were the main opponents of women leaders within the movement. And she felt "these questions of Non-Resistants, Woman's Rights, &c. are only urged to effect a secret purpose," which was to topple Garrison's leadership. Child believed that the conflict would eventually "mightily promote the cause of general freedom." (See Document 39.) In 1840 she was named to the executive committee of the American Anti-Slavery Society and in 1841 became the editor of its weekly, the *National Anti-Slavery Standard.*

All women's antislavery organizations underwent a painful period of reevaluation when the movement split. Many women aligned with Garrison's male critics in believing that perfectionism tainted abolitionism with heretical religious views and unsound political opinions. This was especially true of middle-class women who were members of female moral reform societies. In cities where that group was strong, as in Boston, New York, and Rochester, women's antislavery societies splintered and dissolved. Those outside the middle-class mainstream, such as Hicksite Quakers like Amy Post of Rochester, or elite Bostonians like Maria Weston Chapman, supported Garrison and women's rights as individuals. The Philadelphia society survived, partly because many of its members were Hicksite Quakers.[97] But elite women within Boston's society were not numerous enough to save it. In smaller societies throughout the Northeast, women were at best dispirited. "We are very feeble," wrote one Uxbridge, Massachusetts, woman.[98]

The Boston Female Anti-Slavery Society self-destructed in an acrimonious clash between Garrisonians, who included Lydia Maria Child, and their opponents, led by Mary Parker, the society's president. Women's rights were not mentioned at this meeting. Instead the dispute pivoted around the "new organization" (the American and Foreign Anti-Slavery Society).[99] (See Document 41.) Although most men and women in free black communities remained loyal to Garrisonian organizations, most also regretted the diversion of so much energy from the movement's main goal of ending slavery.

The crisis promoted the growth of women's rights within Garrisonian abolitionism. New leaders emerged to carry women's rights forward, most notably Abby Kelley, who met opponents with the same logic used by the Grimkés: "Whatever ways and means are right for men to adopt in reforming the world, are right also for women to adopt."[100] In the 1840s, Kelley became a popular speaker, carrying Garrison's message of "No Union with Slaveholders" and his denunciation of the Constitution as a "covenant with death."

Dozens of new Garrisonian societies formed in the 1840s. Some, like the Western New York Anti-Slavery Society (WNYASS), were especially vocal in advocating women's rights as well as emancipation. The WNYASS regularly elected women to offices in the society and sent women as delegates to the annual conventions of the AASS. Kelley drew other talented women to the Garrisonian ranks, including Paulina Wright Davis, Lucy Stone, and Susan B. Anthony. In 1845 Kelley helped found and thereafter raised the funds necessary to keep *The Anti-Slavery Bugle* alive in Salem, Ohio. That year she married Stephen Foster, another Garrisonian radical, and, after becoming a mother in 1847, she continued her lecture career while Foster cared for their child. Yet in the mid-1850s, when even Garrisonians began to affiliate with political parties, Garrison supported the new Republican Party, and Kelley and Foster broke with him when they endorsed an abolitionist party.[101]

Because Garrisonian radicalism became a seedbed for the cultivation of radical ideas outside the political mainstream in the 1830s, women's rights could emerge and flourish there. Yet Garrisonian abolitionism was on a trajectory that headed toward party politics in the 1840s—a location that lay beyond the reach of women's activism. In 1848 a group of women drawn from the antislavery movement and other dissenting movements came together to create a new location for women's rights in American political culture.

AN INDEPENDENT WOMEN'S RIGHTS MOVEMENT IS BORN, 1840–1858

A crucial enabling moment for the emergence of an independent women's rights movement was the World's Anti-Slavery Convention in London in 1840. The Garrisonian movement sent seven women delegates, including Lucretia Mott who represented both the Pennsylvania Anti-Slavery Society and the Philadelphia Female Anti-Slavery Society. Their British hosts, the British and Foreign Anti-Slavery Society—in

a step that demonstrated their support of the new anti-Garrison organization, the American and Foreign Anti-Slavery Society—refused to
seat the women. Garrison and Charles Remond, an African American
delegate, sat with the excluded women delegates. The women's ostra-
cism was never officially explained but delegates were told "that it
would be outraging the tastes, habits, customs and prejudices of the
English people, to allow women to sit in this Convention."[102] Sarah Pugh,
also representing both the Pennsylvania Anti-Slavery Society and the
Philadelphia Female Anti-Slavery Society, wrote a polite protest letter
to the conference organizers. And male Garrisonian delegates also published protests on behalf of the excluded women.[103]

Mott and other women delegates were surprised to discover that
British women abolitionists, many of whom were Quakers, supported
the ban on American women delegates. This difference in the gender
politics of the American and British movements arose chiefly from
differences in the political contexts of antislavery struggles in the two
countries.[104] An act of Parliament had abolished slavery in 1833, but
slavery remained an issue in the emerging colony of India, and the
British movement denounced the British textile industry's continued
profits from slave-grown cotton in the United States. The British economy continued to profit from coerced labor, but its distance from that
labor dimmed its apologists' political power. In the United States, where
a large region of the nation was dominated by an expanding slave labor
system and that region was steering the federal government into alli-
ances with other slave powers, it took another generation of protest and
one of the bloodiest wars in human history to end slave labor.[105] Thus,
to oppose slavery in the United States in the 1830s and 1840s required
a radical stance capable of challenging the nation's social, political, and
economic status quo. In that context some activists also challenged the
gendered status quo. British abolitionists did not need to defy the funda-
mentals of their society in this way. Although some British women abolitionists supported American notions of gender equality in the 1840s,
their movement did not become the seedbed for a robust women's
rights convention movement.

Another source of the different views of British and American women
on the question of seating women at the 1840 convention lay in the struggle of British Quakers to gain voting rights for Quaker men. British
laws limited voting rights to men who were members of the Church of
England. This excluded British Quakers, who in a long quest for voting
rights distanced themselves from their radical Puritan origins of the
1640s and adopted many forms of Anglican worship, including creeds

that upheld the divinity of Jesus. This trend also gained ground among American Quakers, producing the schism of 1827, which divided them into "Orthodox" and Hicksite groups. Having no equivalent to Hicksites in England, most British Quakers—men and women—viewed Lucretia Mott as a religious heretic and considered the Garrisonian women's rights agenda as a threat to their goal of achieving suffrage rights for Quaker men. "I fear thy influence on my children!!" one otherwise friendly Quaker told Mott.[106]

In London, a young, newly married advocate for women's rights, Elizabeth Cady Stanton, was accompanying her husband, Henry Stanton, on their honeymoon, he being a delegate affiliated with the "new organization." There she met Mott and learned about politics by observing the grace with which the older woman deflected criticisms of her women's rights beliefs.

Elizabeth Cady Stanton came to the antislavery movement as an outsider raised in her father's legal culture. Her privileged girlhood was shaped by Daniel Cady's successful legal practice and his years in the New York state legislature, in the U.S. Congress, and as a judge. She later wrote that her acquaintance with her father's women clients revealed the law's hostility to women. Her affiliation with the antislavery movement hinged on her relationship with her wealthy cousin, Gerrit Smith, in whose home she met Henry Stanton, then an organizer of the Liberty Party. She agreed to marry Henry after learning of his intention to attend the London conference, putting aside her father's objections to his dim financial prospects and her own previous doubts about the match.[107] Henry had befriended Theodore Weld when both were part of a student antislavery movement that left Lyman Beecher's Lane Theological Seminary in Cincinnati and moved to Oberlin College in 1834. As an agent of the AASS, Henry Stanton worked closely with the Grimké sisters during their 1837 tour, and Angelina judged him "sound" on woman's rights. (See Document 27.) Following the example of Theodore Weld and Angelina Grimké, the word "obey" was omitted from Elizabeth and Henry's wedding vows.[108]

Yet in 1840 Elizabeth did not know what sexual equality looked like in everyday life, and perhaps for that reason soon after their honeymoon she and Henry visited the Weld-Grimké household in New Jersey. Henry's ties with the reform trio led them to expect a comfortable welcome. But if Elizabeth hoped to find a model there for her own married life, she was disappointed. After a long ride on a cool May evening, they hoped for "something hot and stimulating," Elizabeth later recalled, but instead, they were served a health-conscious "Graham diet" of "cold dishes without a whiff of heat, or steam, [which] gave one a feeling of strangeness." Elizabeth found the Weld-Grimké home "destitute of all tasteful, womanly touches, and though neat and orderly, had a cheerless atmosphere."[109] The sisters' zeal served them well in the crucible of innovation around 1837, but they did not inspire imitation in 1840.

Lucretia Mott, by contrast, exemplified a woman who was comfortable with God, with respectable society, and with women's rights. She introduced Stanton to a new dispensation in women's rights—free from the Grimkés' religious fervor but linked to their radical vision of sexual equality. "Her views are many of them so new & strange that my *causality* finds great delight in her society," Elizabeth wrote Angelina and Sarah from London. (See Document 42.) Mott returned the compliment, writing in her diary, "Elizabeth Stanton gaining daily in our affections." And a few months later she praised Stanton as "bright, open, lovely," in a letter to British abolitionists: "I love her now as belonging to us."[110]

Although they came from different backgrounds and Mott was a generation older, she and Stanton agreed on the importance of Mary Wollstonecraft's 1792 book, *Vindication of the Rights of Women.* Stanton had read it before coming to London, and Mott mentioned Wollstonecraft in one of her London talks. Wollstonecraft's unorthodox personal life made this early British feminist just as controversial in 1840 as she was in her own time. Before her marriage to William Godwin in 1797, Wollstonecraft had condemned marriage and was not married when her first child was born. In recognizing her legacy, Mott and Stanton affiliated with a leading figure of the British and French Enlightenment who not only advocated rights for women but also challenged the gendered status quo.[111]

Later Stanton said that in London she and Mott discussed "the propriety of holding a woman's convention."[112] Stanton "made her debut in public" by speaking on temperance in Seneca Falls in the fall of 1841. Mott followed her progress, writing mutual friends in Dublin that Stanton had moved herself to tears and infused into her talk a "homeopathic dose of Woman's Rights." In her talks to audiences that probably included female moral reform society members, Stanton also referred to the sexual double standard that made some things "sinful in woman alone."[113] And she followed the evolution of women's rights within two Garrisonian publications, *The Anti-Slavery Standard* and *The Liberator,* the latter sent to her by Sarah Pugh, Mott's close friend whom she had met in London. Stanton called these periodicals "the only woman's rights food I have for myself & disciples."[114] Yet because Garrisonian groups were calling for a boycott of elections, that movement could not be expected to support the goal of extending voting rights to women.[115] But Henry Stanton's brand of the antislavery movement was also uncongenial; Elizabeth Stanton wrote a friend in 1841, "I do not go to any business meetings with Henry because I know I would have no voice in those meetings."[116]

Elizabeth Cady Stanton began working independently for women's rights in 1843 when, during visits to her father's household in Albany, she joined other women, including Ernestine Rose and Paulina Wright Davis, in circulating petitions to the New York Assembly on behalf of a New York Married Women's Property Act.[117] Beginning with Mississippi in 1836, states were enacting legislation that permitted wives to retain ownership of property that they brought into marriage. New York passed a married women's property act in 1848.[118] Designed to protect women's property from misuse by wastrel or incompetent husbands, such legislation was relevant to Elizabeth Stanton's circumstances, since her homes in Boston and later in Seneca Falls were purchased by her father rather than her husband. During these years Henry did little to sustain their middle-class standard of living, and, taking a dim view of his son-in-law's political enthusiasms, Judge Cady supported the passage of the 1848 law. Until then his daughter lived in a house that was deeded to her in her father's will but owned by her husband.[119]

When Henry and Elizabeth Stanton moved with their three sons from Boston to Seneca Falls in June 1847, they entered one of the most congenial environments for women's rights in the United States. The effects of the Second Great Awakening in central and western New York were especially pronounced a decade earlier, and the region's volatile mix of Hicksite Quakers, evangelical perfectionists, and benevolent activists pursued competing agendas that inspired one another to ever greater efforts. In the 1840s Hicksite Quakers petitioned their chief governing body, the Yearly Meeting, to grant more power to women within local meetings. Evangelical and benevolent women in Rochester's Ladies Washingtonian Total Abstinence Society did more than campaign against drunkenness; in 1846 they collected 1,400 signatures on a petition that bemoaned women's "lack of the ballot." Rochester's Female Moral Reform Society, which claimed 500 members in 1845, mobilized against prostitution and the sexual double standard that condoned male predatory promiscuity.[120]

Coming from Boston, where she had begun to enjoy a rising place among its reform-minded elite, Stanton was unconnected with these upstate New York networks. While her husband traveled on behalf of antislavery political parties during their first year in Seneca Falls, she fought for her sons' lives against recurring bouts of malaria.[121] When invited to spend the day with Lucretia Mott, who was in nearby Waterloo attending the annual New York meeting of Hicksite Quakers in July 1848, she "poured out . . . the torrent of my long-accumulated discontent with such vehemence and indignation that I stirred myself, as well as the rest of the party to do and dare anything."[122] Her listeners were receptive. The Yearly Meeting had just rejected a proposal to grant equal power to women and men in local Quaker meetings. Stanton and Mott and Mott's sister, Martha Coffin Wright, and a neighbor, Mary Ann McClintock, issued a call for "a WOMAN'S RIGHTS CONVENTION . . . to discuss the social, civil, and religious condition and rights of woman" to take place ten days hence, promising Lucretia Mott as a speaker.[123] (See Document 43.)

Stanton's presence among this group of Hicksite women made it easier for them to overcome the Quaker prohibition against joining "popular" non-Quaker reform activities. Despite their rejection by the Quaker meeting, they would have been unlikely to take such a step on their own. As it was, they and one young non-church member worked together effectively. They perused "the reports of Peace, Temperance, and Anti-Slavery conventions" as models for how they might organize their convention and phrase their resolutions. These all seemed too tame. Then one of the group "took up the Declaration of 1776, and read it aloud with much spirit and emphasis, and it was at once decided to adopt the historic document." Several "well-disposed" men helped them compile the grievances listed in their proposed "Declaration of Sentiments." (See Document 43.)

"Crowds in carriages and on foot" responded to the call, filling the Wesleyan chapel to overflowing, about three hundred people in all. The organizers had planned to exclude men the first day of the convention, but when men showed up, they were admitted. In fact, James Mott chaired the meeting. The first day those assembled heard the Declaration of Sentiments and the resolutions that Stanton, Mott, McClintock, and Wright had prepared earlier. That evening Lucretia Mott spoke "on the subject of reforms in general." The second day the convention discussed and adopted the Declaration and resolutions. (See Document 44.)

Historian Judith Wellman found that most of those who came to the convention lived nearby, the majority in Seneca Falls and nearby Waterloo. Others hailed from neighboring counties. Most came with relatives—a sister, parent, child, cousin, or spouse—including Stanton and Mott, whose sisters attended. About a quarter of the attendees were Hicksite Quakers.

Some, including Frederick Douglass, the formerly enslaved, well-known abolitionist editor, came from Rochester. (See Document 44.) The only African American at the convention, Douglass had moved to Rochester in 1843. He and his fledgling newspaper, *The North Star* (founded 1847), were indebted to the support of Rochester's antislavery women, especially Amy Post, a Hicksite Quaker, who also attended the convention. Douglass was a women's rights supporter when he arrived in Seneca Falls; the masthead of *The North Star* declared "Right is of no sex—Truth is of no Color."[124]

Only a few conferees were active in national reform networks, but most would have participated in the region's flourishing social movements and were familiar with the format of conventions that adopted resolutions for future action. This convention's resolutions and Declaration of Sentiments expressed religious, social, and political themes, sometimes separately, sometimes woven together into new statements about women's rights and welfare.

The Declaration enumerated legal issues, presumably shaped by Stanton, and a variety of other topics, probably shaped by Mott, Wright, and McClintock, including women's employment, education, and participation in religious and social reform. Some language echoed the Grimkés' writings and the 1837 women's antislavery convention, especially the rejection of men's "right to assign her a sphere of action, when that belongs to her conscience and to her God." (See Document 44.) Yet while God and the Creator appeared frequently in the convention's resolutions, secular phrases adopted from the Declaration of Independence and from the eighteenth-century Enlightenment prevailed over religious discourse. "Nature" and its "great precept" of happiness was the ultimate authority. In this way Mott and Stanton's collaboration transplanted women's rights into the secular soil of nineteenth-century belief in human progress. The third resolution exemplified this process, asserting "that woman is man's equal," which it supported with two propositions: the Creator intended woman to be man's equal, and "the highest good of the race demands that she should be."[125] (See Document 44.)

The only resolution not unanimously adopted was the ninth that supported women's "sacred right to the elective franchise." This was Stanton's idea, not Mott's, and except for the persistent support of Frederick Douglass, might have been voted down. Eventually a majority at the convention agreed that the right to choose rulers and make laws was crucial because it protected all other rights. In the future, women's rights convention resolutions on the "elective franchise" would become standard fare and pass with little debate.

Press coverage of the Seneca Falls meeting exceeded Stanton and Mott's greatest expectations. The entire proceedings were published in both major and minor newspapers, and every editor seemed to have an opinion about the event.[126] Building on the success of the Seneca Falls example, almost twenty other women's rights conventions met before 1870 in Ohio, Massachusetts, Indiana, Pennsylvania, and New York. Two weeks after Seneca Falls, a convention met in Rochester, where, Stanton and Mott were distressed to learn, participants went further than they thought acceptable by electing a woman to preside. But that "hazardous experiment" did not slow the movement down. In cities like Worcester, Massachusetts, and in towns like Salem, Ohio, the basic format of the Seneca Falls convention was followed: officers were elected; declarations were made; resolutions were discussed and adopted; formal addresses were heard; letters were read from those who could not attend; and delegates responded to ongoing press coverage. Men were active participants on most of these occasions, except the convention at Salem, which permitted only women to speak.[127]

The women's rights convention movement established a foundation for the creation of national women's suffrage associations in 1869. Conventions advanced public debate on women's rights issues, and they cultivated the commitment of a generation of women leaders, many of whom also remained active in other reform movements. Elizabeth Cady Stanton exemplified a trend among some to dedicate themselves solely to women's rights. Lucretia Mott wrote her in the fall of 1848: "You are so wedded to this cause that you must expect to act as pioneer in the work."[128] A few followed Stanton's lead. Many, however, emulated Mott's pattern of continuing to link women's rights with a broader agenda that gave equal or greater weight to abolition.

Perhaps because women's rights did not become a way of life for Mott, Elizabeth Stanton's relationship with her was supplanted in 1852 by a life partnership that she forged with Susan B. Anthony, a younger Quaker woman who never married. Anthony's parents and sister had attended the Rochester convention, where they heard Stanton read the Declaration of Sentiments. After meeting Anthony briefly at an antislavery convention in Seneca Falls, Stanton recruited her to a partnership that lasted fifty years. Stanton wrote speeches that Anthony delivered; Anthony cared for the children while Stanton wrote speeches.[129]

Eleven "national" women's rights conventions were held in northern states between 1848 and 1869, and at least seven local conventions.[130] Thousands of women attended. Many social trends supported their proliferation. The growth of female antislavery societies in the 1830s and 1840s and the eruption of women's rights within the movement problematized women's legal and social rights and created a potential audience for further discussion. By offering a new secular perspective on women's rights, the conventions expanded that audience even further. The conventions raised a big tent that welcomed women from other reform movements, especially temperance and moral reform. Women's rights supporters learned language in the conventions that helped them articulate women's rights issues in other venues, including their families and churches, broadening and deepening the culture's familiarity with women's rights. Some people came because they were curious and stayed because they learned a lot. Just as the women's anti-slavery conventions of 1837–1839 accompanied the annual meetings of the American Anti-Slavery Society, women's rights conventions of the 1850s often coincided with state constitutional conventions; lawyers and politicians who supported married women's property rights often attended women's rights conventions to learn about that issue. And the sea change in family life from traditional to modern relationships made women's rights relevant to the daily lives of women and men.

Abby Price's speech at the first National Women's Rights Convention in 1850 in Worcester, Massachusetts, exemplified the secular discourse of these conventions. Price lived with her husband in the "Practical Christian Republic" of Hopedale, Massachusetts, a utopian community with its own journal, the *Practical Christian*. Later they moved to Brooklyn, New York, where she became a friend of Walt Whitman. Her speech coined a new term that was widely adopted in the women's rights convention movement—"co-equality."[131] (See Document 47.) In the spirit of the Grimkés, Price linked co-equality to the equal creation of the sexes; the creation story remained an indispensable ingredient in women's rights claims: "The natural rights of woman are co-equal with those of man. So God created man in his own image . . . male and female, created he them." But by substituting "co-equal" for the more religious term, "moral being," Price and others brought a more secular valence into the women's rights convention movement.

At Worcester, Abby Price explained that co-equality did not mean that the sexes were the same:

> In contending for this co-equality of woman's with man's rights, it is not necessary to argue, either that the sexes are by nature equally and indiscriminately adapted to the same positions and duties, or that they are absolutely equal in physical and intellectual ability; but only that they are absolutely equal in their rights to life, liberty, and the pursuit of happiness.

Thus, by acknowledging differences between the sexes, co-equality provided the flexibility that "moral being" had given the Grimkés. The term upheld equal rights, but it also recognized the social reality of gender difference. (See Document 47.)

Abby Price's secular language reflected the adoption of perfectionist ideas in American public discourse, such as "the light of the nineteenth century" and "the progressive spirit of the age." What was once considered God's dispensation could now be viewed as human progress. This discourse broadened the appeal of women's rights and helped its language fit more easily into that used by men in legislative halls and political parties.

One difference between women and men that women's rights conventions sought to change was the inferior education of women. Advocates of women's co-equality had a difficult time asserting women's intellectual equality because differences in women's and men's education, especially in the middle and elite classes, meant that men commanded greater intellectual resources. Lucretia Mott wrote in a letter addressed to the Salem, Ohio, women's rights convention:

> Rights are not dependent upon equality of mind; nor do we admit inferiority; leaving that question to be settled by future developments, when a fair opportunity shall be given for the equal cultivation of the intellect, and the stronger powers of the mind shall be called into action.[132]

Women's conventions, like many women's social movements before and after the Civil War, served as educational venues as well as fostering social change. In this way they resembled black women's literary societies of the 1830s.

The women's rights convention movement drew support from the temperance movement because women's auxiliaries already formed a semi-autonomous women's temperance movement. In 1849, *The Lily,* a leading women's temperance periodical, offered a column on "Woman's Rights" that modelled the compatibility between the two movements. (See Document 46.) When the temperance movement rejected women as delegates to "Men's State Conventions" in 1852, and forced women to take their civic interests elsewhere, many attended women's rights conventions, which, in turn, often advocated antiliquor legislation. In the early 1850s Elizabeth Cady Stanton attended women's temperance conventions and frequently chaired meetings.[133]

In the early 1850s women's rights advocates, including Abby Kelley and Frederick Douglass, regularly introduced resolutions about black women's rights in women's rights conventions. A resolution on the rights of black women was noticeably absent from the 1848 Seneca Falls convention. Although Douglass praised that convention in *The North Star,* he did not comment on the absence of women of his own race. But the Rochester convention of 1848 explicitly called for women's equality without regard to "complexion." And a resolution adopted at Worcester in 1850 read:

> Resolved, That the cause we are met to advocate, — the claim for woman of all her natural and civil rights, — bids us remember the million and a half of slave women at the South, the most grossly wronged and foully outraged of all women; and in every effort for an improvement in our civilization, we will bear in our heart of hearts the memory of the trampled womanhood of the plantation, and omit no effort to raise it to a share in the rights we claim for ourselves.[134]

The resolution grimly reminded convention participants of the close association of women's rights with the antislavery movement.

Perhaps for that reason, it generated controversy. Jane Swisshelm (1815–1884), a leading abolitionist and for ten years the editor of Pittsburgh's only abolitionist newspaper, *The Saturday Visiter,* was also a strong supporter of women's rights. Her editorials in support of married women's property rights contributed to their enactment by the Pennsylvania legislature in 1848. Yet in a column about the Worcester convention she declared: "In a Woman's Rights Convention the question of color had no right to a hearing." Parker Pillsbury, a Garrisonian friend of Abby Kelley and Frederick Douglass, criticized Swisshelm's column in a letter to *The North Star.*[135] He admonished Swisshelm to remember that unless black women were specifically mentioned, they would not be thought of at the convention, and reminded her that "scarcely a colored person, man or woman, appeared" at the convention. (See Document 48.) Swisshelm replied that the issues of race and sex should be separated, arguing that the social status of women was set by the men of their class and race. (See Document 49.)

The only black woman who seems to have spoken in the women's rights convention movement was Sojourner Truth. Born around 1797 to enslaved parents on a New York estate and named Isabella, she bore five children fathered by a fellow enslaved person; one died and two were sold away. She ran away in 1827, the year before adult slaves were emancipated in New York state. At an early age she began to have mystical experiences that she identified as the voice of God. During the

1830s she supported herself and two children as a domestic worker in New York City. Responding to voices that told her to take the name "Sojourner Truth" and to travel and preach, she walked through New England and settled in Northampton, Massachusetts, where she joined Garrisonian abolitionists.[136]

Truth made her first documented public speech at the 1850 women's rights convention in Worcester. Speaking in the tradition of "biblical feminism," she encouraged women's public activism: "Woman set the world wrong by eating the forbidden fruit, and now she was going to set it right." On a perfectionist note, she added: "Goodness was from everlasting and would never die, while evil had a beginning and must come to an end." Mott's closing address to the convention warmly repeated Truth's words.[137] After staying for a few months with Amy Post in Rochester, Truth headed to Ohio to attend other women's rights conventions, making her headquarters at the offices of the *Anti-Slavery Bugle* in Salem, Ohio.

In her now-famous speech at the 1851 women's rights convention in Akron, Ohio, Sojourner Truth spoke as a woman who was "as strong as any man." (See Document 50.) Historians have concluded that the most accurate version of Truth's speech was printed in the *Anti-Slavery Bugle,* where it appeared shortly after the event. A more widely read version appeared in 1881 in *History of Woman Suffrage.* That text, edited by Matilda Joslyn Gage, included the famous passage "Ar'n't I a woman?" and was generally more dramatic and poetic. Sojourner Truth was one of the few black woman to attend antebellum women's rights conventions, and as a chronicler of the conventions Gage added dramatic emphasis to Truth's words. Gage's version of the speech became widely known in the 1970s and 1980s, another period when black women's rights resonated between the two movements of women's rights and black rights.[138]

Abby Kelley, Lucretia Mott, and Amy Post continued to support black women's rights in the women's rights convention movement, but black women put their energy into other venues. When Frederick Douglass was elected president of the National Negro Convention Movement in 1848, he sought to promote women's rights there by recruiting a fellow Rochester resident, Mrs. Sanford, to speak at that year's convention, held in Troy, New York, a few months after the Seneca Falls women's rights convention. Part of the convention culture of antebellum public life, the National Negro Convention Movement was founded in Philadelphia in 1830. William Lloyd Garrison attended the 1831 meeting and contributed to the group's orientation away from colonization and toward strengthening black communities in the North, which it did by encouraging education, temperance societies, and the collection of statistical information. In 1843 the movement diversified its antislavery stance by supporting the Liberty Party as well as Garrisonian moral suasion.[139]

Mrs. Sanford's speech reflected women's rights claims as they emerged in the antislavery movement and at Seneca Falls. Anchoring women's equality in religion, she mentioning the birth of Jesus as a liberating moment for women, and added in a more secular voice: "we ask for the Elective Franchise; for rights of property in the marriage covenant, whether earned or bequeathed." In closing, she allied with black men in their struggle to secure "an unqualified citizenship of the United States, and those inalienable rights granted you by an impartial Creator." (See Document 45.) Yet this experiment with a women's rights speaker was not continued in the National Negro Convention Movement. Advocacy of women's rights was not fully respectable and perhaps it conflicted with the National Negro Convention Movement's priority of promoting the respectability of the free black community and the "unqualified citizenship" of free black men.

African American women appeared more often as public speakers against slavery than as women's rights advocates. A good example was Lucy Stanton, who delivered the graduation address of her class at Oberlin College in 1850. Growing up in Cleveland when it was a village with few African Americans, she attended school with white children until a Baptist minister called for her expulsion. Her stepfather, John Brown, then created a school for black children. Brown, a barber and one of the wealthiest black men in Cleveland, was active in the underground railroad during Lucy's childhood, ferrying fugitive slaves across Lake Erie to Canada. At Oberlin, thirty miles away, she was converted to Christianity in a revival conducted by Charles Grandison Finney. With the support of a white antislavery friend, Lucy Stanton was elected president of the Oberlin Ladies Literary Society. And in 1850 she became the first African American woman to graduate from a four-year college. Her speech, "A Plea for the Oppressed," was delivered two weeks before the enactment of the Fugitive Slave Act, during a bleak moment of heightened struggle by the antislavery movement. Stanton emphasized a theme that dominated Weld's 1839 book, *Slavery as It Is*, and soon would become the main drama of Harriet Beecher Stowe's best-selling *Uncle Tom's Cabin*—the intense suffering of enslaved people when their family ties were denied. Stanton called on women to embrace the antislavery cause and predicted: "the arm of the Lord is mighty to save those who trust in him. Truth and right must prevail. The bondsman shall go free." (See Document 51.) After graduation Stanton married and did not continue public speaking.[140]

Although the antislavery movement's campaign against racial prejudice did not continue in the women's rights convention movement, what Angelina Grimké called the "great moral enterprise" of the Moral Reform Society did. Although the Grimkés and other rights activists used euphuisms to refer to ending male control of women's bodies, tributes to moral reform appeared frequently in the rights convention proceedings. Resolution six at Seneca Falls declared: "That the same amount of virtue, delicacy, and refinement of behavior, that is required of woman in the social state, should also be required of man, and the same transgressions should be visited with equal severity on both man and woman." (See Document 44; for other references to moral reform, see Documents 19, 20, 28, 35, and 51.) Along with married women's property rights and temperance, the reshaping of sexual relations between men and women in courtship and marriage were connected to the transition from traditional to modern relationships in family life. These changes made women's rights relevant to the daily lives of most middle-class women.[141]

Fundamental to these changes was a long-term decline in birth rates between 1830 and 1940—among all classes, ethnic groups, and races. This decline bridged the transition between traditional and modern patterns of human reproduction. Called the "demographic transition from high birth and death rates to low birth and death rates," it changed the lives of women profoundly but it has not been extensively studied by historians of women. Declining birth rates meant that, on the average, white, US-born women gave birth to half as many children in 1900 as they did in 1800—3.5 instead of 7—enabling women to give less of their own lives to the life of the species. Giving birth less often, they also reduced their risk of dying from childbirth-related causes. Eventually affecting all modernizing societies, this drop was especially dramatic in the United States because birth rates there were higher than in other nations in 1800 and by 1940 fell lower than most others. Two-thirds of this decrease was accomplished by 1880, before the widespread use of contraceptives; the chief methods were sexual abstinence or *coitus interruptus*. Since the greatest declines occurred between 1840 and 1860, when American society was still overwhelmingly rural, falling birth rates were not caused by industrialization or urbanization. Instead, this remarkable event in human history was achieved by individuals deciding to exercise more control over their destinies by controlling their reproductive lives.[142]

A good example of the Victorian attitudes that reduced sexual activity was Sylvester Graham's 1839 book, *Letters to Young Men,* which, along with dietary recommendations, explained that the expenditure of sperm weakened the male body. He advised limiting the frequency of intercourse to twelve times a year.[143] Elizabeth Stanton seems to have welcomed the "Graham system" on her honeymoon. She wrote the Grimké sisters that Henry, on their voyage to England, attributed "his freedom from seasickness to *his strict observance of the Graham system*" (her emphasis). (See Document 42.) More than Henry's diet was probably involved here.

The "Graham system" and other methods of birth control often produced lengthy intervals between births — generating birth-rate declines in the lives of individual women. Elizabeth Stanton had more children than most of her contemporaries (her eighth and last child was born in 1859) but like many other women of her generation, she created one extraordinarily long birth interval. After giving birth to three boys at traditional intervals of approximately two years, she maintained a five-and-a-half-year interval between 1845 and 1851.[144] During that time she located herself in American public life. Like Harriet Beecher Stowe, who self-consciously maintained a birth interval of six years between 1843 and 1849, during which she established herself as a writer, Stanton resumed bearing children after 1851, integrating them into a life in which they were not the sole symbols of her creativity.[145]

Yet not all men were as modern as Henry Stanton. In many marriages women took the initiative to reduce the frequency of intercourse and thereby increase the intervals between births. Women's ability to control their own bodies and turn away from their husbands' sexual desires marked the dawn of a new era. Victorian sexual ideology supported women's control of their bodies, but that ideology was not established without a struggle. Members of the American Female Moral Reform Society reshaped sexual relations in the vanguard of that struggle with branches in almost every city, town, and village in New England and New York in the 1840s.[146] Most visibly, their campaign against prostitution condemned predatory male sexuality and created institutional support for women to escape prostitution. (See Document 35.)

By the 1850s these changing sexual mores sustained the careers of an array of professionals. The Reverend Henry Clarke Wright, the Grimkés' advance man in Massachusetts, was one of these. Leaving the abolitionist movement in 1849, he joined the Hopedale Community and began a new career lecturing on "marital abuse" and other topics related to the new family order that promoted women's control of marital sexuality. His 1858 book, *Marriage and Parentage; or, the Reproductive Element in*

Man, as a Means to His Elevation and Happiness, aggressively defended married women's rights to control reproduction.[147] In 1838 Sarah Grimké touched on this issue when she referred to the "vast amount of secret suffering endured, from the forced submission of women to the opinions and whims of their husbands."[148] At the national Negro convention in 1848, Mrs. Sanford spoke of pre-Christian women being "the slave of power and passion." (See Document 45.) Lucy Stanton spoke of the "passions" that slavery fostered, making virtue in a slave "a sin counted worthy of death." (See Document 51.) Wright continued these themes in other books—*The Unwelcome Child* (1858) and *The Empire of the Mother over the Character and Destiny of the Race* (1863). These widespread changes in women's possession of their bodies established a personal foundation in their lives that led many to support other forms of women's rights.

The antislavery origins of the women's rights movement of the 1850s was most visible and perhaps most enduring in women's identification with the term "human rights." Angelina Grimké frequently referred to women's "human rights" (see Documents 27, 31, and 32), and Henry Clarke Wright defended women's "human rights" within the AASS (see Document 41). A Seneca Falls resolution referred to "the equality of human rights." (See Document 44.) Perhaps the intersection of multiple forms of rights—freedom from liquor-induced violence; property rights for married women; divorce rights; child custody rights; bodily integrity; and the right to education—made the trope of "human rights" especially relevant to the new movement. "Human rights" became an essential ingredient in the discourse at women's rights conventions. At the 1860 convention in New York City, the "phonographic" transcriber noted audience reactions when one participant declared: "the Women's Rights movement lies deeper than a movement of one sex—it is the Human Rights movement. (A voice—'that's it.') —for one sex cannot be benefitted without benefitting the other. (Cheers.)"[149]

FRANCES ELLEN WATKINS SPEAKS FOR THE AMERICAN ANTI-SLAVERY SOCIETY, 1854–1860

In 1854, when Frances Ellen Watkins began her career as an antislavery lecturer, the abolition movement was being transformed by political events. The Fugitive Slave Act turned the entire United States into slave territory. The "popular sovereignty" principle of the Kansas-Nebraska Act confirmed that the slave or free status of those states would be determined by the armed struggle already underway there, fueled by the commitment of southern leaders to expand "the empire of cotton."

MRS. FRANCIS E. W. HARPER.

See p. 755.

Figure 2. *Portrait of Frances Ellen Watkins Harper.*
Frances Ellen Watkins Harper, a leading abolitionist lecturer to black and racially mixed audiences on the eve of the Civil War, resumed lecturing after the war, emphasizing the need for education, temperance, and family renewal among former slaves. She was outspoken in denouncing racism and violence.
Library of Congress, Prints & Photographs Division, Reproduction number LC-USZ62-75978 (b&w film copy neg.)

Also transformative was the 1852 publication of *Uncle Tom's Cabin; or Life among the Lowly.* The book's focus on anguish in the lives of enslaved families dramatized themes that had appeared in antislavery literature since the 1830s, but that now also drew white readers into the story and led them to identify with that suffering, widely personalizing and popularizing antislavery sentiment.[150]

Speaking as a black woman with a personal knowledge of slavery, and as a poet as well as a lecturer, Frances Ellen Watkins embodied the new antislavery perspective of the 1850s. Local chapters of the American Anti-Slavery Society increasingly represented mainstream opinion in their communities. Nationally the society still brought those communities the most compelling antislavery speakers, now a gifted black woman. Frances Ellen Watkins left her uncle's home in Baltimore at the age of twenty-five in 1850, when the Fugitive Slave Act made the kidnapping of free blacks and their sale as slaves even easier. She worked as a teacher in Ohio and Pennsylvania for three years. Then Maryland law prohibited free blacks from traveling in the state on pain of being imprisoned and sold into slavery, and Watkins learned of the kidnapping and death of a free man who violated this statute; she wrote to a friend: "Upon that grave I pledged myself to the Anti-Slavery Cause." She sought employment as a speaker with the antislavery society in Philadelphia, and when they were slow to respond, she traveled to Boston, where Garrison befriended her and sponsored her appearance at New Bedford — in William Still's words, "the hot bed of the fugitives" in Massachusetts.[151] Most of what we know about Frances Ellen Watkins before 1860 comes from William Still, underground railroad leader in Philadelphia. But we also know that her uncle, William Watkins, in 1853 addressed the Massachusetts state legislative "Committee on the Militia," on behalf of sixty-five "colored petitioners" who wanted "to form an independent military company."[152] Titled "Our Rights as Men," his speech modeled the militancy that his niece adopted in her antislavery lectures for the AASS.

From 1854 to 1860, Frances Ellen Watkins became one of the society's most effective lecturers. Like Angelina Grimké twenty years earlier, she was a compelling speaker whose words carried the added grace of a skilled author. Watkins supported herself as the author of popular poetry books, which she sold at speaking engagements, beginning in 1854 with *Poems of Miscellaneous Subjects*. In letters to William Still, which he excerpted in his 1872 book, she described her public speaking. (See Document 52.) Six hundred attended an 1854 lecture she gave in Providence, Rhode Island. The Maine antislavery society took good care of her while she travelled in that state. Writing and speaking about Free Produce, she exclaimed, "Oh, could slavery exist long if it did not sit on a commercial throne?" Her first view of Canada inspired thoughts about "a land where a poor slave flying from our glorious land of liberty would in a moment find his fetters broken." (See Document 52.) Her 1858 poem, "Bury Me in a Free Land," conveys the power and vision of her language. (See Document 53.) In and around Sandusky, Ohio, Watkins spoke "to an immense audience, with the best effect," as T. R. Davis, secretary of the local antislavery society, wrote Garrison. He continued: "The effect of these lectures upon this part of the country cannot but be most favorable, not only politically, but in dispelling this unreasoning and unreasonable prejudice against the colored people of the country." Arousing support that resembled the response to Angelina Grimké's lectures twenty years earlier, Frances Watkins challenged racial prejudice in ways that were not possible in the 1830s. After Watkins's last lecture, those in attendance composed and adopted resolutions that they sent to Garrison, asking him to publish them. These resolutions conveyed the intensity of antislavery opinion in the region, which would soon send sons to fight and die in the Civil War. One resolution called slavery a "barefaced outrage upon human rights." The document concluded with a resolution praising Watkins: "That it is with feelings of the deepest respect and gratitude, that we regard this timely visit of Miss Watkins to our township, to tell us of the wrongs of the slave, and to increase our zeal and determination to act vigorously and decidedly our part in the truly 'irrepressible conflict' between Freedom and Slavery." (See Document 54.)

By providing a platform for talented women speakers from 1836 to 1860, the Garrisonian antislavery movement brought women into the mainstream of American political culture, sponsoring their voices at political gatherings, where they did much to define the life and death issues of the day. William Nell described the change in a letter to Garrison in 1852: "The seeds sown by you at a time when the public was indifferent have germinated, and now promise an abundant harvest. The fact of woman's equal participation in the lecture room, in the halls of science, and other departments hitherto monopolized by man, has become an every day occurrence."[153] By the late 1850s that change included black women.

WOMEN'S RIGHTS ORGANIZATIONS STRUGGLE WITH RACE IN AMERICAN SOCIETY, 1865–1870

No women's rights conventions were held during the conflagration of Civil War from 1861 to 1865. In 1863 Elizabeth Cady Stanton and Susan B. Anthony organized the Women's Loyal National League, which presented a petition with 400,000 signatures to the U.S. Senate urging the abolition of slavery by a constitutional amendment.[154] In 1866, at the first women's rights convention after the war, women's rights activists formed the American Equal Rights Association (AERA) to continue the antebellum solidarity between women's rights and abolition and to promote universal suffrage—suffrage for black men as well as all women.

At the 1867 meeting of the AERA, Lucretia Mott, its president, looked back on twenty years of women's growing public power. "In the temperance reformation, and in the great reformatory movements of our age, woman's powers have been called into action," she said. "They are beginning to see that another state of things is possible for them, and they are beginning to demand their rights." Noting that they were meeting in one of the wealthiest and most prestigious churches in America—the Church of the Pilgrims in Brooklyn Heights—Mott asked, "Why should this church be granted for such a meeting as this, but for the progress of the cause? Why are so many present, ready to respond to the most ultra and most radical sentiments here, but that woman has grown and is able to assume her rights?" What had been "ultra" and "radical" in the 1830s had almost become respectable by 1867.

Racial differences and animosities were evident in New York City in 1866, at the first post-war women's rights convention. There Frances Ellen Watkins Harper was the most prominent black woman speaker. Watkins had married in 1860 and retired from public life until 1864, when her husband died; she returned to activism as a means of self-support. Watkins Harper recognized the need for black women's rights, but also spoke truth to the power of white women, declaring: "If there is any class of people who need to be lifted out of their airy nothings and selfishness, it is the white women of America." Speaking for the needs of black men, Harper referred to the Dred Scott decision of the U.S. Supreme Court, which in 1857 had found that "men of my race had no rights which the white man was bound to respect." (See Document 55.) This court decision showed her the urgent need for federal protection of the rights of black men. The Fourteenth Amendment to the U.S. Constitution, then being debated in Congress and ultimately ratified in 1868, would be the means by which the Dred Scott decision was overturned and the rights of black men guaranteed. It would also be the means by which the word "male" was first embedded into the Constitution.[155]

Participants in that 1866 convention overcame their differences to create the American Equal Rights Association (AERA), dedicated to universal suffrage and to the support of both black and woman suffrage. Yet at the 1869 meeting of the AERA, the cross-race coalition foundered when debate produced a logjam of disagreement rather than a basis for future cooperation. Competing referenda on woman suffrage and black suffrage in Kansas in 1867 had set those two constituencies against one another; the ratification of the Fourteenth Amendment in 1868, which guaranteed citizenship rights to "male" residents of states, deepened the antagonism. In February 1869, Congress had passed the Fifteenth Amendment, which explicitly enfranchised black men, and that spring the amendment was in the process of being ratified by the states. Stanton and Anthony opposed the amendment; Douglass, Harper, and Stone supported it. Speakers in this debate seem to have realized that their disagreements marked the demise of the AERA.[156] (See Document 56.)

This debate was largely framed in terms of the opposing claims of "the woman" and "the black man." For Frederick Douglass the needs of black women were absorbed into those of black people. Black women were oppressed, he argued, not because they were women, but because they were black. Lucy Stone added that one great ocean of wrong engulfed "the black man," another engulfed "the woman." Paulina Davis, who organized the Worcester women's rights convention in 1850, called for a Sixteenth Amendment that would protect black women in the South against "a race of tyrants raised above her." Elizabeth Cady Stanton argued against enfranchising "ignorant negroes and foreigners" until women were admitted to the polls. Frances Harper commented that "the white women all go for sex, letting race occupy a minor position." Susan Anthony opposed the Fifteenth Amendment because it would put black men "in position of tyrants over" black women "who had until now been the equals of the men at their side." (See Document 56.)

In 1881 the editors of *History of Woman Suffrage* concluded that these debates "proved the futility of any attempt to discuss the wrongs of different classes in one association." (See Document 57.) Although this statement meant to point to the differences between "black men" and "women," it also suggested that differences between black women and white women were too large to be encompassed by one organization at that time in the United States.

In 1869 two woman suffrage organizations were created. The National Woman Suffrage Association, located in New York and headed by Elizabeth Cady Stanton and Susan B. Anthony, opposed the Fifteenth Amendment. The American Woman Suffrage Association, headquartered in Boston and led by Elizabeth Blackwell and Lucy Stone, supported the amendment. Differences between the two groups were finally overcome in 1890, when they united to form the National American Woman Suffrage Association.

After 1869, Sojourner Truth affiliated with Elizabeth Cady Stanton and the National Woman Suffrage Association, and Frances Watkins Harper joined Lucy Stone and the American Woman Suffrage Association.[157] Harper, Lucy Stanton, Sojourner Truth, and other black women activists exemplified the importance of voting rights as part of a larger freedom struggle, which after 1870 meant that their goals were often best advanced by separate black women's suffrage associations, such as the Alpha Suffrage Club, founded by Ida B. Wells-Barnett in Chicago in 1913.[158]

The women's rights movement did not resolve large questions generated by racial prejudice in American society. Just as the "woman question" split the antislavery movement in the late 1830s, so the race question split the women's rights movement in the late 1860s. These fractures reflected important aspects of American civil society. Also significant were the forces that forged coalitions across race differences. Women's rights arose within a relatively small group of women and men who interacted across race differences and expressed a moment of high idealism in American public life. Aspects of that idealism persisted in the movement and drew others into it. What began in the 1830s moved forward into the 1870s as a vital characteristic of American society: the mobilization of women—black and white—within organizations that sought to shape the public life of their communities and their nation.

NOTES

[1] The term "woman's rights" was used more frequently in the nineteenth century than "women's rights," but the preferred twentieth-century term is "women's rights."

[2] See Catherine Anne Brekus, *Strangers and Pilgrims: Female Preaching in America, 1740–1845* (Chapel Hill: University of North Carolina Press, 1998), 7.

[3] See Norma Basch, *In the Eyes of the Law: Women, Marriage, and Property in Nineteenth-Century New York* (Ithaca: Cornell University Press, 1982).

[4] For overviews of the history of antislavery in the United States, see Manisha Sinha, *The Slave's Cause: A History of Abolition* (New Haven: Yale University Press, 2017).

[5] See Kathryn Kish Sklar, "'Women Who Speak for an Entire Nation': American and British Women at the World Anti-Slavery Convention, London, 1840," in *The Abolitionist Sisterhood: Women's Political Culture in Antebellum America,* ed. Jean Fagan Yellin and John C. Van Horne (Ithaca: Cornell University Press, 1994).

[6] See Daniel S. Wright, *"The First of Causes to Our Sex": The Female Moral Reform Movement in the Antebellum Northeast, 1834–1848* (New York: Routledge, 2006).

[7] See John R. McKivigan, *The War against Proslavery Religion: Abolitionism and the Northern Churches, 1830–1865* (Ithaca: Cornell University Press, 1984); and John Ashworth, *Slavery, Capitalism, and Politics in the Antebellum Republic: Vol. 1: Commerce and Compromise, 1820–1850* (New York: Cambridge University Press, 1995), 365.

[8] Brief biographies of Angelina and Sarah Grimké (hereafter AG and SG) and most other women mentioned in this essay can be found in Edward James et al., eds., *Notable American Women: A Biographical Dictionary* (Cambridge, MA: Harvard University Press, 1971). See also footnote 14 below.

[9] "Testimony of Angelina Grimké Weld," in *American Slavery as It Is: Testimony of a Thousand Witnesses,* ed. Theodore D. Weld (New York: American Anti-Slavery Society, 1839), 54–55.

[10]Large portions from AG's diary have been printed in Catherine H. Birney, *The Grimké Sisters: Sarah and Angelina Grimké: The First American Women Advocates of Abolition and Women's Rights* (Philadelphia: Lee and Shepard, 1885), 55–93. The treatment of slaves in the Grimké household can be inferred from passages in "Testimony of Angelina Grimké Weld" and "Narrative and Testimony of Sarah M. Grimké," in Weld, *American Slavery as It Is,* 52–57 and 22–24.

[11]AG, diary entry, June 12, 1828, in Weld-Grimké Family Papers (hereafter WGFP), William L. Clements Library. In the 1840s Henry moved to the plantation with Nancy Weston, an enslaved woman and Henry's common law wife, with whom he had three children. One child, Archibald Grimké, graduated from Harvard Law School and authored an early biography of Garrison, *William Lloyd Garrison: the Abolitionist* (New York: Funk & Wangalls, 1891).

[12]See John Lofton, *Denmark Vesey's Revolt: The Slave Plot That Lit a Fuse to Fort Sumter* (Kent, Ohio: Kent State University Press, 1983).

[13]See Matthew Karp, *This Vast Southern Empire: Slaveholders at the Helm of American Foreign Policy* (Cambridge, MA: Harvard University Press, 2016).

[14]This interpretation of the Grimké sisters draws on my research in primary materials, especially the Weld-Grimké Family Papers. It builds on but is not the same as interpretations found in Birney, *The Grimké Sisters;* Gerda Lerner, *The Grimké Sisters of North Carolina: Pioneers for Women's Rights and Abolitionism* (New York: Oxford, 1967); Gerda Lerner, *The Feminist Thought of Sarah Grimké* (New York: Oxford, 1998); Katharine DePre Lumpkin, *The Emancipation of Angelina Grimké* (Chapel Hill: University of North Carolina Press, 1974); and Larry Ceplair, ed., *The Public Years of Sarah and Angelina Grimké: Selected Writings, 1835–1839* (New York: Columbia University Press, 1989).

[15]See Nathan O. Hatch, *The Democratization of American Christianity* (New Haven: Yale University Press, 1989); and Kathryn Kish Sklar, *Catharine Beecher: A Study in American Domesticity* (New Haven: Yale University Press, 1973).

[16]The literature on this topic is vast. See Robert H. Abzug, *Cosmos Crumbling: American Reform and the Religious Imagination* (New York: Oxford, 1994).

[17]For the power of religious motives in the sisters' lives, see Kathryn Kish Sklar, "'The Throne of My Heart:' Religion, Oratory, and Transatlantic Community in Angelina Grimké's Launching of Women's Rights, 1828–1838," in *Women's Rights and Transatlantic Antislavery in the Era of Emancipation,* ed. Kathryn Kish Sklar and James Brewer Stewart (New Haven: Yale University Press, 2007).

[18]Quakers led the way in the abolition of slavery in the North. In 1758 the Philadelphia Yearly Meeting of the Society of Friends voted to exclude anyone who bought or sold slaves; in 1776 it excluded anyone who owned slaves. Between 1780 and 1800 most Northern states enacted statutes that abolished slavery, though this was usually accomplished gradually. The Pennsylvania "Act for the Gradual Abolition of Slavery" of 1780 immediately emancipated all children born after 1780, but emancipated adults more gradually. See "Abolition Statutes" in Robert H. Bremner et al., eds., *Children and Youth in America: A Documentary History, 1: 1600–1865* (Cambridge, MA: Harvard University Press, 1970), 324–26. In 1830 about 3,500 persons remained in bondage in the North, mostly in New Jersey. See Leon F. Litwack, *North of Slavery: The Negro in the Free States, 1790–1860* (Chicago: University of Chicago Press, 1961), 12–14.

[19]Lumpkin, *Emancipation of Angelina Grimké,* 20.

[20]AG to Elizabeth Bascom, July 23, 1828; and AG to (her sister) Mrs. Anna Frost, March 17, 1828, both in WGFP.

[21]Lerner, *The Grimké Sisters of North Carolina,* 54; Sylvia R. Frey and Betty Wood, *Come Shouting to Zion: African-American Protestantism in the American South and British Caribbean to 1830* (Chapel Hill: University of North Carolina Press, 1998), 182–208.

[22]Although AG later claimed that antislavery motivations impelled her departure from South Carolina, the historical evidence supports a more gradual evolution of her antislavery views.

[23]The sisters' economic independence came from their father's 1818 will, which provided four thousand dollars to each daughter, while sons received that amount plus property. Providing cash rather than land, the gendered discrimination in their father's will did make it easier for the sisters to leave South Carolina. Although the sisters were affiliated with the Free Produce movement, they did not disown this economic support from slave labor. For this contradiction in the lives of contemporary reformers, see Carol Lasser, "Conscience and Contradiction: The Moral Ambiguities of Antebellum Reformers Marcus and Rebecca Buffum Spring," *Journal of the Early Republic* 38 (Spring 2018), 1–35.

[24]For women's spiritual leadership within Quakerism, see Janis Calvo, "Quaker Women Ministers in Nineteenth Century America," *Quaker History* 63, no. 2 (1974): 75–93; and Margaret Hope Bacon, *Mothers of Feminism: The Story of Quaker Women in America* (New York: Harper, 1986).

[25]See Thomas D. Hamm, *The Transformation of American Quakerism: Orthodox Friends, 1800–1907* (Bloomington: Indiana University Press, 1988).

[26]AG to Thomas Grimké (1829); and AG to SG (1836), quoted in Birney, *Grimké Sisters,* 91 and 137.

[27]Another young person who emerged from a moratorium to change society is studied in Erik Erikson, *Young Man Luther* (New York: Norton, 1958).

[28]For the pivotal importance of religion in the birth of immediatism as a social movement, see David Brion Davis, "The Emergence of Immediatism in British and American Antislavery Thought," *Mississippi Valley Historical Review* 49, no. 2 (Sept. 1962), 209–230.

[29]For Garrison and *The Liberator,* see William E. Cain, ed., *William Lloyd Garrison and the Fight against Slavery: Selections from The Liberator* (Boston: Bedford Books, 1995); and Abzug, *Cosmos Crumbling,* 129–62. For Mott, see Beverly Wilson Palmer, ed., *Selected Letters of Lucretia Coffin Mott* (Urbana: University of Illinois Press, 2002); and Carol Faulkner, *Lucretia Mott's Heresy: Abolition and Women's Rights in Nineteenth-Century America* (Philadelphia: University of Pennsylvania Press, 2011).

[30]See Ira V. Brown, "Cradle of Feminism: The Philadelphia Female Anti-Slavery Society, 1833–1840," *Pennsylvania Magazine of History and Biography* 102 (April 1978), 142–166.

[31]Eric Burin, *Slavery and the Peculiar Solution: A History of the American Colonization Society* (Gainesville: University of Florida Press, 2005). The Colonization project attracted the support of some free black men, but few free black women. See Bruce Dorsey, "A Gendered History of African Colonization in the Antebellum United States," *Journal of Social History* 34 (Fall 2000), 77–103.

[32]Mary Beth McQueeny, "Simeon Jocelyn, New Haven Reformer," *New Haven Colony Historical Society Journal* 19, no. 3 (1970): 63–68.

[33]Litwack, *North of Slavery,* 75; Eric Ledell Smith, "The End of Black Voting Rights in Pennsylvania: African Americans and the Pennsylvania Constitutional Convention of 1837–1838," *Pennsylvania History* 65, no. 3 (Summer 1989), 279–299.

[34]See Julie Winch, *Between Slavery and Freedom: Free People of Color in America from Settlement to the Civil War* (Lanham, MD: Rowman & Littlefield, 2014); and Don E. Fehrenbacher, *The Dred Scott Case Its Significance in American Law and Politics* (New York: Oxford, 1978).

[35]Gerda Lerner, "The Grimké Sisters and the Struggle against Race Prejudice," *Journal of Negro History* 26 (October 1963): 277–91; and Carolyn L. Karcher, ed., *A Lydia Maria Child Reader* (Durham, N.C.: Duke University Press, 1997).

³⁶[William Watkins], "Colored Baltimorian," *Freedom's Journal*, September 28, 1827, and October 5, 1827, quoted in R. J. M. Blackett, *Building an Antislavery Wall: Black Americans in the Atlantic Abolitionist Movement, 1830–1860* (Baton Rouge: Louisiana State University Press, 1983), 150–151. See also Jacqueline Bacon, *Freedom's Journal: The First African-American Newspaper* (Lanham, MD: Lexington Books, 2007). In 1820 the free black population nationally numbered 230,000. By 1860 that number had doubled. The enslaved population more than doubled during those decades, increasing from 1,538,038 to 3,953,760, or 150 percent. Due to immigration, the white population increased even more, from almost 8 million in 1820 to almost 26 million in 1860, an increase of more than 300 percent. https://www.census.gov/history/www/through _the_decades/overview/1860.html.

³⁷Porter, *Early Negro Writing,* 200–215; and Erica L. Ball, *To Live an Antislavery Life: Personal Politics and the Antebellum Black Middle Class* (Athens: University of Georgia Press, 2012), 100; and Howard H. Bell, "The American Moral Reform Society, 1836–1841," *Journal of Negro Education* 27, no. 1 (Winter 1958), 34–40. [Not to be confused with the Female Moral Reform Society.] For Frances Watkins's childhood, see Melba Joyce Boyd, *Discarded Legacy: Politics and Poetics in the Life of Frances E. W. Harper, 1825–1911* (Detroit: Wayne State University Press, 1994), 33–40. See also Frances Smith Foster, "Introduction," in *A Brighter Coming Day: A Frances Ellen Watkins Harper Reader* (New York: Feminist Press, 1990), 5–8; and Bettye Collier-Thomas, "Frances Ellen Watkins Harper: Abolitionist and Feminist Reformer, 1825–1911," in Ann D. Gordon, et al., *African American Women and the Vote, 1837–1965* (Amherst: University of Massachusetts Press, 1997), 41–65.

³⁸For more on antebellum black women's organizations, see Teresa Zackodnik, *Press, Platform, Pulpit: Black Feminist Publics in the Era of Reform* (Knoxville: University of Tennessee Press, 2011); Gayle T. Tate, *Unknown Tongues: Black Women's Political Activism in the Antebellum Eras, 1830–1860* (East Lansing: Michigan State University Press, 2003); Shirley J. Yee, *Black Women Abolitionists: A Study in Activism, 1828–1860* (Knoxville: University of Tennessee Press, 1992); and Anne M. Boylan, "Benevolence and Antislavery Activity among African American Women in New York and Boston, 1820–1840, in *Abolitionist Sisterhood,* ed. Yellin and Van Horne.

³⁹Dorothy B. Porter, "The Organized Educational Activities of Negro Literary Societies, 1828–1846," *Journal of Negro Education* 5, No. 4 (Oct. 1936), 557–58; Elizabeth McHenry, *Forgotten Readers: Recovering the Lost History of African American Literary Societies* (Durham: Duke University Press, 2002), 57–83; and Marie Lindhorst, "Politics in a Box: Sarah Mapps Douglass and the Female Literary Association, 1831–1833," *Pennsylvania History* 65, no. 3 (Summer 1998), 263–278. The equivalent forging of gendered social identities for white women occurred in local meetings of the American Female Moral Reform Society, which problematized sexual relations rather than race.

⁴⁰Margaret Hope Bacon, "New Light on Sarah Mapps Douglass and Her Reconciliation with Friends," *Quaker History* 90, No. 1 (Spring 2001), 28–49.

⁴¹Kidnapping of free blacks, see Carol Wilson, *Freedom at Risk: The Kidnapping of Free Blacks in America, 1780–1865* (Lexington: University of Kentucky Press, 1994).

⁴²For the liminal quality of black women's activism in literary societies, see Carla L. Peterson, *"Doers of the Word": African-American Women Speakers and Writers in the North,* 1830–1880 (New York: Oxford, 1995), 17–23. See also Ball, *To Live an Antislavery Life,* 62–80.

⁴³See Marilyn Richardson, ed., *Maria W. Stewart, America's First Black Woman Political Writer: Essays and Speeches* (Bloomington: University of Indiana Press, 1987); and Peterson, *Doers of the Word,* 56–73.

⁴⁴James Oliver Horton and Lois E. Horton, *Black Bostonians: Family Life and Community Struggle in the Antebellum North* (New York: Holmes and Meyer, 1979),

70–71, 88–89, 96; and Peter Hinks, *To Awaken My Afflicted Brethren: David Walker and the Problem of Antebellum Slave Resistance* (University Park: Pennsylvania State University Press, 1996).

[45]William Lloyd Garrison to Maria W. Stewart, quoted in Richardson, *Maria W. Stewart,* 11.

[46]Letter from William Cooper Nell to William Lloyd Garrison, Feb. 19, 1852, published in *Liberator,* March 5, 1852. Portions excerpted in Richardson, *Maria W. Stewart,* 90. Nell was the author of *Services of Colored Americans in the Wars of 1776 and 1812* (1851); and *The Colored Patriots of the American Revolution* (1855). See Patrick R. J. Browne, "'To Defend Mr. Garrison': William Cooper Nell and the Personal Politics of Antislavery," *New England Quarterly* 70, no. 3 (Sept. 1997), 415–442.

[47]Maria W. Stewart, *Productions of Mrs. Maria W. Stewart, Presented to the First African Baptist Church and Society of the City of Boston* (Boston: Friends of Freedom and Virtue, 1835). Letter from Alexander Crummell, 1879, quoted in Richardson, *Maria W. Stewart,* 94.

[48]For the abolition of slavery by Parliament, see Clare Midgley, *Women against Slavery: The British Campaigns, 1780–1870* (London: Routledge, 1992). See also Seymour Drescher, "Women's Mobilization in the Era of Slave Emancipation: Some Anglo-French Comparisons," in Sklar and Stewart, *Women's Rights and Transatlantic Antislavery.*

[49]A Member of the Boston Female Anti-Slavery Society, "Ladies' Department," *Liberator,* October 24, 1835. See also Wendell Phillips Garrison and Francis Jackson Garrison, *William Lloyd Garrison, 1805–1879; the Story of His Life Told by His Children* (Boston: Houghton, Mifflin, 1894), 15–16; James Brewer Stewart, *Holy Warriors: The Abolitionists and American Slavery* (New York: Hill and Wang, 1997); and Leonard L. Richards, *"Gentlemen of Property and Standing": Anti-Abolition Mobs in Jacksonian America* (New York: Oxford, 1970). For the destabilizing influence of British emancipation on Southern cotton producers, see Karp, *This Vast Southern Empire,* 17.

[50]William Lloyd Garrison, *Thoughts on African Colonization: or an impartial exhibition of the doctrines, principles and purposes of the American Colonization Society, together with the resolutions, addresses and remonstraces of the free people of color* (Boston: Garrison and Knapp, 1832), 142–143.

[51]Bertram Wyatt-Brown, "The Abolitionists' Postal Campaign of 1835," *Journal of Negro History* 50 (Oct. 1963): 227–38.

[52]AG to William Lloyd Garrison, Aug. 30, 1835, printed in *Liberator,* Sept. 19, 1835; also in Ceplair, *The Public Years,* 24–27, quote 26. For AG's state of mind, see AG to SG, Sept. 27, 1835, quoted in Birney, *Grimké Sisters,* 127.

[53]Diary of SG, Sept. 25, 1835; and AG to SG, Sept. 27, 1835, both quoted in Birney, *Grimké Sisters,* 128–29.

[54]Richard John, "Taking Sabbatarianism Seriously: The Postal System, the Sabbath, and the Transformation of American Political Culture," *Journal of the Early Republic* 10 (1990): 517–67; Mary Hershberger, "Mobilizing Women, Anticipating Abolition: The Struggle against Indian Removal in the 1830s," *Journal of American History* 86, no. 1 (June 1999): 15–40; Kathryn Kish Sklar, "How Did the Removal of the Cherokee Nation from Georgia Shape Women's Activism in the North, 1817–1838," online in *Women and Social Movements in the United States,* Vol. 8 (June 2004).

[55]Garrison and Garrison, *William Lloyd Garrison,* 482. For the growth of women's antislavery societies, see Beth A. Salerno, *Sister Societies: Women's Antislavery Organizations in Antebellum America* (DeKalb: Northern Illinois University Press, 2005); Debra Gold Hansen, *Strained Sisterhood: Gender and Class in the Boston Female Anti-Slavery Society* (Amherst: University of Massachusetts Press, 1993); and Blanche Glassman

Hersh, *The Slavery of Sex: Feminist-Abolitionists in America* (Urbana: University of Illinois Press, 1978.

[56]For the petition campaign, see Susan Zaeske, *Signatures of Citizenship: Petitioning, Antislavery, and Women's Political Identity* (Chapel Hill: University of North Carolina Press, 2003); Gerda Lerner, "The Political Activities of Antislavery Women," in Lerner, *The Majority Finds Its Past: Placing Women in History* (New York: Oxford, 1979); and Deborah Bingham Van Broekhoven, "'Let Your Names Be Enrolled': Method and Ideology in Women's Antislavery Petitioning," in *Abolitionist Sisterhood,* ed. Yellin and Van Horne.

[57]Theodore Weld's later account, quoted in Birney, *Grimké Sisters,* 149.

[58]AG to SG (Shrewsbury, Summer 1836), quoted in Birney, *Grimké Sisters,* 141. See also Stanley Harrold, *The Abolitionists and the South, 1831–1861* (Lexington: University Press of Kentucky, 1995).

[59]Diary of Sarah Grimké, Aug. 3, 1836; and AG to SG, n.d., both quoted in Birney, *Grimké Sisters,* 144–45.

[60]AG to Jane Smith, Nov. 11, 1836; and AG to Jane Smith, Nov. 1836, both quoted in Birney, *Grimké Sisters,* 159.

[61]Sarah Forten's niece, Charlotte Forten, kept a diary of her antebellum life in Philadelphia and postbellum work among freedmen in the South: Ray Allen Billington, ed., *The Journal of Charlotte L. Forten* (New York: Macmillan, 1961). In 1878 Charlotte married Francis Grimké, who was the son of AG and SG's brother, Henry Grimké, and Nancy Weston, an enslaved woman with whom he lived as his wife. See footnote 11 above.

[62]See Ira V. Brown, "'Am I Not a Woman and a Sister?' The Anti-Slavery Convention of American Women, 1837–1839," *Pennsylvania History: A Journal of Mid-Atlantic Studies* 50, no. 1 (January 1983), 1–19.

[63]The full proceedings of the convention have been published as *Turning the World Upside Down: The Anti-Slavery Convention of American Women, Held in New York City, May 9–12, 1837* (New York: Feminist Press, 1987). For the online proceedings of all three women's antislavery conventions, see "Women and Antislavery Outline," in *Women and Social Movements in the United States.*

[64]Quoted in Dorothy Sterling, *Ahead of Her Time: Abby Kelley and the Politics of Antislavery* (New York: Norton, 1991), 44.

[65]AG to Jane Smith, New York, May 20, 1837, in Ceplair, *The Public Years,* 133.

[66]For the southern strategies that Beecher feared, see Karp, *This Vast Southern Empire.*

[67]See Lee V. Chambers, *The Weston Sisters: An American Abolitionist Family* (Chapel Hill: University of North Carolina Press, 2014), 19–28.

[68]Lumkin, *Emancipation of Angelina Grimké,* 128.

[69]Birney, *Grimké Sisters,* 190.

[70][Theodore D. Weld], *In Memory of Angelina Grimké Weld* (Boston: George Ellis, 1880). For an example of AG's speaking style, see Document 36, the only one of her lectures to be recorded by shorthand.

[71]Gilbert Hobbs Barnes, *The Antislavery Impulse, 1830–1844* (New York: Appleton-Century, 1933; reprint Smith, 1957), 134–35; and Louis Filler, *The Crusade against Slavery, 1830–1860* (New York: Harper, 1960), 67.

[72]See Dorothy Sterling, *Ahead of Her Time: Abby Kelley and the Politics of Antislavery* (New York: Norton, 1991).

[73]See John R. McKivigan, *The War against Proslavery Religion: Abolitionism and the Northern Churches, 1830–1865* (Ithaca: Cornell University Press, 1984).

[74]See Ruth M. Alexander, "'We Are Engaged as a Band of Sisters': Class and Domesticity in the Washingtonian Temperance Movement, 1840–1850," *Journal of American History* 75 (Dec. 1988), 763–85. For moral reform, see Wright, *The First of Causes to Our Sex;* and Carroll Smith Rosenberg, "Beauty, the Beast, and the Militant Woman: A Case Study in Sex Roles and Social Stress in Jacksonian America," *American Quarterly* 23 (1971), 562–84. See also Daniel Wright, "What Was the Appeal of Moral Reform to Antebellum Northern Women?" online in "Women and Social Movements in the United States."

[75]Kelly Olds, "Privatizing the Church: Disestablishment in Connecticut and Massachusetts," *Journal of Political Economy* 102, no. 2 (1994), 277–297.

[76]AG to Jane Smith, June 26, July 16, and July 25, 1837, quoted in Ceplair, *The Public Years,* 140.

[77]Wright's diary, quoted in Ceplair, *The Public Years,* 140.

[78]AG to Theodore Weld, Fitchburg (Mass.), Sept. 20, 1837, in *Letters of Theodore Dwight Weld, Angelina Grimké Weld and Sarah Grimké, 1822–1844,* ed. Gilbert H. and Dwight L. Dumond (New York: Appleton-Century-Crofts, 1934; reprint Gloucester, MA: Smith, 1965), 1:451. [Hereafter *Weld-Grimké Letters.*]

[79]Theodore Weld to Sarah and Angelina Grimké, Hartford, Conn., May 22, 1837, in Barnes and Dumond, *Weld-Grimké Letters,* 1:389. For Child, Chapman, and Mott, see Hersh, *Slavery of Sex.*

[80]AG to Jane Smith, Holliston, Mass., Oct. 26, 1837, WGFP.

[81]Sarah M. Grimké, *Letters on the Equality of the Sexes, and the Condition of Woman, Addressed to Mary S. Parker, President of the Boston Female Anti-Slavery Society* (Boston: Knapp, 1838); and Angelina E. Grimké, *Letters to Catherine E. Beecher, in Reply to An Essay on Slavery and Abolitionism, Addressed to A. E. Grimké. Revised by the author.* (Boston: Knapp, 1838). The versions reprinted here are those that originally appeared in *The Liberator.* They have the virtue of the immediacy of the moment; Theodore Weld later aided in the revisions that appeared in the book. See also Sarah Grimké, *Letters on the Equality of the Sexes and Other Essays,* ed. Elizabeth Ann Bartlett (New Haven: Yale University Press, 1988).

[82]Sarah's *Letters on the Equality of the Sexes* struggled more explicitly with scripture. Her efforts inspired a more thorough work: Elizabeth Wilson, *A Scriptural View of Woman's Rights and Duties in All the Important Relations of Life* (Philadelphia: Young, 1849). For an appraisal of biblical criticism by SG and Lucretia Mott, see Marla J. Selvidge, *Notorious Voices: Feminist Biblical Interpretation, 1500–1920* (New York: Continuum, 1996), 44–62; and Cullen Murphy, *The Word According to Eve: Women and the Bible in Ancient Times and Our Own* (Boston: Houghton Mifflin, 1998), 25–29.

[83]For similar debates within feminist theory, see Mary Lyndon Shanley and Uma Narayan, *Reconstructing Political Theory: Feminist Perspectives* (University Park: University of Pennsylvania Press, 1995).

[84]Typed copy, John F. Grimké, Last Will and Testament, 1818, Grimké Family Papers, Special Collections, Addlestone Library, College of Charleston, Charleston, South Carolina.

[85]Ephesians 5:22.

[86]AG to Sarah Douglass, Brookline (Mass.), Feb. 25, 1838, in Barnes and Dumond, *Weld-Grimké Letters,* 1:574.

[87]Theodore Weld to AG, New York, Feb. 8, 1838, and AG to Theodore Weld, Brookline (Mass.), Feb. 11, 1838, in Barnes and Dumond, *Weld-Grimké Letters,* 2:533–34 and 536–37.

[88]AG to TW. Feb. 11, 1838, Barnes and Dumond, *Weld-Grimké Letters,* 2:536–38.

[89]Weld, ed., *American Slavery as It Is.*

[90]*History of Pennsylvania Hall, Which Was Destroyed by a Mob, on the 17th of May, 1838* (Philadelphia: Merrihew and Gunn, 1838; reprint New York: Negro University Press, 1969), 135; David Grimsted, *American Mobbing, 1828–1861: Toward Civil War* (New York: Oxford, 2003); Lerner, *Grimké Sisters*, 247.

[91]*Liberator,* Dec. 15, 1837.

[92]AG to Henry Clarke Wright, Brookline (Mass.), Aug. 27, 1837, in Barnes and Dumond, *Weld-Grimké Letters,* 1:436.

[93]AG to Jane Smith, Brookline (Mass.), Aug. 26, 1837, in Ceplair, *The Public Years,* 285.

[94]On the larger context of the movement's split, see Aileen S. Kraditor, *Means and Ends in American Abolitionism: Garrison and His Critics on Strategy and Tactics, 1834–1850* (New York: Random House, 1967); Lewis Perry, *Radical Abolitionism: Anarchy and the Government of God in Antislavery Thought* (Knoxville: University of Tennessee Press, 1995); and Corey M. Brooks, *Liberty Power: Antislavery Third Parties and the Transformation of American Politics* (Chicago: University of Chicago Press, 2016).

[95]"Address to the American and Foreign A.S. Society," *Liberator,* June 19, 1840; "Address of the Executive Committee of the American Anti-Slavery Society," *Liberator,* July 31, 1840.

[96]Lydia Maria Child, *Appeal in Favor of That Class of Americans Called Africans* (Boston: Allen and Ticknor, 1833). See also Karcher, *Lydia Maria Child Reader.*

[97]Brown, "The Philadelphia Female Anti-Slavery Society;" Nancy A. Hewitt, *Radical Friend: Amy Kirby Post and Her Activist Worlds* (Chapel Hill: University of North Carolina Press, 2018).

[98]Quoted in Jeffrey, *The Great Silent Army of Abolitionism,* 98.

[99]For more on the Boston society, see Hansen, *Strained Sisterhood.*

[100]*Connecticut Observer,* March 7, 1840, 38; quoted in Keith Melder, "Abby Kelley Foster," *Notable American Women.* See also Sterling, *Ahead of Her Time.*

[101]See Brooks, *Liberty Power.*

[102]"Proceedings of the General Anti-Slavery Convention," quoted in Sklar, "Women Who Speak for an Entire Nation," in Yellin and Van Horne, *Abolitionist Sisterhood,* 311.

[103]Pugh's protest and her account of the convention are in [n.a.], *Memorial of Sarah Pugh: A Tribute of Respect from her Cousins* (Philadelphia: Lippincott, 1888), 23–30. See also "News from England," *Liberator,* July 24, 1840; "The Rejected Protest," *Liberator,* London, July 3, 1840.

[104]See Sklar, "Women Who Speak for an Entire Nation."

[105]For slave-owner dominated foreign policy, see Karp, *This Vast Southern Empire.*

[106]Elizabeth Cady Stanton, Susan B. Anthony, and Matilda Joslyn Gage, *History of Woman Suffrage, 1: 1848–1861* (New York: Fowler & Wells, 1881), 423.

[107]Theodore Stanton and Harriot Stanton Blatch, eds., *Elizabeth Cady Stanton, As Revealed in Her Letters, Diary and Reminiscences* (New York: Harper & Bros., 1922), 67.

[108]See Elisabeth Griffith, *In Her Own Right: The Life of Elizabeth Cady Stanton* (New York: Oxford, 1984), 33.

[109]Stanton and Blatch, *Elizabeth Cady Stanton,* 392.

[110]Frederick B. Tolles, ed., "'Slavery and The Woman Question': Lucretia Mott's Diary of Her Visit to Great Britain to Attend the World's Anti-Slavery Convention of 1840," *Journal of the Friends Historical Society,* suppl. 23 (1952): 41; LM to Richard D. Webb and Hannah Webb, Philadelphia, April 2. 1841, in Palmer, *Selected Letters of Lucretia Coffin Mott,* 93.

[111]Stanton, Anthony, and Gage, *History of Woman Suffrage,* 1:421, 423–24. See also Moira Ferguson, "Mary Wollstonecraft and the Problematic of Slavery," in *Mary Wollstonecraft and 200 Years of Feminisms,* ed. Eileen Janes Yeo (London: Rivers Oram, 1997), 89–103.

[112]Stanton, Anthony, and Gage, History of Woman Suffrage, 1:67–69.

[113]Lucretia Mott to Richard and Hannah Webb, Philadelphia, Feb. 25, 1842, in *James and Lucretia Mott: Life and Letters,* ed. Anna Davis Hallowell (Boston: Houghton Mifflin, 1884), 228.

[114]Elizabeth Cady Stanton [hereafter ECS] to Elizabeth J. Neall, Johnstown, November 26, 1841, in Ann D. Gordon, ed., *The Selected Papers of Elizabeth Cady Stanton and Susan B. Anthony, 1: In the School of Anti-Slavery, 1840–1866* (New Brunswick, NJ: Rutgers University Press, 1997), 25. [Hereafter Gordon, *Papers of Stanton and Anthony.*]

[115]*Liberator,* Oct. 28, 1842.

[116]ECS to Elizabeth Neall, Nov. 26, 1841, in Gordon, *Papers of Stanton and Anthony,* 25.

[117]Stanton et al., *History of Woman Suffrage,* 1:63–67.

[118]See Norma Basch, *In the Eyes of the Law: Women, Marriage, and Property in Nineteenth-Century New York* (Ithaca: Cornell University Press, 1982).

[119]Griffith, *In Her Own Right,* 44–49.

[120]Nancy A. Hewitt, *Women's Activism and Social Change: Rochester, New York, 1822–1872* (Ithaca: Cornell University Press, 1984), 107–113.

[121]Griffith, *In Her Own Right,* 48–50.

[122]Elizabeth Cady Stanton, *Eighty Years and More: Reminiscences, 1815–1897* (New York: European Publishing Company, 1898), 148.

[123]For the Hicksite influence on this gathering, see Judith Wellman, "The Seneca Falls Women's Rights Convention: A Study of Social Networks," *Journal of Women's History* 3, no. 1 (Spring 1991); and Nancy A. Hewitt, "Feminist Friends: Agrarian Quakers and the Emergence of Woman's Rights in America," *Feminist Studies* 12 (Spring 1986): 27–49.

[124]*The North Star,* Rochester, NY, Dec. 3, 1847. See also Philip S. Foner, ed., *Frederick Douglass on Women's Rights* (Westport, CT: Greenwood Press, 1976); and William S. McFeely, *Frederick Douglass* (New York: Simon & Schuster, 1991), 149–56.

[125]Nineteenth-century authors referred to the human "race" in usage that changed in the twentieth century to human "species."

[126]Press coverage is described in Stanton et al., *History of Woman Suffrage,* 1:802–04. In the *New York Tribune,* Horace Greeley provided the women's rights conventions with sympathetic newspaper coverage throughout the 1850s.

[127]Stanton et al., *History of Woman Suffrage,* 1:74–79, 101–70.

[128]Lucretia Mott to ECS, Oct. 3, 1848, in Palmer, *Selected Letters of Lucretia Coffin Mott,* 172. On microfilm: *The Papers of Elizabeth Cady Stanton and Susan B. Anthony* (Wilmington, DE: Scholarly Resources, 1991), reel 6, frame 828.

[129]For this relationship, see Ellen Carol DuBois, ed., *The Elizabeth Cady Stanton-Susan B. Anthony Reader: Correspondence, Writings, Speeches* (New York: Schocken, 1981); Kathleen Barry, *Susan B. Anthony: A Biography* (New York: New York University Press, 1988); and Gordon, *Papers of Stanton and Anthony.*

[130]Historians have not yet systematically studied the women's rights convention movement, but the published proceedings are available online in *Women and Social Movements in the United States.* See also Nancy Isenberg, *Sex and Citizenship in Antebellum America* (Chapel Hill: University of North Carolina Press, 1998).

[131]See McClymer, *This High and Holy Moment.* See also Isenberg, *Sex and Citizenship.* The term seems to have evolved from *coeval,* a word used in the 1848 Seneca Falls resolutions.

[132]"From Lucretia Mott to the 'Woman's Convention' to Be Held in Salem, Ohio," *Liberator,* May 17, 1850.

[133]Stanton, *History of Woman Suffrage,* 1:472–512. See also Dexter C. Bloomer, ed., *Life and Writings of Amelia Bloomer* (Boston: Arena, 1895).

[134]*Proceedings,* Worcester Women's Rights Convention, quoted in McClymer, *This High and Holy Moment,* 132.

[135]See Stacey M. Robertson, *Parker Pillsbury: Radical Abolitionist, Male Feminist* (Ithaca: Cornell University Press, 2000); and Sylvia Hoffert, *Jane Grey Swisshelm, an Unconventional Life, 1815–1882* (Chapel Hill: University of North Carolina Press, 2004).

[136]See Margaret Washington, *Sojourner Truth's America* (Urbana: University of Illinois Press, 2009); and Sojourner Truth and Margaret Washington, *Narrative of Sojourner Truth* (New York: Vintage, 1993).

[137]John McClymer, ed., *This High and Holy Moment: The First National Woman's Rights Convention, Worcester, 1850* (New York: Harcourt Brace, 1999).

[138]Carleton Mabee, *Sojourner Truth: Slave, Prophet, Legend* (New York: New York University Press, 1993), 67–82.

[139]Howard Holman Bell, *A Survey of the Negro Convention Movement, 1830–1861* (Evanston, IL: Howard Holman Bell, 1953; reprint New York: Arno, 1969), 31–34, 72, 98.

[140]Ellen NicKenzie Lawson, *The Three Sarahs: Documents of Antebellum Black College Women* (New York: Edwin Mellen, 1984), 189–195.

[141]See Robert G. Wells, *Uncle Sam's Family: Issues in and Perspectives on American Demographic History* (Albany: State University of New York Press, 1985).

[142]See Daniel Scott Smith, "Family Limitation, Sexual Control, and Domestic Feminism in Victorian America," in *Controlling Reproduction: An American History,* ed. Andrea Tone (Wilmington, DE: SR Books, 1997); and Janet Farrell Brodie, *Contraception and Abortion in 19th-Century America* (Ithaca: Cornell University Press, 1994).

[143]Stephen Nissenbaum, *Sex, Diet, and Debility in Jacksonian America: Sylvester Graham and Health Reform* (Westport, CT: Greenwood Press, 1980).

[144]Historians have looked for but not found evidence to support the possibility that Stanton had miscarriages that would help account for this interval. See Judith Wellman, "The Seneca Falls Women's Rights Convention: A Study of Social Networks," *Journal of Women's History* 3, no. 1 (Spring 1991): 31, note 10.

[145]See Kathryn Kish Sklar, "Victorian Women and Domestic Life: Mary Todd Lincoln, Elizabeth Cady Stanton, and Harriet Beecher Stowe," in *The Public and the Private Lincoln,* ed. Cullom Davis et al. (Carbondale: Southern Illinois University Press, 1980).

[146]See Smith-Rosenberg, "Beauty, the Beast, and the Militant Woman"; Barbara J. Berg, *The Remembered Gate: Origins of American Feminism: The Woman and the City, 1800–1860* (New York: Oxford, 1978); and Wright, *First of Causes to Our Sex.*

[147]Henry Clark Wright, *Marriage and Parentage; or, the Reproductive Element in Man, as a Means to His Elevation and Happiness* (Boston: Marsh, 1855). The book was reprinted in many editions. See Lewis Perry, *Childhood, Marriage, and Reform: Henry Clarke Wright, 1797–1870* (Chicago: University of Chicago Press, 1980), 349.

[148]See Bartlett, ed., *Letters on the Equality of the Sexes,* 79.

[149]Kathryn Kish Sklar, "Human Rights Discourse in the Proceedings of Women's Rights Conferences in the United States, 1848–1869," in *Revisiting the Origins of Human Rights,* ed. Miia Halme-Tuomisaari and Pamela Slotte (Cambridge: Cambridge University Press, 2015).

[150]See Harriet Beecher Stowe and Henry Louis Gates, *The Annotated Uncle Tom's Cabin* (New York: Norton, 2006).

[151]For Still, see Eric Foner, *Gateway to Freedom: The Hidden History of the Underground Railroad* (New York: Norton, 2016).

[152]William J. Watkins, "Our Rights as Men: An Address Delivered in Boston, before the Legislative Committee on the Militia, February 24, 1853, by William J. Watkins, in Behalf of Sixty-Five Colored Petitioners, Praying for a Charter to Form an Independent Military Company," in *Negro Protest Pamphlets*, ed. Dorothy Porter (New York: Arno, 1969), cited in Ball, *To Live an Antislavery Life*, 166.

[153]William Cooper Nell to William Lloyd Garrison, Feb. 19, 1852, *Liberator,* March 5, 1852.

[154]Ellen Carol DuBois, *Feminism and Suffrage: The Emergence of an Independent Women's Movement in America, 1848–1869* (Ithaca: Cornell University Press, 1978), 53. See also Faye E. Dudden, *Fighting Chance: The Struggle over Woman Suffrage and Black Suffrage in Reconstruction America* (New York: Oxford, 2011), 51–58.

[155]For more on Harper's speech, see Alison M. Parker, *Articulating Rights: Nineteenth-Century American Women on Race, Reform, and the State* (DeKalb: Northern Illinois University Press, 2010), 114–124; and Rosalyn Terborg-Penn, *African American Women in the Struggle for the Vote, 1850–1920* (Bloomington: Indiana University Press, 1998), 13–35.

[156]See DuBois, *Feminism and Suffrage,* 162–202; and Andrea Moore Kerr, *Lucy Stone: Speaking Out for Equality* (New Brunswick, NJ: Rutgers University Press, 1992), 138–59.

[157]Peterson, *"Doers of the Word,"* 120, 199, 224, 228–29.

[158]See Terborg-Penn, *African American Women in the Struggle for the Vote,* 36–54. See also Louise Michele Newman, *White Woman's Rights: The Racial Origins of Feminism in the United States* (New York: Oxford, 1999).

PART TWO

The Documents

Women Emerge in Public Life as Writers and Speakers against Slavery and Racial Prejudice, 1831–1833

1

THE FEMALE LITERARY ASSOCIATION OF PHILADELPHIA

Preamble to Constitution

1831

Free black women organized literary societies to advance members' writing and speaking skills, shape their individual and collective identities, and combat racial prejudice. Sarah Mapps Douglass sent the constitution of this Philadelphia group to William Lloyd Garrison, who immediately published it and soon thereafter created a "Ladies' Department" in The Liberator. *The Preamble stated the group's goals.*

Conscious that among the various pursuits that have engaged the attention of mankind in the different eras of the world, none have ever been considered by persons of judgment and penetration, as superior to the cultivation of the intellectual powers, bestowed upon us by the God of nature; it therefore becomes a duty incumbent upon us as women, as daughters of a despised race, to use our utmost endeavors to enlighten the understanding, to cultivate the talents entrusted to our keeping, that by so doing, we may in a great measure, break down the strong barrier of prejudice, and raise ourselves to an equality with those of our fellow

"Preamble," *The Liberator*, Dec. 3, 1831, 196.

beings, who differ from us in complexion, but who are with ourselves, children of one Eternal Parent, and by his immutable law, we are entitled to the same rights and privileges; therefore, we, whose names are here-unto subscribed, do agree to form ourselves into a society for the promotion of this great object, to be called "The Female Literary Association of Philadelphia."

2

MARIA STEWART

Religion and the Pure Principles of Morality

Boston, January 7, 1832

Maria Stewart, a free black Bostonian, wrote this essay, which Garrison's press printed as a pamphlet, and which he also excerpted in the first "Ladies' Department" in The Liberator. *Stewart urged black women to unite, promote education, claim their rights, and combat racial prejudice.*

I am of a strong opinion, that the day on which we unite, heart and soul, and turn our attention to knowledge and improvement, that day the hissing and reproach amongst the nations of the earth against us will cease. And even those who now point at us with the finger of scorn, will aid and befriend us. It is of no use for us to sit with our hands folded, hanging our heads like bulrushes, lamenting our wretched condition' but let us make a mighty effort and arise; and if no one will promote or respect us, let us promote and respect ourselves.

The American ladies have the honor conferred on them, that by prudence and economy in their domestic concerns, and their unwearied attention in forming the minds and manners of their children, they laid the foundation of their becoming what they now are . . . and shall we not imitate their examples, as far as they are worthy of imitation? Why cannot we do something to distinguish ourselves, and contribute some of our hard earnings that would reflect honor upon our memories, and cause our children to arise and call us blessed? Shall it any longer be said of the daughters of Africa, they have no ambition, they have no force? By no means. Let every female heart become united and let us raise a fund ourselves; and at the end of one year and a half, we might be able to lay the corner-stone for the building of a High School, that the higher branches of knowledge might be enjoyed by us; and God would raise us up, and enough to aid us in our laudable designs. Let each one strive to excel in good housewifery, knowing that prudence and economy are the road to wealth. Let us not say, we know this, or we know that, and practice nothing; but let us practice what we do know.

How long shall the fair daughters of Africa be compelled to bury their minds and talents beneath a load of iron pots and kettles? Until union, knowledge and love begin to flow amongst us. How long shall a mean set of men flatter us with their smiles, and enrich themselves with our hard earnings,—their wives' fingers sparkling with rings, and they themselves laughing at our folly? Until we begin to promote and patronize each other. Shall we be a by-word among the nations any longer? Shall they laugh us to scorn forever? Do you ask, what can you do? Unite, and build a store of your own, if you cannot procure a license. Fill one side with dry goods, and the other with groceries. Do you ask, where is the money? We have spent more than enough for nonsense, to do what building we should want. We have never had an opportunity of displaying our talents, therefore the world thinks we know nothing. And we have been possessed of by far too mean and cowardly a disposition, though I highly disapprove of an insolent or impertinent one. Do you ask the disposition I would have you possess? Possess the spirit of independence. The Americans do, and why should not you? Possess the spirit of men, bold and enterprising, fearless and undaunted. Sue for your rights and privileges. Know the reason that you cannot attain them. Weary them with your importunities. You can but die, if you make the attempt; and we shall certainly die if you do not. The Americans have practiced nothing but head work these 200 years, and we have done their drudgery. And is it not high time for us to imitate their examples and practice head-work too, and keep what we have got, and get what we can? We need never to think that any body is going to feel interested for us, if we do not feel interested for ourselves. That day we, as a people, hearken unto the voice of the Lord our God, and walk in his ways and ordinances, and become distinguished for our ease, elegance and grace, combined with other virtues,—that day the Lord will raise us up, and enough to aid and befriend us, and we shall begin to flourish.

3

MARIA W. STEWART

Address before the Afric-American Female Intelligence Society of Boston

April 1832

In her first public speech, Stewart addressed a women's group. She praised the importance of women, but her sharp criticisms of the African American community seem to have undercut her leadership. Garrison printed her speech, excerpted here, in the "Ladies' Department" of The Liberator, *but his editorial note* * *on an earlier page explained that he was responding to Stewart's request, not the Society's.*

The frowns of the world shall never discourage me, nor its smiles flatter me; for with the help of God I am resolved to withstand the fiery darts of the devil, and the assaults of wicked men. The righteous are as bold as a lion, but the wicked flee where no man pursueth. . . .

And why is it, my friends, that we are despised above all the nations upon the earth? Is it merely because our skins are tinged with a sable hue? No, nor will I ever believe that it is. What then is it? Oh, it is because that we and our fathers have dealt treacherously one with another, and because many of us now possess that envious and malicious disposition, that we had rather die than see each other rise an inch above a beggar. No gentle methods are used to promote love and friendship amongst us, but much is done to destroy it. Shall we be a hissing and a reproach amongst the nations of the earth any longer? Shall they laugh us to scorn forever?

Ingratitude is one of the worst passions that reigns in the human breast; it is this that cuts the tender fibres of the soul; for it is impossible for us to love those who are ungrateful towards us. "Behold," says the wise man Solomon, counting one by one, "a man have I found in a thousand, but a woman among all these have I not found." . . .

Mrs. Maria W. Stewart, "An Address Delivered Before the Afric-American Female Intelligence Society of Boston," *The Liberator,* April 28, 1832, 67 and William Lloyd Garrison, "Editorial Note," *The Liberator,* April 28, 1832, 86.

A lady of high distinction among us, observed to me, that I might never expect your homage. God forbid! I ask it not. But I beseech you to deal with gentleness and godly sincerity towards me; and there is not one of you, my dear friends, who has given me a cup of cold water in the name of the Lord, or soothed the sorrows of my wounded heart, but God will bless, not only you, but your children for it. Cruel indeed are those that indulge such an opinion respecting me as that. . . .

O woman, woman! Upon you I call; for upon your exertions almost entirely depends whether the rising generation shall be any thing more than we have been or not. O woman, woman! Your example is powerful, your influence great; it extends over your husbands and over your children, and throughout the circle of your acquaintance. Then let me exhort you to cultivate among yourselves a spirit of Christian love and unity, having charity one for another, without which all our goodness is as sounding brass, and as a tinkling cymbal. And O, my God I beseech thee to grant that the nations of the earth may hiss at us no longer! O suffer them not to laugh us to scorn forever!

*It is proper to state that the Address of Mrs. Stewart, in our Ladies' Department to-day, is published at her own request, and not by desire of the Society before whom it was delivered. Mrs. S. uses very plain, some may call it severe language; but we are satisfied that she is actuated by good motives, and that her only aim is to rouse a spirit of virtuous emulation in the breasts of her associates, and to elevate the whole colored population. "Faithful are the wounds of a friend, but the kisses of an enemy are deceitful."

4

SARAH MAPPS DOUGLASS

"Ladies' Department, Mental Feast"

Philadelphia, July 21, 1832

This column in The Liberator *has four parts. It began with the women's antislavery emblem, the first use of what became a standard feature of* The Liberator's *"Ladies' Department" column. Then, Garrison introduced "our brother Jocelyn" as the originator of the idea of a "Mental*

Sarah Mapps Douglass, "Ladies' Department, Mental Feast," *The Liberator*, July 21, 1832, 114.

Feast" meeting by women of color. Simeon Jocelyn, the white pastor of the Congregational church for African Americans in New Haven, was raising money to create a "Negro College" there. The plan's unpopularity led to his house being wrecked by a mob in 1837. The column also included a letter about the "Mental Feast" gathering. Finally, the evening's address by Sarah Mapps Douglass, schoolteacher daughter of a free black Philadelphia artisan family, depicted her changing views of slavery.

It gives us pleasure to learn that the excellent suggestions made by our brother Jocelyn of New-Haven, to a number of respectable colored females in Philadelphia, during his late visit to that city, in regard to their holding a Mental Feast monthly, has been then carried into effect. He proposed that they should meet alternately at their own dwellings, for the purpose of moral and religious meditation, conversation, reading and speaking, sympathising over the fate of unhappy slaves, improving their own minds, &c. &c.; and, in order to make the meeting truly a *Mental* Feast and unburthensome to the entertainer, that the visiters should receive the simplest fare. We hope something of this kind will be attempted by the colored females of this city, and in other places.

The following extract of a letter from a lady who was invited to attend the meeting alluded to, we think will prove interesting to our readers:

Figure 3. "Am I not a Woman and a Sister?," *The Liberator*, July 21, 1832, 114.
Bettmann/Getty Images

"Soon after all were quietly seated, a short address, prepared for the occasion, was read by the authoress (Sarah Douglass,*) a copy of which is herewith sent: it speaks its own praise, therefore comment from me is unnecessary. The fifty-fourth beautiful and encouraging chapter of Isaiah was then read. After sitting a short time under a solemn and impressive silence that ensued the reading of the chapter, one of the company vocally petitioned our heavenly Father for a continuance of his favor, &c. The remainder of the evening was occupied principally by their severally reading and relating affecting slave tales, calculated to bring forcibly into view the deplorable situation of our fellow-creatures at the south—both the oppressor and the oppressed. This interesting interview was closed with singing an appropriate hymn. The precious covering which was spread around bespoke that divine *goodness* was near; and I am bound to believe that He graciously condescends to regard, in a very peculiar manner, the sincere attempts made by this greatly injured people to serve Him, the true and living God. Ah! does He not design to raise from among them a peculiar people for his own praise? Methinks he does. Whether it will be separately by themselves, or collectively with white people, I will not presume to say."

ADDRESS

MY FRIENDS—MY SISTERS:

How important is the occasion for which we have assembled ourselves together this evening, to hold a feast, to feed our never-dying minds, to excite each other to deeds of mercy, words of peace; to stir up in the bosom of each, gratitude to God for his increasing goodness, and fueling of deep sympathy for our brethren and sisters, who are in this land of Christian light and liberty held in bondage the most cruel and degrading—to make their cause our own!

An English writer has said, "We must feel deeply before we can act rightly; from that absorbing, heart-rending compassion for ourselves springs a deeper sympathy for others, and from a sense of our weakness and our own upbraidings arises a disposition to be indulgent, to

---

*To this accomplished young colored lady we are indebted for several original and truly beautifully articles which have appeared in the Ladies' Department of *The Liberator.*—Ed.

forbear, to forgive." This is my experience. One short year ago, how different were my feelings on the subject of slavery! It is true, the wail of the captive sometimes came to my ear in the midst of my happiness, and caused my heart to bleed for his wrongs; but, alas! the impression was as evanescent as the early cloud and morning dew. I had formed a little world of my own, and cared not to move beyond its precincts. But how was the scene changed when I beheld the oppressor lurking on the border of my own peaceful home! I saw his iron hand stretched forth to seize me as his pretty, and the cause of the slave became my own. I started up, and with one mighty effort threw from me the lethargy which had covered me as a mantle for years; and determined, by the help of the Almighty, to use every exertion in my power to elevate the character of my wronged and neglected race. One year ago, I detested the slaveholder; now I can pity and pray for him. Has not this been your experience, my sisters? Have you not felt as I have felt upon this thrilling subject? My heart assures me some of you have.

And now, my sisters, I would earnestly and affectionately press upon you the necessity of placing your whole dependence on God; poor, weak, finite creatures as we are, we can do nothing for ourselves. He is all-powerful; He is waiting to be gracious to us as a people. Do you feel your inability to do good? Come to Him who giveth liberally and upbraideth not; bring your wrongs and fears to Him, as you would to a tender parent—He will sympathise with you. I know from blessed, heart-cheering experience the excellency of having a God to trust to in seasons of trial and conflict. What but this can support us should the pestilence which has devastated Asia be borne to us by the summer breezes? What but this can uphold our fainting footsteps in the swellings of Jordan? It is the only thing worth living for—the only thing that can disarm death of his sting. I am earnestly solicitous that each of us may adopt this language:

"I have no hope in man, but much in God—Much in the rock of ages."

In conclusion, I would respectfully recommend that our mental feast should commence by reading a portion of the Holy Scriptures.

5

MARIA STEWART

Lecture Delivered at the Franklin Hall

Boston, September 21, 1832

*In this address delivered on September 21, Stewart became one of the
first women in the United States to speak to a public assembly of men
and women. She called on religious authority to protect her presentation,
urged mutual support and cultural change in the black community, and
concluded with a call for compassion from whites. Franklin Hall was
the meeting place of the New England Anti-Slavery Society, founded by
Garrison and others in 1831.*

Methinks I heard a spiritual interrogation—"Who shall go forward, and
take off the reproach that is cast upon the people of color? Shall it be a
woman?" And my heart made this reply—"If it is thy will, be it even so,
Lord Jesus!". . .

I have asked several individuals of my sex, who transact business for
themselves, if providing our girls were to give them the most satisfactory references, they would not be willing to grant them an equal opportunity with others? Their reply has been—for their own part, they had
no objection; but as it was not the custom, were they to take them into
their employ, they would be in danger of losing the public patronage.

And such is the powerful force of prejudice. Let our girls possess
whatever amiable qualities of soul they may; let their characters be fair
and spotless as innocence itself; let their natural taste and ingenuity
be what they may; it is impossible for scarce an individual of them to
rise above the condition of servants. Ah! why is this cruel and unfeel-
ing distinction? Is it merely because God has made our complexion to
vary? If it be, O shame to soft relenting humanity! . . . Yet, after all,
methinks were the American free people of color to turn their attention
more assiduously to moral worth and intellectual improvement, this
would be the result: prejudice would gradually diminish, and the whites
would be compelled to say, unloose those fetters! . . .

Maria Stewart, *Meditations*, 55–59.

O, ye fairer sisters, whose hands are never soiled, whose nerves and muscles are never strained, go learn by experience! Had we had the opportunity that you had had, to improve our moral and mental faculties, what would have hindered our intellects from being as bright, and our manners from being as dignified as yours? Had it been our lot to have been nursed in the lap of affluence and ease, should we not have naturally supposed that we were never made to toil? And why are not our forms as delicate, and our constitutions as slender, as yours? Is not the workmanship as curious and complete? Have pity upon us, have pity upon us, O ye who have hearts to feel for other's woes; for the hand of God has touched us.

6

MARIA STEWART

Farewell Address to Her Friends in the City of Boston
September 1833

Stewart's farewell address in September 1833 expressed her belief that her leadership was rejected by the African American community because she was a woman. She defended her ability to speak against the "strong current of prejudice" that blocked the progress of African Americans.

On my arrival here, not finding scarce an individual who felt interested in these subjects [the welfare of the black community], and but few of the whites, except Mr. Garrison, and his friend, Mr. Knapp; and hearing that those gentlemen had observed that female influence was powerful; my soul became fired with a holy zeal for your cause. . . . The spirit of God came before me, and I spake before many. When going home, reflecting on what I had said, I felt ashamed, and knew not where I should hide myself. A something said within my breast, "Press forward, I will be with thee." And my heart made this reply, "Lord, if thou wilt be with me, then I will speak for thee as long as I live.". . .

Maria Stewart, *Meditations*, 74–82.

What if I am a woman; is not the God of ancient times the God of these modern days? Did he not raise up Deborah, to be a mother, and a judge in Israel? Did not queen Esther save the lives of the Jews? And Mary Magdalene first declare the resurrection of Christ from the dead? . . . St. Paul declared that it was a shame for a woman to speak in public. . . . Did St. Paul but know of our wrongs and deprivations, I presume he would make no objections to our pleading in public for our rights. . . .

If such women as are here described have once existed, be no longer astonished then, my brethren and friends, that God at this eventful period should raise up your own females to strive, by their example both in public and private, to assist those who are endeavoring to stop the strong current of prejudice that flows so profusely against us at present. No longer ridicule their efforts, it will be counted for sin. For God makes use of feeble means sometimes, to bring about his most exalted purposes. . . .

Dearly beloved, I have made myself contemptible in the eyes of many, that I might win some. But it has been like labor in vain. . . . The bitterness of my soul has departed from those who endeavored to discourage and hinder me in my Christian progress; and I can now forgive my enemies, bless those who have hated me, and cheerfully pray for those who have despitefully used and persecuted me.

FARE YOU WELL, FAREWELL.

MARIA STEWART

7

Declaration of Sentiments at the Founding of the American Anti-Slavery Society

Philadelphia, December 6, 1833

On December 6, 1833, three African American men, four white women, and sixty white men responded to a call by William Lloyd Garrison to meet in Philadelphia, and they founded the American Anti-Slavery Society (AASS). They prefaced the society's constitution with a

"Declaration of the National Anti-Slavery Convention," *The Liberator.* Dec. 14, 1833, 198.

"Declaration of Sentiments," the concluding paragraph of which summa-
rized the group's dual goals of the immediate and unconditional abolition
of slavery and an end to racial prejudice. Their goals were vilified as
incendiary attacks on American institutions.

More than fifty-seven years have elapsed, since a band of patriots convened in this place, to devise measures for the deliverance of this country from a foreign yoke. The corner-stone upon which they founded the Temple of Freedom was broadly this—"that all men are created equal; that they are endowed by their Creator with certain inalienable rights; that among these are life, LIBERTY, and the pursuit of happiness." . . .

Their grievances, great as they were, were trifling in comparison with the wrongs and sufferings of those for whom we plead. Our fathers were never slaves—never bought and sold like cattle—never shut out from the light of knowledge and religion—never subjected to the lash of brutal taskmasters.

But those, for whose emancipation we are striving—constituting at the present time at least one-sixth part of our countrymen—are recognized by law, and treated by their fellow-beings, as marketable commodities, as goods and chattels, as brute beasts; are plundered daily of the fruits of their toil without redress; really enjoy no constitutional nor legal protection from licentious and murderous outrages upon their persons; and are ruthlessly torn asunder—the tender babe from the arms of its frantic mother—the heart-broken wife from her weeping husband—at the caprice or pleasure of irresponsible tyrants. For the crime of having a dark complexion, they suffer the pangs of hunger, the infliction of stripes, the ignominy of brutal servitude. They are kept in heathenish darkness by laws expressly enacted to make their instruction a criminal offence. . . .

Hence we maintain—that, in view of the civil and religious privileges of this nation, the guilt of its oppression is unequalled by any other on the face of the earth; and, therefore, that it is bound to repent instantly, to undo the heavy burdens, and to let the oppressed go free. . . .

We further believe and affirm—that all persons of color, who possess the qualifications which are demanded of others, ought to be admitted forthwith to the enjoyment of the same privileges, and the exercise of the same prerogatives, as others; and that the paths of preferment, of wealth, and of intelligence, should be opened as widely to them as to persons of a white complexion.

8

Preamble, Constitution of the Philadelphia Female Anti-Slavery Society

1833

The society's constitution reflected its dual priorities of ending slavery and ending racial prejudice. Sarah Mapps Douglas served as the society's recording secretary.

Whereas, more than two millions of our fellow countrymen, of these United States, are held in abject bondage; and whereas, we believe that slavery and prejudice against color are contrary to the laws of God, and to the principles of the our far-famed Declaration of Independence, and recognising the right of the slave to immediate emancipation; we deem it our duty to manifest our abhorrence of the flagrant injustice and deep sin of slavery, by united and vigorous exertions for its speedy removal, and for the restoration of the people of color to their inalienable rights. For these purposes, we, the undersigned, agree to associate ourselves under the name of the "The Philadelphia Female Anti-Slavery Society."

"Ladies' Department, Constitution of the Female Anti-Slavery Society of Philadelphia," *The Liberator,* April 19, 1834, 61.

9

LUCRETIA MOTT

Life and Letters

1833

Lucretia Mott, abolitionist and Quaker minister, later recalled her participation in the founding of the women's antislavery society. She highlighted the newness of such public activity for herself and for other women, even though, as a Quaker, Mott was accustomed to speaking in religious services.

At that time I had no idea of the meaning of preambles, and resolutions, and votings. Women had never been in any assemblies of the kind. I had attended only one convention — a convention of colored people — before that; and that was the first time in my life I had ever heard a vote taken, being accustomed to our Quaker way of getting the prevailing sentiment of the meeting. When, a short time after, we came together to form the Female Anti-Slavery Society, there was not a woman capable of taking the chair and organizing that meeting in due order; and we had to call on James McCrummel, a colored man, to give us aid in the work.

Anna Davis Hallowell, ed., *James and Lucretia Mott, Life and Letters* (Boston: Houghton-Mifflin, 1884), 121.

Women Claim and Debate the Right to Speak and Act against Slavery and Race Prejudice, July 1836–May 1837

10

AMERICAN ANTI-SLAVERY SOCIETY

Petition Form for Women

1834

By 1834 women had become active in the petition campaign to Congress to end slavery in the District of Columbia. The AASS printed a special form for women, which asserted that women's petitions were appropriate to the political moment. Hundreds of women who signed these forms thronged to hear the Grimké sisters speak in 1836 and 1837.

FATHERS AND RULERS OF OUR COUNTRY:
Suffer us, we pray you, with the sympathies which we are constrained to feel as wives, as mothers, and as daughters, to plead with you in behalf of a long oppressed and deeply injured class of native Americans [i.e., American-born slaves], residing in that portion of our country which is under your exclusive control. We should poorly estimate the

Gilbert H. Barnes and Dwight L. Dumond, eds., *Letters of Theodore Dwight Weld, Angelina Grimké Weld and Sarah Grimké, 1822–1844* (New York: Appleton-Century-Crofts, 1934; reprint Gloucester, MA: Smith, 1965), 1:175–76.

virtues which ought ever to distinguish your honorable body could we anticipate any other than a favorable hearing when our appeal is to men, to philanthropists, to patriots, to the legislators and guardians of a Christian people. We should be less than women, if the nameless and unnumbered wrongs of which the slaves of our sex are made the defenseless victims, did not fill us with horror and constrain us, in earnestness and agony of spirit to pray for their deliverance. By day and by night, their woes and wrongs rise up before us, throwing shades of mournful contrast over the joys of domestic life, and filling our hearts with sadness at the recollection of those whose hearths are desolate.

Nor do we forget, in the contemplation of their other sufferings, the intellectual and moral degradation to which they are doomed; how the soul formed for companionship with angels, is despoiled and brutified, and consigned to ignorance, pollution, and ruin.

Surely then, as the representatives of a people professedly christian, you will bear with us when we express our solemn apprehensions in the language of the patriotic Jefferson "we tremble for our country when we remember that God is just, and that his justice cannot sleep forever," and when in obedience to a divine command "we remember them who are in bonds as bound with them." Impelled by these sentiments, we solemnly purpose, the grace of God assisting, to importune high Heaven with prayer, and our national Legislature with appeals, until this christian people abjure forever a traffic in the souls of men, and the groans of the oppressed no longer ascend to God from the dust where they now welter.

We do not ask your honorable body to transcend your constitutional powers, by legislating on the subject of slavery within the boundaries of any slaveholding State; but we do conjure you to abolish slavery in the District of Columbia where you exercise exclusive jurisdiction. In the name of humanity, justice, equal rights and impartial law, our country's weal, her honor and her cherished hopes we earnestly implore for this our humble petition, your favorable regard. If both in christian and in heathen lands, Kings have revoked their edicts, at the intercession of woman, and tyrants have relented when she appeared a suppliant for mercy, surely we may hope that the Legislators of a free, enlightened and christian people will lend their ear to our appeals, when the only boon we crave is the restoration of rights unjustly wrested from the innocent and defenseless.—And as in duty bound your petitioners will ever pray.

11

ANGELINA GRIMKÉ

Appeal to the Christian Women of the South
1836

In her first publication, Angelina Grimké expressed themes that characterized women's abolitionist efforts, especially their appeal to women as women and their encouragement of women's activism in public life.

RESPECTED FRIENDS:

It is because I feel a deep and tender interest in your present and eternal welfare that I am willing thus publicly to address you. Some of you have loved me as a relative, and some have felt bound to me in Christian sympathy, and Gospel friendship. . . . It is because you have known me that I write thus unto you. . . .

If you really suppose *you* can do nothing to overthrow slavery, you are greatly mistaken. You can do much in every way: four things I will name. 1st. You can read on this subject. 2d. You can pray over this subject. 3d. You can speak on this subject. 4th. You can *act* on this subject. . . .

3. Speak on this subject. It is through the tongue, the pen, and the press, that truth is principally propagated. Speak then to your relatives, your friends, your acquaintances on the subject of slavery; be not afraid if you are conscientiously convinced it is sinful, to say so openly, but calmly, and let your sentiments be known. If you are served by the slaves of others, try to ameliorate their condition as much as possible; never aggravate their faults, and thus add fuel to the fire of anger already kindled in a master and mistress's bosom. . . . Discountenance *all* cruelty to them, all starvation, all corporal chastisement; these may brutalize and *break* their spirits, but will never bond them to willing, cheerful obedience. If possible, see that they are comfortably and *seasonably*

Angelina E. Grimké, *Appeal to the Christian Women of the South,* New York: [American Anti-Slavery Society], 1836.

fed, whether in the house or the field; it is unreasonable and cruel to expect slaves to wait for their breakfast until eleven o'clock, when they rise at five or six. Do all you can, to induce their owners to clothe them well, and to allow them many little indulgences which would contribute to their comfort. Above all, try to persuade your husband, father, brothers and sons that *slavery is a crime against God and man* . . . be faithful in pleading the cause of the oppressed.

> Will you behold unheeding,
>
> Life's holiest feeling crushed,
>
> Where *woman's* heart is bleeding,
>
> Shall *woman's* heart be hushed? . . .

4. Act on this subject. Some of you *own* slaves yourselves. If you believe slavery is *Sinful,* set them at liberty, "undo the heavy burdens and let the oppressed go free." If they wish to remain with you, pay them wages, if not let them leave you. Should they remain teach them and have them taught the common branches of an English education; they have minds and those minds *ought to be improved.* So precious a talent as intellect, never was given to be wrapt in a napkin and buried in the earth. It is the *duty* of all, as far as they can, to improve their own mental faculties, because we are commanded to love God with *all our minds,* as well as with all our hearts, and we commit a great sin, if we *forbid or prevent* that cultivation of the mind in others, which would enable them to perform this duty. . . .

I know that this doctrine of obeying *God,* rather than man, will be considered as dangerous and heretical by many, but I am not afraid openly to avow it, because it is the doctrine of the Bible. . . . If a law commands me to sin I will break it. . . . The doctrine of blind obedience and unqualified submission to *any human* power, whether civil or ecclesiastical, is the doctrine of despotism, and ought to have no place among Republicans and Christians.

But you will perhaps say, such a course of conduct would inevitably expose us to great suffering. Yes! my christian friends, I believe it would, but this will *not* excuse you or anyone else for the neglect of *duty.* If Prophets and Apostles, Martyrs, and reformers had not been willing to suffer for truth's sake, where would the world have been now? If they had said, we cannot speak the truth, we cannot do what we believe is right, because *the laws of our country or public opinion are against us,* where would our holy religion have been now? . . . Why were the Presbyterians chased like the partridge over the highlands of Scotland—the Methodists pumped, and stoned, and pelted with rotten eggs—the Quakers incarcerated in filthy prisons, beaten, whipped at the cart's tail, banished and hung? Because they dared to *speak* the *truth,* to *break* the unrighteous *laws* of their country, and chose rather to suffer affliction with the people of God, "not accepting deliverance," even under the gallows.

But you may say we are *women,* how can *our* hearts endure persecution? And why not? Have not women stood up in all the dignity and strength of moral courage to be the leaders of the people, and to bear a faithful testimony for the truth whenever the providence of God has called them to do so?. . .

Let [the Christian women of the South] embody themselves in societies, and send petitions up to their different legislatures, entreating their husbands, fathers, brothers, and sons, to abolish the institution of slavery; no longer to subject *woman* to the scourge and the chain, to mental darkness and moral degradation, no longer to tear husbands from their wives, and children from their parents; no longer to make their lives bitter in hard bondage; no longer to reduce *American citizens* to the abject condition of *slaves,* of "chattels personal"; no longer to barter the *image of God* in human shambles for corruptible things such as silver and gold. . . .

If you could obtain but six signatures to such a petition in only one state, I would say, send up that petition, and be not in the least discouraged by the scoffs and jeers of the heartless, or the resolution of the house to lay it on the table. It will be a great thing if the subject can be introduced into your legislatures in any way, even by *women,* and *they* will be the most likely to introduce it there in the best possible manner, as a matter of *morals* and *religion,* not of expediency or politics. . . .

I have appealed to your sympathies as women, to your sense of duty as *Christian women.* . . . Count me not your "enemy because I have told you the truth," but believe me in unfeigned affection,

YOUR SYMPATHIZING FRIEND,
ANGELINA E. GRIMKÉ

12

ANGELINA GRIMKÉ

Letter to Jane Smith

New York, December 17, 1836

*In a series of personal letters to Jane Smith, her close friend, Angelina
Grimké expressed her hopes and fears about her public speaking in
New York. Smith was a Quaker who joined the Philadelphia Female
Anti-Slavery Society in 1838.*

MY BELOVED JANE:

Thou deservest a good long letter & I feel far more capable of writing
such a one today than I have for some weeks past & now I am going
to tell thee all my heart. After the privilege of attending the convention (during which time my feelings were too much occupied with the
business & taking notes to have much time to think of myself), I began
to feel afresh my *utter inability* to do any thing in the work I had undertaken. The more I looked at it, with the eye of reason, the more unnatural it seemed, & if I had dared to return to Philadelphia & lay down my
commission, most gladly would I have done so. But one little grain of
faith yet remains. I remember the deep travail of spirit thro' which I had
passed at Shrewsbury & could not but believe that He who had sent me
out would go before & prepare the way of the poor instruments he was
pleased to employ.

Last week a Baptist minister of the name of Dunbar proposed our
having a meeting in his Session room. . . . This was a great relief to our
minds, for we both felt that this was just the right thing & readily closed
in with the offer. The Female A S Sy embraced the opportunity of making this the commencement of Quarterly Meetings for their Sy, & it was
accordingly given out in 4 churches on the Sabbath, but our names *not*
mentioned. Well, after this was done we felt almost in despair about the
meeting, for we know that some persons here were exceedingly afraid
that if we addressed our sisters, it would be called Quaker preaching

Weld-Grimké Papers, Clements Library, University of Michigan, Ann Arbor.

& that the prejudice here against women speaking in public life was so great that if such a view was taken, our precious cause would be injured.

The Throne of Grace was our only refuge & to it we often fled in united supplication for divine help. On 4th day morning, our dear brother in the Lord, G. Smith, came to Henry Ludlow's (where we are now staying) to breakfast, & when we gathered round the family altar, our hearts were melted together as he poured out his soul in prayer for *us,* particularly, that we might be directed, strengthened & comforted in our work of mercy, & as soon as we rose from our places, the bell rung & a printed notice of the meeting was handed in, & in it our names were mentioned as intending to address the meeting. It was too much for us, & in christian freedom we opened our hearts to our dear friends. Truly we felt as if such a thing was humanly impossible. We talked the matter over & found that G Smith had another fear, that it would be called a Fanny Wright meeting & so on, & advised us not to make addresses except in parlors.

Well, we did not know what to do. The meeting was appointed & there was no business at all to come before it. When he left us, I went to my room. I laid my difficulty at the feet of Jesus. I called upon him in my trouble & he harkened unto my cry, renewed my strength & confidence in God, & from that time I felt sure of his help in the hour of need. My burden was rolled off upon his everlasting arm, & I could rejoice in a full assurance of his mercy & power to be mouth & wisdom, tongue & utterance to us both.

Yesterday morning, T d Weld came up like a brother to sympathize with us & encourage our hearts in the Lord. He is a precious christian, bid us not to fear, but to trust in God &c. In a previous conversation on our holding meetings, he had expressed his full unity with our doing so, and grieved over that factitious state of society which bound up the energies of woman, instead of allowing her to exercise them to the glory of God and the good of her fellow creatures. In the cause of the slaves, he believes, she has a *great* work to do & *must* be awakened to her responsibility &c.

His visit was really a strength to us, & I felt *no* fear about the consequences, went to the meeting at 3 O clock & found about 300 persons. It was opened with prayer by H Ludlow. We were warmly welcomed by brother Dunbar. They soon left us &, after an opening minute, I spoke for about 40 minutes, I think, feeling perfectly unembarrassed, about which Dear Sister [Sarah] did her part better than I did. We then read some extracts from papers & letters & answered a few questions, when at 5 the meeting closed, after the question had been put whether our sisters wished another meeting to be held. A good many rose & H L says he is sure he can get his Session room for us. . . . Many came up and spoke to us after the meeting was over. . . .

I know nothing of the effects on *others*. We went home with Julia Tap-pan to tea, & brother Weld was all anxiety to know about it. She undertook to give some account & among other things mentioned that a warm-hearted Abolitionist had found *his* way into the back pack of the meeting & that H L had escorted him out. Weld's countenance was instantly lighted up, & he exclaimed how extremely ridiculous to think of a man's being shouldered out of a meeting for fear he should hear a woman speak. *We* smiled & said we did not know how it seemed to others, but it looked very strange in our eyes. . . .

[Gerrit Smith] is one of the noblest, loveliest men I ever met. He seemed just like a brother to us and invited us very kindly to go to their house as a resting place after our winter work was over. No doubt thou will want to know when we expect to leave N Y. We don't know. Sister is now writing an Address to Southern Clergymen & we think this had best be finished before we go hence. She has already written 24 p & it is not yet done. Then it must all be copied, so that we cannot tell any thing about our movements. . . . We hope that now beginning has been made, that we shall be able to hold a series of meetings here with our sisters, &, as the brethren think it will not do to have public lectures in N Y, it seems the more necessary for us to do what we can. . . .

VERY AFFY A E GÉ

13

ANGELINA GRIMKÉ

Letter to Jane Smith
New York, January 20, 1837

To Jane Smith, Angelina Grimké described her growing power as a public speaker, the deepening effect the sisters were having on their audiences, and her love for this antislavery work.

Weld-Grimké Papers, Clements Library, University of Michigan, Ann Arbor.

MY DEAR JANE:

For the three weeks previous we had lectured on the Laws of the Slave States & illustrated each by example to show those laws were not a dead letter.[1] Yesterday we had intended to close this part of the subject by this testimony, then by showing that Slavery is cruel to the body, heart, mind and soul of the slave. But I could not get thro' more than the two first, so that the degradation of the mind and destruction of the soul remain for next week. We now hold our meetings regularly at Henry G. Ludlow's session room every 5th day [Thursday] afternoon at 3 O'Clock. By the by, as the room was so crowded and oppressively warm he gave out that we should have the Church itself hereafter—there must have been *more* than 300 out yesterday & we are told, a more influential class than at first attended. Our publications were eagerly received by the hands which were raised to catch them as we threw them into the crowd. A deepening interest we think is evidently exhibited. It really seems as if the Lord was moving by his Spirit on the hearts of the people and that the tide of feeling is beginning to rise, which under the Divine Blessing may yet move this city to rise up in the dignity of moral power against the crying sin of our Land.

But dear friend, thou will doubtless want to know whether I find it an *easy* thing to hold such meetings—I, no! I can truly say that the day I have to speak is always a day of suffering, & I now understand what friends mean when they say, they speak for *the relief of their own minds.* I feel like a totally different being after the meeting is over, for I assure thee I do know that a fresh caption [source of energy] is needed for every appearance in public. It is really delightful to see dear Sister so happy in this work. I have not the shadow of a doubt she is in her right place & will be made instrumental of great good. . . .

Thou mayest remark I speak of our *talks* as *lectures.* Well this is the name that *others* have given our poor effort, & I don't know in fact what to call such novel proceedings. How little! how *very little* I supposed, when I used to say "I wish I was a man, that I might go out and lecture," that I would ever do such a thing. The idea never crossed my mind that *as a woman* such work could possibly be assigned me. But the Lord is "wonderful counsel, excellent in working," making a way for his people when there seems to be *no* way. Dear Jane, I love the work. I count myself greatly favored in being called to it, & I often feel as if the only earthly blessing I have to ask for is to be made the unworthy instrument of arousing the slumbering energy & dormant sympathy of my northern sisters on this deeply painful & interesting subject.

[1]Hence AG countered the claims of proslavery advocates that cruel slave laws were not enforced.

ANGELINA GRIMKÉ

Letter to Jane Smith

New York, February 4, 1837

This letter contains Angelina Grimké's first mention of women's rights content in her lectures.

MY DEAR JANE:

. . . [Our meeting last week] was the largest we have had, about 400, I should think. . . . We had one male auditor, who refused to go out when H. G. L[udlow] told him it was exclusively for ladys, & so there he sat & somehow I did not feel his presence at all embarrassing & went on just as 'tho he was not there. Some one said he took notes, & I think he was a Southern spy & shall not be at all surprized if he publishes us in some Southern paper, for we have heard nothing of him here. . . .

Some friends think *I* make too many gestures, one thinking females ought to be *motionless* when speaking in public, another fearing that *other* denominations might be offended by them, because they were unaccustomed to hear women speak in public. But I think the more a speaker can yield himself entirely to the native impulses of feeling, the better, & this is just what I do. . . .

Last 5th day I think not more than 200 were out. Sister spoke one hour on the effects on the soul, & I finished off with some remarks on the popular objection Slavery is a political subject, therefore *women* should not intermeddle. I admitted it was, but endeavored to show that women were citizens & had duties to perform to their country as well as men. . . . I tried to enlighten our sisters a little in their rights & duties. . . .

PRAY FOR US —

A.E.GÉ

Weld-Grimké Papers, Clements Library, University of Michigan, Ann Arbor.

SARAH AND ANGELINA GRIMKÉ

Letter to Sarah Douglass

Newark, New Jersey, February 22, 1837

Sarah Douglass headed the only academy for African American girls in Philadelphia. She and her mother, Grace, were founding members of the Philadelphia Female Anti-Slavery Society. Yet racial prejudice among Philadelphia Quakers meant that the Douglasses sat on the "colored bench" in the Grimkés' Quaker meeting house. In this first of two joint letters to Sarah Douglass, Sarah and Angelina describe their meetings with African American abolitionists in New York and New Jersey as they sought to build a cross-race antislavery coalition.

MY DEAR SARAH:

. . . It is a great comfort to us that our dear sisters in Philadelphia pray for us. We need your prayers & I believe they help us. We have had the privilege of attending several female prayer meetings among the colored people in New York & uniting with them in supplicating the Lord of Hosts to open a door of deliverance for our colored brethren. I have faith to believe God will answer our petitions, but sometimes my heart trembles for my country & I fear she will persist in sin until she brings down upon her guilty head the thunders of his wrath. Oh then let us pray that she may repent quickly.

Our meetings in New York have been better attended than we expected, but it is a hard place to labor in; ten thousand cords of interest are linked with the southern slaveholder. Still there are some warm-hearted abolitionists there, & I believe the fire of Emancipation will increase until our Jubilee is proclaimed.

We came to Bloomfield [N.J.] . . . last week, held two meetings with the ladies there, & they formed a society. We have had two interesting meetings also at this place [Newark] & a society was formed here;

Gilbert H. Barnes and Dwight L. Dumond, eds., *Letters of Theodore Dwight Weld, Angelina Grimké Weld and Sarah Grimké, 1822–1844* (New York: Appleton-Century-Crofts, 1934; reprint Gloucester, MA: Smith, 1965), 1:362.

many ladies here are much engaged on behalf of the slave & this is a very important place. Southern interest is powerful; shoes & carriages, etc. made in Newark are bartered for the gold of the South, which is gotten by the unrequited Toil of the slave. Many children attended our meetings, which rejoiced us because they will soon come on the stage of action & if they are only thoro'ly abolitionized, the bastille of slavery will fall. . . .[1]

I feel deeply for thee in thy sufferings on account of the cruel & unchristian prejudice which thou hast suffered so much from. Perhaps for the present generation we can do little on this subject especially in large cities; but if we are willing to suffer, our children will reap the reward of our afflictions & toil, & we shall meet a glorious reward hereafter.

It is so much the fashion to publish anti-slavery movements that I will just mention that our friends in N.Y. think the less said at present about what we are doing the better. Let us move quietly on for a while & the two "fanatical women," as the Richmond papers call us, may, thro' divine help, do a little good. . . .

AFFY THY FRIEND
SARAH M. GRIMKÉ

MY DEAR SARAH:

. . . We feel as yet unprepared to go fully into our delightful work, because the subject of Slavery is one of such length and breadth, height & depth that our time has been, & ought to be for some time to come, spent in reading on & studying it in its various bearings, I long to be fully harnessed for it, & often feel as if I had no petition to ask for at a throne of Grace, but to be made a blessing to the free & bond colored people of our land. The more I mingle with your people, the more I feel for their oppressions & desire to sympathize in their sorrows. . . .

ANGELINA E. GRIMKÉ

---

[1]Bastille: the notorious French prison that symbolized despotism was liberated by Revolutionary groups on July 14, 1789.

ANGELINA GRIMKÉ

Letter to Jane Smith

New York, March 22, 1837

Angelina Grimké describes the "sinful prejudice" that blocked the progress of antislavery women in New York.

MY DEAR JANE,

I do not think we shall form a National Female Society at the Convention & for this reason, but it must *not be* mentioned. The Ladys [Anti-Slavery] Sy is realy doing nothing, it is utterly inefficient & must continue so until our Sisters here are willing to giv up sinful prejudice. It is a canker worm among them & paralyzes every effort. They are doing literaly nothing as a Sy for the colored people. We attended their last Monthly mg. of Managers. I believed it right to throw before them our views on the state of things among them, particularly on prejudice. No colord Sister has ever been in the board, & they hav hardly any colored members even & will not admit any such in the working Sy. What we said to them was from a sense of duty in love & tears, but it was hard work, & I believ as much as they could possibly hear from us. But some were reachd, I do believ, for tears were shed, & when it was moved that a vote of thanks should be tendered to us for our kind & sisterly counsel, it was seconded with great feeling by a female who sat opposite to us. . . .

O Jane, how this Anti Slavery does grind us in the dust, hurls us from the proud elevation of *rank* in Society & throws us right down among those who sit, as it were, on the dung pile & among the pots. This is the best, the *only* way to get our wings coverd with silver & our feathers with yellow gold. Now it does seem to us that we had better hav no National Society until we can hav one of the *right stamp,* & I do not think one can flourish in this city while Prejudice banishes our colored sisters from an equal & full participation in its deliberations & labors. I am greatly in hopes that the Boston Society will send colord Delegates

---

Weld-Grimké Papers, Courtesy of William L. Clements Library, University of Michigan, Ann Arbor.

to the Convention & that something may be done to break down this
adamantine wall in this proud city. . . .

I AM THY A E GÉ

17 ⑫

ANGELINA AND SARAH GRIMKÉ

Letter to Sarah Douglass
New York City, April 3, 1837

*While organizing the upcoming convention of antislavery women, the
sisters urged African American friends to attend the meeting, noting the
harsh truth that racial prejudice would make the meeting difficult for
them, but encouraging them to believe that the benefits of their presence
would outweigh the pain. Angelina Grimké hoped that African American
delegates would help draft documents related to their race. Sarah
Grimké asked Sarah Douglass to help her understand the effects of racial
prejudice. Sarah and Grace Douglass did attend the 1837 Anti-Slavery
Convention of American Women in New York City, with Grace serving as
a vice president and Sarah serving on the Committee of Arrangements.*

DEAR SARAH:
. . . Whenever allusion is made to that distinction which American prejudice has made between those who wear a darker skin than we do,
I feel ashamed for my Country, ashamed for the church, but the time is
coming when such "respect of persons" will no more be known in our
land, & the children of the Lord will think no more of a difference in the
color of the skin than of that of the hair or the eyes. I was very glad to
hear from Sydney Ann Lewis that thy Mother & thyself tho't of coming
to our Female Convention. I am very, very glad of it, and would say all
I could to urge you to do so without fail. You, my dear Sisters, have a
work to do in rooting out this wicked feeling, as well as we. You *must be*

Weld-Grimké Papers, Clements Library, University of Michigan, Ann Arbor.

willing to come amongst us, tho' it *may be* your feelings *may* be wounded by the "putting forth of the finger," the avoidance of a seat by you, or the glancing of the eye. To suffer these things is the sacrifice which is called for at *your hands,* & I earnestly desire that you may be willing to bear these mortifications with christian meekness, gentleness & love. They will tend to your growth in grace, & will help your paler sisters *more* than anything else to overcome their own sinful feelings. Come, then, I would say, for we need your help. I cannot help hoping that a place will be found for the Fortens too. . . . If an Address to the colored people is passed by our Convention, it will be absolutely necessary that some of them should be on the Committee to examine it before it is printed.

. . . [W]e spent yesterday week in Poughkeepsie, & brother [Gerrit] Smith & ourselves had a meeting with the colored people in the evening. About 300 attended, & it was a very satisfactory meeting I believe to all parties & for the first time in my life I spoke in a promiscuous assembly, but I found that the men were no more to me then, than the women. Some of the females present were very desirous we should hold a meeting with the ladies, & we would gladly have done so, had we not expected to leave town early the next morning.

> I REMAIN THY SISTER IN THE LORD
> A E GRIMKÉ

MY BELOVED SISTER:

I suppose thou still attends our meeting. I feel as if the seat you occupy there is a reproach to us, & I think the Lord must send you there to be a memorial to us of our pride & our prejudice. Yet we heed it not; like many of his other lessons we let it pass unimproved. . . . I feel as if I had taken my stand by the side of the colored American, willing to share with him the odium of a darker skin, & trust, if I am permitted again to take my seat in Arch St. Mtg. House, it will be beside thee & thy dear mother. Will it be too painful for thee to give me a description of thy feelings under the effect of steel hearted prejudice? Dear Sarah, does it sink thy spirits, does it destroy thy comfort? I pray that I may feel more & more deeply for you, that thro' the grace of God my soul may be in your soul's stead. . . .

> [SARAH GRIMKÉ]

The Anti-Slavery Convention
of American Women, 1837

18 ⑬

SARAH FORTEN

Letter to Angelina Grimké
Philadelphia, April 15, 1837

Sarah Forten responded to Angelina's desire to learn about the effects of racial prejudice. Forten evaluated both the positive effects of the antislavery movement and the negative effects of racial prejudice on her life. She explained why she despised the colonization movement. Daughter of one of Philadelphia's wealthiest African American families, Sarah Forten wrote poetry and essays for the antislavery press and was an active member of the Philadelphia Female Anti-Slavery Society. A poem she wrote for the 1837 Anti-Slavery Convention of American Women was read to the gathering.

Esteemed Friend:

I have to thank you for the interest which has led you to address a letter to me on subject which claims so large a share of your attention. In making a reply to the question proposed by you, I might truly advance the excuse of inability; but you well know how to compassionate the weakness of one who has written but little on the subject, and who has until very lately lived and acted more for herself than for the good of others.

Gilbert H. Barnes and Dwight L. Dumond, eds., *Letters of Theodore Dwight Weld, Angelina Grimké Weld and Sarah Grimké, 1822–1844* (New York: Appleton-Century-Crofts, 1934; reprint Gloucester, MA: Smith, 1965), 1:379.

I confess that I am wholly indebted to the Abolition cause for arousing me from apathy and indifference, shedding light into a mind which has been too long wrapt in selfish darkness.

In reply to your question—of the "effect of Prejudice" on myself, I must acknowledge that it has often embittered my feelings, particularly when I recollect that we are the innocent victims of it; for you are well aware that it originates from dislike to the color of the skin, as much as from the degradation of Slavery. I am peculiarly sensitive on this point, and consequently seek to avoid as much as possible mingling with those who exist under its influence. I must also own that *it* has often engendered feelings of discontent and mortification in my breast when I saw that many were preferred before me, who by education, birth, or worldly circumstances were no better than myself. THEIR sole claim to notice depending on the superior advantage of being *White;* but I am striving to live above such heart burnings, and will learn to "bear and forbear" believing that a spirit of forbearance under such evils is all that we as a people can well exert.

Colonization is, as you well know, the offspring of Prejudice. It has doubtless had a baneful influence on our People. I despise the aim of that Institution most heartily, and have never yet met one man or woman of Color who thought better of it than I do. I believe, with all just and good persons, that it originated more immediately from prejudice than from philanthropy. The longing desire of a separation induces this belief, and the spirit of "this is not your Country" is made manifest by many obstacles it throws in the way of their advancement mentally and morally. No doubt but there has always existed the same amount of prejudice in the minds of Americans towards the descendants of Africa; it wanted only the spirit of colonization to call it into action. It can be seen in the exclusion of the colored people from their churches, or placing them in obscure corners. We see it in their being barred from a participation with others in acquiring any useful knowledge; public lectures are not usually free to the colored people; they may not avail themselves of the right to drink at the fountain of learning, or gain an insight into the arts and science of our favored land. All this and more do they feel acutely. I only marvel that they are in possession of any knowledge at all, circumscribed as they have been by an all powerful prejudice. Even our professed friends have not yet rid themselves of it—to some of them it clings like a dark mantle obscuring their many virtues and choking up the avenues to higher and nobler sentiments. I recollect the words of one of the one of the best and least prejudiced men in the Abolition ranks. "Ah," said he, "I can recall the time when in walking with a colored brother, the darker the night, the better Abolitionist was I." He does not say so now, but my friend, how much of this leaven still lingers in the hearts of our white brethern and sisters is oftentimes made manifest to us; but when we recollect what great sacrifices to public sentiment they are called upon to make, we cannot wholly blame them. Many, very many are anxious to take up the cross, but how few are strong enough to bear it. For our own family, we have to thank a kind Providence for placing us in a situation that has hitherto prevented us from falling under the weight of this evil; we feel it but in a slight degree compared with many others. We are not much dependent upon the tender mercies of our enemies, always having resources within ourselves to which we can apply. We are not disturbed in our social relations; we never travel far from home and seldom go to public places unless quite sure that admission is free to all; therefore we meet with none of these mortifications which might otherwise ensue. I would recommend to my colored friends to follow our example and they would be spared some very painful realities. . . .

Do you know whether the Ladies have fixed on the day for holding their Convention? Do you not think it would be best to hold it the day before the men's meeting, for most of us would be desirous to be present at both meetings. Could you not suggest this plan? There will probably be a large delegation from our society. My sisters propose going but not as Delegates. I presume there will be a sale of fancy articles there, as we were requested to send some of our work. We are all quite busy preparing something pretty and useful. Several of our schools will have specimens of work and penmanship to be sent. . . .

My Parents and Sisters unite with me in affection to you and your excellent sister.

YOURS AFFECTIONATELY
SARAH L. FORTEN

19

ANGELINA GRIMKÉ

An Appeal to the Women of the Nominally Free States

1837

Published by the 1837 Anti-Slavery Convention of American Women, Angelina Grimké's second publication asserted women's right to act on behalf of emancipation and exhorted women to incorporate their antislavery beliefs into their daily actions. Her cogent defense of women's rights reflected the confidence that flowed from her successful public speaking.

BELOVED SISTERS:

. . . The women of the North have high and holy duties to perform in the work of emancipation—duties to themselves, to the suffering slave, to the slaveholder, to the church, to their country, and to the world at large, and, above all to their God. Duties, which if not performed now, may never be performed at all. . . .

Every citizen should feel an intense interest in the political concerns of the country, because the honor, happiness, and well being of every class, are bound up in its politics, government and laws. Are we aliens because we are women? Are we bereft of citizenship because we are the *mothers, wives,* and *daughters* of a mighty people? Have *women* no country—no interest stakes in public weal—no liabilities in common peril—no partnership in a nation's guilt and shame?—Has *woman* no home nor household altars, nor endearing ties of kindred, nor sway with man, nor power at a mercy seat, nor voice to cheer, nor hand to raise the drooping, and to bind the broken? . . .

What then is Slavery? It is that crime, which casts man down from that exaltation where God has placed him, "a little lower than the angels," and sinks him to a level with the beasts of the field. This intelligent and immortal being is confounded with the brutes that perish; he whose spirit was formed to rise in aspirations of gratitude and praise

Angelina E. Grimké, *An Appeal to the Women of the Nominally Free States, Issued by an Anti-Slavery Convention of American Women* (New York: W. S. Dorr, 1837).

whilst here, and to spend an eternity with God in heaven, is herded with the beasts, whose spirits go downward with their bodies of clay, to the dust of which they were made. Slavery is that crime by which man is robbed of his inalienable right to liberty, and the pursuit of happiness, the diadem of glory, and honor, with which he was crowned, and that sceptre of dominion which was placed in his hand when he was ushered upon the theatre of creation. . . .

It is gravely urged that as it is a *political subject, women* have no concernment with it; this doctrine of the North is a sycophantic response to the declaration of a Southern representative, that women have no right to send up petitions to Congress. We know, dear sisters, that the open and the secret enemies of freedom in our country have dreaded our influence, and therefore have reprobated our interference, and in order to blind us to our responsibilities, have thrown dust into our eyes, well knowing that if the organ of vision is only clear, the whole body, the moving and acting faculties will become full of light, and will soon be thrown into powerful action. Some, who pretend to be very jealous for the honor of our sex, and are very anxious that *we* should scrupulously maintain the dignity and delicacy of female propriety, continually urge this objection to female effort. We grant that it is a political, as well as a moral subject: does this exonerate women from their duties as subjects of the government, as members of the great human family? Have women never wisely and laudably exercised political responsibilities? . . .

And, dear sisters, in a country where women are degraded and brutalized, and where their exposed persons bleed under the lash—where they are sold in the shambles of "negro brokers"—robbed of their hard earnings—torn from their husbands, and forcibly plundered of their virtue and their offspring; surely, in *such* a country, it is very natural that *women* should wish to know "the reason *why*"—especially when these outrages of blood and nameless horror are practised in violation of the principles of our national Bill of Rights and the Preamble of our Constitution. We do not, then, and cannot concede the position, that because this is a *political subject* women ought to fold their hands in idleness, and close their eyes and ears to the "horrible things" that are practised in our land. The denial of our duty to act, is a bold denial of our right to act; and if we have no right to act, then may *we* well be termed "the white slaves of the North"—for, like our brethren in bonds, we must seal our lips in silence and despair. . . . *All moral beings have essentially the same rights and the same duties,* whether they be male or female. . . .

Out of the millions of slaves who have been stolen from Africa, a very great number must have been women, who were torn from the arms of their fathers and husbands, brothers, and children, and subjected to all the horrors of the middle passage and the still greater sufferings of slavery in a foreign land.[1] . . . The great mass of female slaves in the southern states are the descendants of these hapless strangers: 1,000,000 of them now wear the iron yoke of slavery in this land of boasted liberty and law. They are our countrywomen — *they are our sisters,* and to us, as women, they have a right to look for sympathy with their sorrows, and effort and prayer for their rescue. Upon those of us especially, who have named the name of Christ, they have peculiar claims, and claims which *we must answer or we shall incur a heavy load of guilt.*

Women, too, are constituted by nature the peculiar guardians of children, and children are the victims of this horrible system. Helpless infancy is robbed of the tender care of the mother, and the protection of the father. . . .

And now, dear sisters, let us not forget that *Northern* women are participators in the crime of Slavery — too many of *us* have surrendered our hearts and hands to the wealthy planters of the South, and gone down with them to live on the unrequited toil of the Slave. Too many of *us* have ourselves become slaveholders, our hearts have been hardened under the searing influence of the system, and we too, have learned to be tyrants in the school of despots. . . .

But let it be so no longer. Let us henceforward resolve, that the women of the free states never again will barter their principles for the blood bought luxuries of the South — never again will regard with complacency, much less with the tender sentiments of love, any man "who buildeth his house by unrighteousness and his chambers by wrong, that useth his neighbor's service *without* wages, and giveth him *not* for his work.". . .

Multitudes of Northern women are daily making use of the products of slave labor. They are clothing themselves and their families in the cotton, and eating the rice and the sugar, which they well know has cost the slave his unrequited toil, his blood and his tears; and if the maxim in law be founded in justice and truth, that "the receiver is *as bad* as the thief," how much *greater* the condemnation of those, who, not merely receive the stolen products of the slave's labor, but *voluntarily* purchase them, and *continually appropriate them to their own use.* . . .

In consequence of the odium which the degradation of slavery has attached to *color* even in the free states, our *colored sisters* are dreadfully

---

[1]Middle passage: the long voyage from Africa to the slave colonies of North and South America, during which many African captives died.

oppressed here. Our seminaries of learning are closed to them, they are almost entirely banished from our lecture rooms, and even in the house of God they are separated from their white brethren and sisters as though we were afraid to come in contact with a colored skin. . . . Yes, our sisters, little as we may be willing to admit it, yet it is assuredly true, that whenever we treat a colored brother and sister in a way different from that in which we would treat them, were they white, we do virtually *reproach our Maker* for having dyed their skins of a sable hue. . . .

Much may be done, too, by sympathizing with our oppressed colored sisters, who are suffering in our very midst. Extend to them the right hand of fellowship on the broad principles of humanity and Christianity — treat them as *equals* — visit them as *equals* — invite them to cooperate with you in Anti-Slavery and Temperance, and Moral reform Societies — in Maternal Associations, and Prayer Meetings, and Reading Companies. . . . Opportunities frequently occur in travelling, and in other public situations, when your countenance, your influence, and your hand, might shield a sister from contempt and insult, and procure for her comfortable accommodations. . . . Multitudes of instances will continually occur in which you will have the opportunity of identifying yourselves with this injured class of our fellow-beings; embrace these opportunities at all times and in all places. . . . In this way, and in this way alone, will you be enabled to subdue that deep-rooted prejudice which is doing the work of oppression in the Free States to a most dreadful extent.

20

THE ANTI-SLAVERY CONVENTION
OF AMERICAN WOMEN

Proceedings

New York City, May 9–12, 1837

Resolutions passed at this unprecedented convention highlight the public priorities of Garrisonian women and the place that women's rights was beginning to occupy in their ranks.

Proceedings of the Anti-Slavery Convention of American Women, Held in the City of New York, May 9–12, 1837 (New York: W. S. Dorr, 1837).

WEDNESDAY, MAY 10.

The Convention was called to order at 3 o'clock, p.m.

A portion of the Scriptures was read, and prayer offered.

The Committee of Arrangements made a report recommending the following subjects for the consideration of the Convention.

1. Appeal to the Women of the *nominally* Free States;
2. Address to Free Colored Americans;
3. Letter to the Women of Great Britain;
4. Circular to the Female Anti-Slavery Societies in the United States;
5. Letter to Juvenile Anti-Slavery Societies;
6. Letter to John Quincy Adams.

. . . On motion of A. E. Grimké the following resolutions were adopted: Resolved, That we regard the combination of interest which exists between the North and the South, in their political, commercial, and domestic relations, as the true, but hidden cause of the unprincipled and violent efforts which have been made, (at the North, but made in vain,) to smother free discussion, impugn the motive, and traduce the characters of abolitionists.

Resolved, That the right of petition is natural and inalienable, derived immediately from God and guaranteed by the Constitution of the United States, and that we regard every effort in Congress to abridge this sacred right, whether it be exercised by man or woman, the bond or the free, as a high-handed usurpation of power, and an attempt to strike a deathblow at the freedom of the people. And therefore that it is the duty of every woman in the United States, whether northerner or southerner, annually to petition Congress with the faith of an Esther, and the untiring perseverance of the importunate widow, for the immediate abolition of slavery in the District of Columbia and the Territory of Florida, and the extermination of the inter-state slave trade.

On motion of S. M. Grimké the following resolution was adopted:

Resolved, That we regard those northern men and women, who marry southern slaveholders, either at the South or the North, as identifying themselves with a system which desecrates the marriage relation among a large portion of the white inhabitants of the southern states, and utterly destroys it among the victims of their oppression.

The movers of the previous resolutions, sustained them by some remarks. . . .

A. E. Grimké offered the following resolution:

Resolved, That as certain rights and duties are common to all moral beings, the time has come for woman to move in that sphere which

Providence has assigned her, and no longer remain satisfied in the circumscribed limits with which corrupt custom and a perverted application of Scripture has encircled her; therefore that it is the duty of woman, and the province of woman, to plead her cause of the oppressed in our land and to do all that she can by her voice, and her pen, and her purse, and the influence of her example, to overthrow the horrible system of American slavery.

The resolution was sustained by the mover, and by Lucretia Mott. Amendments were offered by Mary Grew and Mrs. A. L. Cox, which called forth an animated and interesting debate respecting the rights and duties of women. The resolution was finally adopted, without amendments, though *not unanimously.*

Adjourned to Thursday morning, 10 o'clock.

Among those who voted against the adoption of this resolution, the following wished to have their names recorded in the minutes, as disapproving of some parts of it: — Mrs. Brower, Mrs. A. L. Cox, Mrs. Sophronia Johnson, Mrs. R. W. Lambden, Mrs. A. J. Lane, Mrs. R. G. Williams, Mrs. G. F. Martyn, Mrs. O. Willcox, Miss A. Rankin, Miss A. J. Dunbar, Miss H. Willcox, and Ruby Knight.

Selected Resolutions on Thursday, May 11:

On motion of Mrs. A. L. Cox, seconded by Rebecca B. Spring,

Resolved, That there is no class of women to whom the anti-slavery cause makes so direct and powerful an appeal as to *mothers*; and that they are solemnly urged by all the blessings of their own and their children's freedom, and by all the contrasted bitterness of the slave-mother's condition, to lift up their hearts to God on behalf of the captive, as often as they pour them out over their own children in a joy with which "no stranger may intermeddle"; and that they are equally bound to guard with jealous care the minds of their children from the ruining influences of the spirit of pro-slavery and prejudice, let those influences come in what name, or through what connections they may.

A. W. Weston offered the following resolution, viz:

Resolved, That we feel bound solemnly to protest against the principles of the American Colonization Society, as anti-Republican and anti-Christian, that we believe them to have had a most sorrowful influence in removing the chains of the slave by recognizing him as the property of his master, and in strengthening the unreasonable and unholy prejudice against our oppressed brethren and sisters, by declaring them "almost too debased to be reached by the heavenly light," that to the slave, the Society offers exile or bondage; to the free man, persecution or banishment, and that we view it as an expatriation Society.

On motion of A. E. Grimké,

Resolved, That this Convention do firmly believe that the existence of an unnatural prejudice against our colored population, is one of the chief pillars of American slavery—therefore, that the more we mingle with our oppressed brethren and sisters, the more deeply are we convinced of the sinfulness of that anti-Christian prejudice which is crushing them to the earth in our nominally Free States—sealing up the fountains of knowledge from their panting spirits, and driving them into infidelity, and that we deem it a solemn duty for every woman to pray to be delivered from such an unholy feeling, and to act out the principles of Christian equality by associating with them as though the color of the skin was of no more consequence than that of the hair, or the eyes.

21

CATHARINE E. BEECHER

Essay on Slavery and Abolitionism, with Reference to the Duty of American Females
1837

Responding to Angelina Grimké's Appeal to the Christian Women of the South (1836; see Document 11), Catharine Beecher defended different forms of female power. Her goal of feminizing the teaching profession drew on and led her to promote women's power in family life. Opposing slavery, but fearful of civil war, Beecher hoped for change through slow reforms and education.

MY DEAR FRIEND:

Your public address to Christian females at the South has reached me, and I have been urged to aid in circulating it at the North. I have also been informed, that you contemplate a tour, during the ensuing year, for the purpose of exerting your influence to form Abolition Societies among ladies of the non-slave-holding States.

Catharine E. Beecher, *Essay on Slavery and Abolitionism, with Reference to the Duty of American Females* (Philadelphia: Perkins, 1837).

Our acquaintance and friendship give me a claim to your private ear; but there are reasons why it seems more desirable to address you, who now stand before the public as an advocate of Abolition measures, in a more public manner.

The object I have in view, is to present some reasons why it seems unwise and inexpedient for ladies of the non-slave-holding States to unite themselves in Abolition Societies; and thus, at the same time, to exhibit the inexpediency of the course you propose to adopt. . . .

Now Abolitionists are before the community, and declare that all slavery is sin, which ought to be immediately forsaken; and that it is their object and intention to promote the *immediate emancipation* of all the slaves in this nation. . . . [R]eproaches, rebukes, and sneers, were employed to convince the whites that their prejudices were sinful. . . .

[T]he severing of the Union by the present mode of agitating the question . . . may be one of the results, and, if so, what are the probabilities for a Southern republic that has torn itself off for the purpose of excluding foreign interference, and for the purpose of perpetuating slavery? . . .

Heaven has appointed to one sex the superior, and to the other the subordinate station, and this without any reference to the character or conduct of either. It is therefore as much for the dignity as it is for the interest of females, in all respects to conform to the duties of this relation. . . . But while woman holds a subordinate relation in society to the other sex, it is not because it was designed that her duties or her influence should be any the less important, or all-pervading. But it was designed that the mode of gaining influence and of exercising power should be altogether different and peculiar. . . .

Woman is to win every thing by peace and love; by making herself so much respected, esteemed and loved, that to yield to her opinions and to gratify her wishes, will be the free-will offering of the heart. But this is to be all accomplished in the domestic and social circle. . . . But the moment woman begins to feel the promptings of ambition, or the thirst for power, her aegis of defence is gone. All the sacred protection of religion, all the generous promptings of chivalry, all the poetry of romantic gallantry, depend upon woman's retaining her place as dependent and defenceless, and making no claims, and maintaining no right but what are the gifts of honour, rectitude and love.

A woman may seek the aid of co-operation and combination among her own sex, to assist her in her appropriate offices of piety, charity, maternal and domestic duty; but whatever, in any measure, throws a woman into the attitude of a combatant, either for herself or others—whatever binds her in a party conflict—whatever obliges her in any way to exert coercive influences, throws her out of her appropriate sphere. . . .

If it is asked, "May not woman appropriately come forward as a suppliant for a portion of her sex who are bound in cruel bondage?" It is replied, that, the rectitude and propriety of any such measure, depend entirely on its probable results. If petitions from females will operate to exasperate; if they will be deemed obtrusive, indecorous, and unwise, by those to whom they are addressed; . . . if they will be the opening wedge, that will eventually bring females as petitioners and partisans into every political measure that may tend to injure and oppress their sex . . . then it is neither appropriate nor wise, nor right, for a woman to petition for the relief of oppressed females. . . .

In this country, petitions to congress, in reference to the official duties of legislators, seem, IN ALL CASES, to fall entirely without the sphere of female duty. Men are the proper persons to make appeals to the rulers whom they appoint, and if their female friends, by arguments and persuasions, can induce them to petition, all the good that can be done by such measures will be secured. But if females cannot influence their nearest friends, to urge forward a public measure in this way, they surely are out of their place, in attempting to do it themselves. . . .

It is allowed by all reflecting minds, that the safety and happiness of this nation depends upon having the *children* educated, and not only intellectually, but morally and religiously. There are now nearly two millions of children and adults in this country who cannot read, and who have no schools of any kind. To give only a small supply of teachers to these destitute children, who are generally where the population is sparse, will demand *thirty thousand teachers* at the moment and an addition of *two thousand every year.* Where is this army of teachers to be found? Is it at all probable that the other sex will afford even a moderate portion of this supply? . . . Men will be educators in the college, in the high school, in some of the most honourable and lucrative common schools, but the *children,* the *little children* of this nation must, to a wide extent, be taught by females, or remain untaught. . . . And as the value of education rises in the public mind . . . women will more and more be furnished with those intellectual advantages which they need to fit them for such duties.

The result will be, that America will be distinguished above all other nations, for well-educated females and for the influence they will exert on the general interests of society. But if females, as they approach the other sex, in intellectual elevation, begin to claim, or to exercise in any manner, the peculiar prerogatives of that sex, education will prove a doubtful and dangerous blessing. But this will never be the result. For the more intelligent a woman becomes, the more she can appreciate the wisdom of that ordinance that appointed her subordinate station.

But it may be asked, is there nothing to be done to bring this national sin of slavery to an end? Must the internal slave-trade, a trade now ranked as piracy among all civilized nations, still prosper in our bounds? Must the very seat of our government stand as one of the chief slave-markets of the land; and must not Christian females open their lips, nor lift a finger, to bring such a shame and sin to an end? To this it may be replied, that Christian females may, and can say and do much to bring these evils to an end; and the present is a time and an occasion when it seems most desirable that they should know, and appreciate, and *exercise* the power which they do possess for so desirable an end. . . .

In the present aspect of affairs among us, when everything seems to be tending to disunion and distraction, it surely has become the duty of every female instantly to relinquish the attitude of a partisan, in every matter of clashing interests, and to assume the office of a mediator, and an advocate of peace. And to do this, it is not necessary that a woman should in any manner relinquish her opinion as to the evils or the benefits, the right or the wrong, of any principle of practice. But, while quietly holding her own opinions, and calmly avowing them, when conscience and integrity make the duty imperative, every female can employ her influence, not for the purpose of exciting or regulating public sentiment, but rather for the purpose of promoting a spirit of candour, forbearance, charity, and peace.

The Grimké Sisters Redefine the Rights of Women as Antislavery Speakers, Massachusetts, Summer 1837

22

ANGELINA GRIMKÉ

Letter to Jane Smith

Boston, May 29, 1837

In this letter Angelina reflected on her public embrace of "the rights of women." Amazed by her success, she began to seek support for the untrodden path she was entering. She also expressed interest in another radical notion emerging within the abolitionist movement: "non-resistance," or the repudiation of civil government.

MY DEAR JANE:
. . . [At the convention of the American Anti-Slavery Society] a peace resolution was brought up, but this occasioned some difficulty, on account of non-resistance here meaning a repudiation of civil Government, & of course we cannot expect many to be willing to do this. There was no difficulty as to war itself. Indeed my own mind is all in a mist & I desire earnestly to know what is the truth about it, whether all civil government is an usurpation of Gods authority or not. Hast thou ever tho't about it, & what is thy opinion?

It has really been delightful to mingle with our brethren & sisters in this city. On 5th day evening we had a pleasant meeting of Abolitionists at Francis Jackson's, in the rooms where the Female Anti-Slavery

Weld-Grimké Papers, Clements Library, University of Michigan, Ann Arbor.

Meeting was held. On 6th day evening, we had just another such at Friend Chapman's, Ann's father. Here I had a long talk with the brethren on the rights of women & found a very general sentiment prevailing that it was time our fetters were broken. Goodell said he was well aware that women could not perform their duties as moral beings, under the existing state of public sentiment. M Child & M Chapman support the same views. Indeed very many seem to think that a new order of things is very desirable in this respect.

And now, my dear friend, in view of these things, I feel as if it is not the cause of the slave only which we plead, but the cause of woman as a responsible moral being, & I am ready to exclaim, "Who is sufficient for these things?" These holy causes must be injured if they are not helped by us. What an untrodden path we have entered upon! Sometimes I feel almost bewildered, amazed, confounded & wonder by what strange concatenation of events I came to be where I am & what I am. And if I look forward, I am no less bewildered. I see not to what point, all these things are leading me. I wonder whether I shall make shipwreck of the faith—I cannot tell—but one thing comforts me, I do feel as tho' the Lord had sent us, & as if I was leaning on the arm of my beloved. I do not believe we are going into this warfare at our own charges (spiritually), tho' I rejoice the Lord has provided for our doing so in a pecuniary point of view.

Tomorrow, we begin our public labor at Dorchester. . . . Pray for us, dear Jane. We need it *more* than ever. We see only in a glass darkly what results are to grow out of this experiment. I tremble for fear. . . . Sister is to speak at the Moral Reform Society this afternoon. I will leave this open & say something about it.

We have just returned from the meeting, & the Lord was there to help us, for I, too, opened my mouth, tho' I had refused to engage to do so. About 300, I guess, were present & appeared interested in the remarks made. We broached one part of the subject, which I doubt not was new to many, i. e., that this reform was to begin in *ourselves.* We were polluted by it, our moral being was seared & scathed by it. Look at our feelings in the society of *men,* why the restraint & embarrassment? If we regarded each other as *moral* & intellectual beings merely, how pure & elevated & dignified would be our feelings towards, & intercourse with them. How is the solemn & sacred subject of marriage regarded & talked about? My heart is pained, my womanhood is insulted, my moral being is outraged continually, & I told them so. After we had finished, many women came up & expressed their pleasure & satisfaction at this part particularly of our remarks. They were their own feelings, but had never heard them expressed before.

No doubt, thou wilt wish to know whether the Boston women have answered our high expectations—they have: Maria Chapman, particularly, is one of the noblest women I ever saw. She has been 3 times to see us: there is real antislavery here: a heart to work, a tongue to speak. We feel ourselves surrounded by an elastic atmosphere which yields to the stroke of the wings of effort & sends up the soaring spirit still higher & swifter in its upward flight. In New York we were allowed to sit down & do nothing. Here, invitations to labor pour in from all sides. . . .

Farewell my dear Jane. May we often meet where spirits blend in prayer is the desire of Thy Angelina.

23

MARIA CHAPMAN

"To Female Anti-Slavery Societies throughout New England"
Boston, June 7, 1837

Urging women abolitionists to support the Grimké sisters, Maria Chapman, a leader in the Boston Female Anti-Slavery Society, highlighted the sisters' advocacy of women's rights as an integral part of their antislavery message.

CHRISTIAN FRIENDS:

The purpose of this letter is to entreat, in the name of the Boston Female Anti-Slavery Society, that you will afford every facility in your power to Sarah M. and Angelina E. Grimké, for the prosecution of their labours in the cause of emancipation.

With their names and characters, with their noble sacrifices and with their published works, you are well acquainted, and therefore there is no need that we should dwell on all the circumstances growing out of these which so peculiarly fit them to dispense the truth respecting the conflicting principles of Freedom and slavery.

Gilbert H. Barnes and Dwight L. Dumond, eds., *Letters of Theodore Dwight Weld, Angelina Grimké Weld and Sarah Grimké, 1822–1844* (New York: Appleton-Century-Crofts, 1934; reprint Gloucester, MA: Smith, 1965), 1:395.

One thing we cannot omit to mention, which marks them eminently qualified for the promulgation of Anti-Slavery principles;—the elevated and Christian point of view from which they behold the condition of woman; her duties and her consequent rights. It is of paramount importance that both men and women should understand their true positions and mighty responsibilities to this and to coming generations. In all spiritual things their functions are identical. Both are created to be parents and educators; both for all the duties growing out of that spiritual equality here and for communion with their maker during their immortal life hereafter; Neither for helplessness or dependence; neither for arbitrary dictation; each to obey the commands of God as responsible to him alone. Such is our view of the primary duties of our race. With respect to secondary pursuits, whether mercantile, mechanical, domestic, or professional—the machinery of mortal existence—"the tools to whosoever can use them." All are alike bound to the strenuous exercise of such faculties as God has given them. . . .

Dear friends, let us urge on you the importance of making available to the cause of Freedom the scattered energies of your respective neighborhoods by gathering together and seeking the cooperation of all whose interest in suffering humanity is leading them to ask "what shall we *do?*" The numbers of such, in every place, are small in comparison with those who will undertake to dictate to *you* what you shall *not* do.

We are not entirely without experience. Trust us when we say that we have found those the most effectual helpers who come to us least encumbered by the trappings of this world, and unfettered from the thraldom of its ways.

Let there be no exclusive system adopted in our societies. Ask no one's sect, rank or colour. Whosoever *will,* let them come. If our worship be sincere of the God who created our race free, and the Savior who came to redeem them from bondage, it will so appear in our active exertions for our enslaved countrymen, that the selfish, the hypocritical and the unfaithful, will be compelled to hold themselves aloof from our ranks. There is no danger to be apprehended from the companionship of any others, for a holy cause purifies the heart, and refines and exalts the ideal of all who embrace it in sincerity.

We renewedly commend to you these our beloved friends, nothing doubting that they will receive from you that hospitality of the heart which will be to them an assurance that they have not consecrated their lives and fortunes to the cause of Christian Freedom in vain.

IN BEHALF OF THE BOSTON FEMALE ANTI-SLAVERY SOCIETY.
MARIA WESTON CHAPMAN. SEC.

24

ANGELINA GRIMKÉ

Letter to Jane Smith

Danvers, Massachusetts, June 1837

By June the sisters were speaking almost every day to large audiences, most of which included men as well as women. They had become highly skilled professionals.

I do not know, My Beloved Jane, why it is that I have not heard from you since I left New York, but I am sure that thou wantest to hear something of our getting along since my last, written from Boston near three weeks ago. I will, therefore, copy a leaf from our day book since the time I wrote. 7th of 6th month. Spoke before the Anti Slavery Society in Boston, in Washington Hall, where they had been mobbed 18 months before.[1] About 400 present; many could not get in. 5 life members. 33 annual subscribers. 8th. Held a meeting at Brookline, in the house of Saml Phil-brick. 75 present, first A S meeting ever held in the town, much opposition to be felt & very hard to speak to such strong hearts. 9th. Addressed the A S Society at North Weymouth, about 120 present—great apathy—hard to speak. 9 new subscribers—near 30 men present. . . . 16th. Attended a Peace meeting in the Vestry of the Old South Ch[urch] in Boston, about 250 out. took the *ultra* ground, on law & civil government also. 18th. Addressed the A S Sy of So Weymouth, about 150 out. tho' it was very rainy. 19th. A S Sy in Boston. 550 women. 50 men. very easy to speak because there was great openness to hear, about 50 new subscribers added. 21st. Attended the Anniversary of the Lynn A S Sy. Spoke on the Report & Resolutions—about 500 women present.

In the evening of the same day, addressed our first large mixed audience. about 1000 present. Great openness to hear & ease in speaking. 22d. Held another in Lynn, but in a smaller house, so that it was crowded to excess, about 600 seated, many went away, about 100 stood around

---

[1]Refers to a mob that in October 1835 dragged William Lloyd Garrison out of a meeting of the Boston Female Anti-Slavery Society and threatened to hang him.

Weld-Grimké Papers, Clements Library, University of Michigan, Ann Arbor.

the door, & we were told that on each window on the outside stood three men with their heads above the lowered sash, very easy speaking indeed. 23d. Held a meeting here [Danvers]. About 200 out—a few of the brethren, very hard speaking: I gave them a complete scolding, which I afterwards found they deserved. Think it likely we shall not have much more than half as many this afternoon in consequence of it, but the truth must be told.

And now thou will want to know how we feel about all these things. . . . Whilst in the act of speaking I am favored to forget little "I" entirely & to feel altogether hid behind the great cause I am pleading. Were it not for this feeling, I know not how I could face such audiences without embarrassment.

It is wonderful to us how the way has been opened for us to address mixed audiences, for most sects here are greatly opposed to public speaking for women, but curiosity in many & real interest in the AS cause in others induce the attendance of our meetings. When they are over, we feel as if we had nothing to do with the results. We cast our burden upon the Lord, & feel an inexpressible relief until the approach of another meeting produces an exercise & sense of responsibility which becomes at times almost insupportable. At some of the meetings I have really felt sick until I rose to speak. But our health has been good & we bear the exertion of body & exercise of mind wonderfully. Our compass of voice has astonished us, for we can fill a house containing 1000 persons with ease. . . . It seems that the Salem meeting house was granted for us . . . so that we are to speak in it on 2nd day afternoon. I almost feel sorry for I am afraid I shall feel the influence of Quaker restrictions & be ill at ease. . . . Our headquarters [in Newburyport] is to be with Henry C. Wright, one of the best men I ever met with & there he says we must rest, but if we continue to bear one meeting a day as well as we have done, we shall not want to rest at all.

Hast thou read CE Beecher's book? I am answering it by letter in *The Liberator* & requested that they might be sent to thee by post. I have not spared her at all, as thou wilt perceive. It was one of the most subtle things I ever saw. . . . I do not know how I shall find language strong enough to express my indignation at the view she takes of the woman's character & duty. . . .

Sister enjoys more real comfort of mind than I ever saw her enjoy before & it is delightful to be there yoked with her in this work, but we often wish we could divide ourselves in order to do far more work than we can at present. . . .

THY EVER AFFECTIONATE A. E. GRIMKÉ

25

ANGELINA GRIMKÉ

Letter to Jane Smith

New Rowley, Massachusetts, July 25, 1837

Angelina's increasing radicalism on the question of civil government accompanied her growing militancy on women's rights.

MY DEAR JANE:

I am truly glad thou wilt have an opportunity of becoming acquainted with brother Wright. He will tell thee all about his views of civil government & be not afraid to be converted. I can truly say that until I embraced them I never understood the full extent of that Liberty wherewith Christ makes his followers *free*. It is indeed delightful to realize that He is our King, our lawgiver & our judge. Without these views I know not *how* I could press forward in the path of difficulty which lies before me. . . .

Some of these places are only villages, so that the few hundred who have come out have been a good many for the size of them. But our *womanhood*—it is as great offense to some as our Abolitionism. I will let H C W [Henry Clarke Wright] tell thee what a war is waged against it. The whole land seems roused to discussion on the *province of woman,* & I am glad of it. We are willing to bear the brunt of the storm, if we can only be the means of making a breach in the wall of public opinion, which lies right in the way of woman's true dignity, honor & usefulness. Sister Sarah does preach up woman's rights most nobly & fearlessly, & we find that many of our New England sisters are ready to receive these strange doctrines, feeling as they do, that our whole sex needs an emancipation from the thraldom of public opinion. What doest thou think of some of them walking 2, 4, 6 & 8 miles to attend our meetings?

But I must forbear—as Sisters voice failed her on account of cold. I have had to bear the brunt of the meeting for two days, speaking an hour & a half today & an hour and three quarters yesterday & as it is 1/2 past 9 I must say Fare thee well to night my dear friend.

A E GÉ

Weld-Grimké Papers, Clements Library, University of Michigan, Ann Arbor.

26

Pastoral Letter: The General Association of Massachusetts to Churches under Their Care

July 1837

Issued by the highest authority in the Congregational Church, the most powerful church in Massachusetts, this letter rebuked the Grimkés' assertion of women's rights with words like "permanent injury," "shame and dishonor," and "degeneracy and ruin."

Brethren and Friends, — Having assembled to consult upon the interests of religion within the Commonwealth, we would now, as pastors and teachers, in accordance with the custom of this Association, address you on some of the subjects which at the present time appear to us to have an important bearing upon the cause of Christ. . . .

We invite your attention to the dangers which at present seem to threaten the female character, with wide spread and permanent injury.

The appropriate duties and influence of women are clearly stated in the New Testament. Those duties and that influence are unobtrusive and private, but the sources of mighty power. When the mild, dependent, softening influence of woman upon the sternness of man's opinion is fully exercised, society feels the effects of it in a thousand forms. The power of woman is in her dependence, flowing from the consciousness of that weakness which God has given her for her protection, and which keeps her in those departments of life that form the character of individuals and of the nation. There are social influences which females use in promoting piety and the great objects of Christian benevolence which we cannot too highly commend. We appreciate the unostentatious prayers and efforts of woman in advancing the cause of religion at home and abroad; in Sabbath schools; in leading religious inquirers to the pastors for instruction; and in all such associated efforts as becomes the modesty of her sex; and earnestly hope that she may abound more and more in these labors of piety and love.

"Pastoral Letter: The General Association of Massachusetts to Churches under Their Care," *New England Spectator*, July 12, 1837, 106.

But when she assumes the place and tone of man as a public reformer, our care and protection of her seem unnecessary; we put ourselves in self-defence against her; she yields the power which God has given her for protection, and her character becomes unnatural. If the vine, whose strength and beauty is to lean upon the trellis work and half conceal its clusters, thinks to assume the independence and the overshading nature of the elm, it will not only cease to bear fruit, but fall in shame and dishonor into the dust. We cannot, therefore, but regret the mistaken conduct of those who encourage females to bear an obtrusive and osten-tatious part in measures of reform, and countenance any of that sex who so far forget themselves as to itinerate in the character of public lec-turers and teachers. — We especially deplore the intimate acquaintance and promiscuous conversation of females with regard to things which ought not to be named; by which that modesty and delicacy which is the charm of domestic life, and which constitutes the true influence of woman in society is consumed, and the way opened, as we apprehend, for degeneracy and ruin.[1] We say these things, not to discourage proper influence against sin, but to secure such reformation as we believe is Scriptural, and will be permanent.

[1]"Things which ought not to be named" probably referred to the sisters' discussions of sexual relations (both forced and consensual) between masters and female slaves. In this phrase the Pastoral Letter also indirectly denounced the practice by which Female Moral Reform Society members publicized the names of men who frequented prostitutes.

27

ANGELINA GRIMKÉ

Letter to Jane Smith

Groton, Massachusetts, August 10, 1837

Pushing ahead despite growing opposition to their women's rights stance and to their insistence on lecturing before men as well as women, the Grimkés often encountered hostile audiences, especially at Andover, seat of New England's most prominent theological seminary. But at Lowell,

Weld-Grimké Papers, Clements Library, University of Michigan, Ann Arbor.

they attracted a crowd of 1,500, including a large number of working
girls and women, and they spoke with great success beneath the blazing
chandeliers of the city hall.

MY DEAR JANE:

. . . I wonder not that some think there is danger of my thinking "more highly of myself than I ought to think." There is danger, & therefore I believe the Lord is mercifully preparing an opposition to our labor which I trust will tend to humble & keep us at the foot of the Cross. No doubt H C W [Henry Clarke Wright] told you that a storm was gathering all around against our *womanhood;* the Ministers especially are in great trepidation, & I should not be at all surprised, if in 3 months, almost every pulpit was closed against us. . . .

My only fear is that some of the anti-slavery brethern will commit themselves, in this excitement, against *woman's rights & duties,* before they examine the subject, & will, in a few years, regret the steps they may take. This will soon be an absorbing topic.

It must be discussed whether women are moral & responsible beings, and whether there is such a thing as *male and female virtue & male and female* duties &c. My opinion is that there *are none* & that this false idea has driven the plowshare of ruin over the whole field of morality. My idea is that whatever is morally right for a man to do is morally right for a woman to do. I recognize no rights but human rights. I know nothing of men's rights and women's rights; for in Christ Jesus there is neither male nor female. . . . I am persuaded that woman is not to be as she has been, a mere secondhand agent in the regeneration of a fallen world, but the acknowledged equal and co-worker with man in this glorious work. . . .

Hubbard Winslow[1] of Boston has preached & published a sermon to set forth the *proper sphere of our sex,* which I think I shall review when I can get time. I am truly glad that men are not ashamed to come out boldly & tell us just what is in their hearts.

But I must take up the account of our labors now as I know you want to hear about them. On the 28th we had our second meeting at Andover, a heavy thunderstorm was coming up when we went but the meeting house was full, about 800 present, a good many of the students were out.

---

[1]Hubbard Winslow (1799–1864) was a Congregational minister who denounced women abolitionists in a sermon that he later expanded into a book, *The Appropriate Sphere of Woman* (Boston: Jordan Weeks & Co., 1837).

I never felt as if I was speaking before such a formidable array of talent & learning & prejudice against my womanhood. I felt miserable in view of the meeting, but the Lord helped me through. I spoke on these subjects, the South never was preparing for Emancipation, therefore we could not have rolled it back & the effects of Abolitionism on the South. 29th went to Methuen in the rain, felt pretty nearly worn out, things looked gloomy, did not feel much like speaking that evening. After dinner the weather cleared off beautifully—about 1000 people were out, the largest audience it was that had ever been collected there. Remarks desultory. Rested on the Sabbath, staying at home as usual. 31st went to Lowell in the afternoon thinking it was only a manufacturing place. I thot the meetings would not be of very great consequence, but found to my surprise that it contained 15,000 inhabitants & that the friends expected a large meeting & had engaged the *city hall.* I was fairly frightened when I found myself in a city audience of 1500, surrounded with a blaze of light from chandeliers & lamps. I hardly knew what would become of me. Sister says I looked just before I rose, as tho' I was saying to myself, the time has arrived & the *sacrifice must be offered,* & I felt just so. The Lord stood at my right hand & sustained & carried me through. . . .

On the 2d came to this lovely little village [Groton]. . . . Here Anne Weston of Boston had come to meet us. She says the Boston women will stand by us in the contest for woman's rights, that they were very glad to find we had accepted the challenge of a discussion at Amesbury, on account of its bearings on the province of *woman &c.*[2]

On the 3d brother Stanton came here, found he was sound on the subject of woman's rights. He went to meeting with us in the evening, opened it with a precious prayer & sat with us in the pulpit. About 500 out, the largest Anti-Slavery audience that has yet attended in this place. He says he wants very much so to arrange some meeting, so that *we & he* may speak at it together. This would be an *irretrievable commitment,* but I doubt whether the time has fully come for such an anomaly in Massachusetts. . . .

MOST AFFY WITH SISTERS LOVE TO ALL OF YOU.
A E GÉ

---

[2]At Amesbury the sisters had agreed to debate two men who challenged their views on slavery.

28

ANGELINA GRIMKÉ

Letter to Theodore Weld

Groton, Massachusetts, August 12, 1837

Angelina's letter to Theodore crossed his letter to her in the mail. She expressed anxiety about what steps the AASS leadership might take against her and Sarah. Acknowledging that their advocacy of women's rights affected men in "the tenderest relations of life," she invited Weld to tell her his views on equality within marriage.

MY DEAR BROTHER:

No doubt thou hast heard by this time of all the fuss that is now making in this region about our stepping so far out of the bounds of female propriety as to lecture to promiscuous assemblies. My auditors literally sit some times with "mouths agape and eyes astare," so that I cannot help smiling in the midst of "rhetorical flourishes" to witness their perfect amazement at hearing a woman speak in the churches. I wish thou couldst see Brother Phelp's letter to us on this subject and sister's admirable reply. I suppose he will soon come out with a conscientious protest against us. I am waiting in some anxiety to see what the Executive Committee mean to do in these troublous times, whether to renounce us or not.

But seriously speaking, we are placed very unexpectedly in a very trying situation, in the forefront of an entirely new contest—a contest for the *rights of woman* as a moral, intelligent & responsible being. Harriet Martineau says "God & man know that the time has not come for women to make their injuries even heard of";[1] but it seems as tho' it had come *now* & that the exigency must be met with the firmness & faith of

---

[1] Harriet Martineau (1802–1876), a British abolitionist and author of *Society in America* (1837), described the struggles of American women abolitionists in "The Martyr Age in the United States of America," in the *London and Westminister Review*, Dec. 1838.

Gilbert H. Barnes and Dwight L. Dumond, eds., *Letters of Theodore Dwight Weld, Angelina Grimké Weld and Sarah Grimké, 1822–1844* (New York: Appleton-Century-Crofts, 1934; reprint Gloucester, MA: Smith, 1965), 1:414.

woman in by gone ages. I cannot help feeling some regret that this shld have come up *before* the AntiSlavery question was settled, so fearful am I that it may injure that blessed cause, & then again I think this must be the Lord's time & therefore the *best* time, for it seems to have been brought about by concatenation of circumstances over which we had no control. The fact is it involves the interests of every minister of our land, & therefore they will stand almost in a solid phalanx against woman's rights, & I am afraid the discussion of this question will divide in Jacob and scatter in Israel:[2] it will also touch every man's interests at home, in the tenderest relation of life; it will go down into the very depths of his soul & cause great searchings of heart. I am glad H Winslow of Boston has come out so boldly & told us just what I believe is in the hearts of thousands of men in our land.

I must confess my womanhood is insulted, my moral feelings outraged when I reflect on these things, & I am sure *I know just* how the free colored people feel towards the whites when they pay them more than common attention; it is *not paid as a RIGHT, but given as a BOUNTY*. . . . There is not one man in 500 who really understands what kind of attention is alone acceptable to a woman of pure & exalted moral & intellectual worth. Hast thou read Sister's letters in the Spectator? I want thee to read them and let us know what thou thinkest of them. That a wife is not to be subject to her husband in any other sense than I am to her or she to me, seems to be strange and *alarming* doctrine indeed, but how can it be otherwise unless *she surrenders her moral responsibility,* which *no woman has a right* to do? . . .

WHO will stand by woman in the great struggle? As to our being Quakers being an excuse for our speaking in public, we do *not* stand on this ground at all; we ask no favors for ourselves, but *claim* rights for our *sex*. If it is wrong for woman to lecture or preach then let the Quakers give up their false views, and let the other sects refuse to hear their women, but if it is *right* then let *all* women who have gifts "mind their calling" and enjoy "the liberty wherewith Christ hath made them free," in that declaration of Paul, "in Christ Jesus there is neither male nor female." O! if in our intercourse with each other we realized this great truth, how delightful, ennobling and dignified it would be, but as I told the Moral Reform Society of Boston in my address, *this* reformation *must begin with ourselves.* . . .

Yesterday the sabbath, rode 12 miles to lecture at Boxboro, brother Gross having written us a pressing invitation to come and plead the

[2]Genesis 49:7.

cause of God's perishing poor in *his pulpit*. It so happened that yesterday was the only day we could do so before we left for Boston. Found his meeting crammed to overflowing. O! what a feeling, to see such a congregation waiting for the words that shall fall from MY unworthy lips. Thou knowest it dear brother, and can understand all about it *except that I am a woman*. I spoke an hour and a half and then stopped and took some refreshment with his family. He says J. Woodbury[3] is against our womanhood and that as *all* the Congregational ministers except himself (about here I mean) are opposed, he expects to have to fight a battle at their next meeting; and that he means to throw down the gauntlet about women's preaching. We pointed out some texts he had not tho't of and tried to throw our views before his mind. May the Lord open his heart more and more on this subject and sustain him in the sore conflict he will have to wage, if he is faithful in pleading for woman's essential rights.

I have no doubt that posterity will read withal *women* were *not* permitted to preach the gospel, with as much amazement and indignation as we do that no *colored* man in No. Ca[rolina] is allowed this *holy right*. Now we want thee to sustain us on the high ground of MORAL RIGHT, *not* of Quaker peculiarity. This question must be met now; let us do it as *moral* beings, & not try to turn a SECTARIAN *peculiarity* to the best account for the benefit of Abolitionism. We do not stand on Quaker ground, but on Bible ground & *moral right*. What we claim for ourselves, we claim for *every* woman who God has called & qualified with gifts & graces. Can't *thou* stand *just here* side by side with us? . . .

Mary Parker sent us word that the Boston women would stand by us if *every* body else forsook us. A[nne] Weston has been here with us & is very strong. . . .

THY SISTER IN THE BONDS OF WOMAN AND THE SLAVE.
A E GÉ

---

[3]James Woodbury (1803–1861) was a Congregational minister in Connecticut who had trained with the Grimkés in New York.

THEODORE WELD

Letter to Sarah and Angelina Grimké
August 15, 1837

Declaring his unqualified support of women's rights, Weld urged the sisters to put the antislavery cause first. Any women could defend women's rights, he insisted; as southerners, they were needed and were in a powerful position to speak for enslaved people.

MY DEAR SISTERS:

. . . As to the *rights* and *wrongs* of women, it is an old theme with me. It was the *first* subject I ever *discussed.* In a little debating society when a boy, I took the ground that *sex* neither *qualified* nor *disqualified* for the discharge of any functions mental, moral, or spiritual; that there is no reason why *woman* should not make laws, administer justice, sit in the chair of state, plead at the bar or in the pulpit, if she has the qualifications, just as much as tho she belonged to the other sex. Further, that the proposition of marriage may with just the same propriety be made by the *woman* as the *man,* and that the existing usage on that subject, pronouncing it *alone* the province of the *man,* and *indelicacy* and almost, if not quite *immoral* for *woman* to make the first advances, overlooks or rather *perverts* the sacred design of the institution and debases it into the mire of earthliness and gross sensuality, smothering the spirit under the flesh. . . . [W]e *fully agree in principle.* . . .

Now notwithstanding this, I do most deeply regret that you have begun a series of articles in the Papers on the rights of woman. Why, my dear sisters, the best possible advocacy which you can make is just what you are making day by day. Thousands hear you every week who have all their lives held that woman must not speak in public. Such a practical refutation of the dogma as your speaking furnishes has already converted multitudes. . . . Besides you are *Southerners,* have been slave-holders; your dearest friends are all in the sin and shame and peril.

Gilbert H. Barnes and Dwight L. Dumond, eds., *Letters of Theodore Dwight Weld, Angelina Grimké Weld and Sarah Grimké, 1822–1844* (New York: Appleton-Century-Crofts, 1934; reprint Gloucester, MA: Smith, 1965), 1:425.

All these things give you great access to northern mind, great *sway* over it. You can do ten times as much on the subject of *slavery* as Mrs. Child or Mrs. Chapman. Why? Not because your powers are superior to theirs, but because you are *southerners*. You can do more at convincing the North than twenty *northern* females, tho' they could speak as well as you. Now this peculiar advantage you *lose* the moment you take *another* subject. . . . *Any* women of your powers will produce as much effect as you on the north in advocating the rights of *free* women (I mean in contradistinction to *slave* women). . . . Let us all *first* wake up the nation to lift millions of slaves of both sexes from the dust, and turn them into MEN and then . . . it will be an easy matter to take millions of females from their knees and set them on their feet. . . . All our opposers . . . will chuckle if only a part of your energies . . . can be diverted into one which will make you so obnoxious as to cripple your influence on the subject of slavery. . . .

YOUR BROTHER T. D. WELD

30

JOHN GREENLEAF WHITTIER

Letter to Angelina and Sarah Grimké

New York City, August 14, 1837

Calling the women's rights issue a "paltry grievance" when compared to needs of slaves, Whittier wrote from the head office of the American Anti-Slavery Society. He supported the sisters' right to speak to "promiscu-ous" audiences (comprising both men and women) but expressed anxiety about the "startling opinions" that were emerging within the movement, and he urged them not to divert their energies into writing about women's rights.

Gilbert H. Barnes and Dwight L. Dumond, eds., *Letters of Theodore Dwight Weld, Angelina Grimké Weld and Sarah Grimké, 1822–1844* (New York: Appleton-Century-Crofts, 1934; reprint Gloucester, MA: Smith, 1965), 1:423.

MY DEAR SISTERS:

. . . I am anxious, too, to hold a long conversation with you on the subject of war, human government, and church and family government. The more I reflect on this subject, the more difficulty I find, and the more decidedly am I of the opinion that we ought to hold all these matters far aloof from the cause of abolition. Our good friend, H. C. Wright, with the best intentions in the world, is doing great injury by a different course. He is making the anti-slavery party responsible in a great degree, for his, to say the least, startling opinions. . . . But let him keep them distinct from the cause of emancipation. This is his duty.

In regard to another subject, *"the rights of woman,"* you are now doing much and nobly to vindicate and assert the rights of woman. Your lectures to crowded and promiscuous audiences on a subject manifestly, in many of its aspects, *political,* interwoven with the framework of the government, are practical and powerful assertions of the right and the duty of woman to labor side by side with her brother for the welfare and redemption of the world.

Why, then, let me ask, is it necessary for you to enter the lists as controversial writers on this question? Does it not *look,* dear sisters, like abandoning in some degree the cause of the poor and miserable slave, sighing from the cotton plantations of the Mississippi, and whose cries and groans are forever sounding in our ears, for the purpose of arguing and disputing about some trifling oppression, political or social, which we may ourselves suffer? Is it not forgetting the great and dreadful wrongs of the slave in a selfish crusade against some paltry grievance of our own? . . . The Massachusetts Congregational Association can do you no harm if you do not allow its splenetic and idle manifesto to divert your attention from the great and holy purpose of your souls. . . .

YOUR FRIEND AND BROTHER,
JON. G. WHITTIER

ANGELINA GRIMKÉ

Letter to Theodore Dwight Weld and John Greenleaf Whittier

Brookline, Massachusetts, August 20, 1837

Seeing herself in the ancient role of a prophet overturning the power of priests, Angelina scathingly denounced the clerical origins of the power arrayed against her vindication of women's rights. She saw past the strategy of silencing women and addressed the issue of men's power, their fear of losing power, and their desire to keep it. She also defended the "rain bow" of "moral reformations" emerging within the antislavery movement, and she continued her colloquy with Weld on the topic of courtship and marriage.

To Theodore D. Weld and J.G. Whittier Brethren Beloved in the Lord: As your letters came to hand at the same time & both are devoted mainly to the same subject, we have concluded to answer them on one sheet & jointly. You seem greatly alarmed at the idea of our advocating the *rights of woman*. . . . These letters have not been the means of *arousing* the public attention to the subject of Woman's rights; it was the Pastoral Letter which did the mischief. The ministers seemed panic struck at once & commenced a most violent attack upon us. I do not say *absurd,* for in truth if it can be fairly established that women *can lecture,* then why may they not preach, & if *they* can preach, then woe! woe be unto the Clerical Domination which now rules the world under the various names of Genl Assemblies, Congregational Associations, etc. *This Letter,* then roused the attention of the whole country to inquire what *right* we had to open our mouths for the dumb; the people were continually told "it is a *shame* for a *woman* to speak in the churches. Paul suffered not a *woman to teach* but commanded *her* to be in silence. The pulpit is too *sacred a place for woman's* foot &c."

Gilbert H. Barnes and Dwight L. Dumond, eds., *Letters of Theodore Dwight Weld, Angelina Grimké Weld and Sarah Grimké, 1822–1844* (New York: Appleton-Century-Crofts, 1934; reprint Gloucester, MA: Smith, 1965), 1:427.

Now, my dear brothers, *this invasion of our rights* was just such an attack upon *us,* as that made upon Abolitionists generally, when they were told a few years ago that *they had no right* to discuss the subject of Slavery. Did *you* take no notice of this assertion? Why no! With one heart & one voice, you said, *We will* settle *this right before* we go one step further. *The time* to assert a right is *the* time when *that* right is denied. *We must establish this right,* for if we do not, it will be impossible for *us* to go on *with the work of Emancipation. . . .*

You certainly *must* know that the leaven which the ministers are so assiduously working into the minds of the people *must* take effect in process of time, & *will close every church to us,* if we give the community no reasons to counteract the sophistry of priests & levites. In this State, particularly, there is an utter ignorance on the subject. Some few noble minds bursting thro' the trammels of educational prejudice FEEL that woman does stand on the same platform of human rights with man, but even these cannot sustain their ground by argument, & as soon as they open their lips to assert her *rights,* their opponents throw perverted scripture into their faces & call O yea, clamor for proof, PROOF, PROOF! & this *they cannot* give & are beaten off the field in disgrace. Now, we are confident that there are scores of such minds panting after light onto this subject: "the children *ask* bread & no MAN giveth it unto them." There is an eagerness to understand our views. Now, is it wrong to give those views in a series of letters in a paper NOT devoted to Abolition?

And can you not see that women *could* do, & *would* do a hundred times more for the slave if she were not fettered? Why! we are gravely told that we are out of our sphere even when we circulate petitions; out of our "appropriate sphere" when we speak to women only; & out of them when we *sing* in the churches. Silence is *our* province, submission *our* duty. If, then, we "give *no reason* for the hope that is in us," that we have *equal rights* with our brethren, how can we expect to be permitted *much longer to exercise those rights?* IF I know in my own heart, I am NOT actuated by any selfish considerations . . . but we are actuated by the full conviction that if we are to do any good in the Anti Slavery cause, our *right* to labor in it *must* be firmly established; *not* on the ground of Quakerism, but on the firm basis of human rights, the Bible. Indeed, I contend brethren that *this* is not *Quaker* doctrine; it is no more like *their* doctrine on Women than our Anti Slavery is like their Abolition—just about the same difference. I will explain myself. Women are regarded as equal to men on the ground of *spiritual gifts, not* on the broad ground of *humanity.* Woman may *preach;* this is a *gift;* but woman must not make the discipline by which *she herself* is to be governed.

O that you were here that we might have a good long, long talk over matters and things; then I could explain myself far better, & I think we could convince you that we cannot push Abolitionism forward *until* we take up the stumbling block out of the road. We cannot see with brother Weld in this matter. We acknowledge the excellence of his reasons for urging us to labor in this cause of the Slave, our being Southerners, &c. But then we say how can we expect to be able to hold these meetings much longer, when people are so diligently taught to *despise* us for thus stepping out of the "sphere of woman"!

Look at this instance: after we had left Groton, the *Abolition* minister there, at a Lyceum meeting, poured out his sarcasm & ridicule upon our heads, & among other things said, he would as soon be caught robbing a hen roost as encouraging a woman to lecture. Now, brethren, if the leaders of the people thus speak of our labors, *how long* will we be allowed to prosecute them? Answer me this question. You may depend on it, tho' to meet *this* question *may appear* to be turning out of our road, that *it is not.* IT IS NOT: we must meet it & meet it *now* & meet it like *women* in the fear of the Lord. . . . If we dare to stand upright & do our duty according to the dictates of *our own* consciences, why then we are compared to Fanny Wright, &c.

Why, my dear brothers, can you not see the deep laid scheme of the clergy against us as lecturers? They know full well that if they can persuade the people it is a *shame* for us to speak in public, & that every time we open our mouths for the dumb we are breaking a divine command, that even if we spoke with the tongues of *men* or angels, we should have no *hearers.* They are springing a deep mine beneath our feet, & we shall very soon be compelled to retreat for we shall have no ground to stand on. If we surrender the right to *speak* to the public this year, we must surrender the right to petition next year & the right to write the year after &c. What *then* can *woman* do for the slave, when she herself is under the feet of man & shamed into *silence?* Now we entreat you to weigh candidly the *whole subject,* & then we are sure you will see this is no more than an abandonment of our first love than the effort made by Anti Slavery men to establish the right of *free* discussion.

With regard to brother Weld's ultraism on the subject of marriage, he is quite mistaken if he fancies he has got far *ahead of us* in the human rights reform. We do *not* think his doctrine at all shocking: it is *altogether right.* But I am afraid I am too *proud* ever to exercise the right. The fact is we are living in such an artificial state of society that there are some feelings about which we dare not speak out, or act out the most natural & best feelings of our hearts. O! *when* shall we be "delivered from the *bondage of corruption* into the glorious liberty of the sons of God!" By the bye, it will be very important to establish this right, for the men of Mass[achusetts] stoutly declare that women who hold such sentiments of *equality* can never expect to be courted. They seem to hold out this as a kind of threat to deter us from asserting our rights, not *knowing where-unto this will grow.* But jesting is inconvenient says the Apostle: to business then. . . .

The fact is I believe—but don't be alarmed, for it is only I—that Men & Women will have to go out on their own responsibility, just like the prophets of old & declare the *whole* counsel of God to the people. The whole Church Government must come down; the clergy stand right in the way of reform, & I do not know but this stumbling block too must be removed *before* Slavery can be abolished, for the system is supported by *them;* it could not exist without the Church, as it is called. This grand principle must be mooted, discussed & established, viz. the Ministers of the Gospel are the successors of the *Prophets,* not of the *priests.* . . . The Church is built *not* upon the priests at all but upon the *prophets and apostles,* Jesus Christ being the chief corner stone.

This develops three important inferences; 1. True ministers are called, like Elisha from the plough & Amos from gathering sycamore fruit, Matthew from the receipt of custom & Peter and John from their fishing nets. 2. As prophets *never were paid,* so ministers ought not to be. 3. As there were *prophetesses* as well as prophets, so there *ought* to be now *female* as well as male ministers. Just let this one principle be established, & what will become of the power and sacredness of the pastoral office? Is brother Weld frightened at *my ultraism?* . . .

We never mention women's rights in our *lectures,* except so far as is necessary to urge them to meet their responsibilities. We speak of their *responsibilities* & leave *them* to *infer* their *rights.* I could cross this letter all over but must not encroach on your time.[1]

> MAY THE LORD BLESS YOU MY DEAR BROTHERS
> IS THE PRAYER OF YOUR SISTER IN JESUS,
> A.E.G.

---

[1] To save paper, after they had filled one side of the paper nineteenth-century correspondents often turned the page sideways and wrote across lines already written.

ANGELINA GRIMKÉ

"Human Rights Not Founded on Sex":
Letter to Catharine Beecher

August 2, 1837

Answering Beecher's Essay on Slavery and Abolitionism (see Document 21), which appeared in March 1837, Angelina in the summer of 1837 composed a series of letters that defended the activism of antislavery women. Her twelfth letter addressed the issue of women's rights. Published individually in The Liberator, *her letters appeared in book form in 1838.*

DEAR FRIEND:

Since I engaged in the investigation of the rights of the slave, I have necessarily been led to a better understanding of my own; for I have found the Anti-Slavery cause to be the high school of morals in our land — the school in which human rights are more fully investigated, and better understood and taught, than in any other benevolent enterprise. Here one great fundamental principle is disinterred, which, as soon as it is uplifted to public view, leads the mind into a thousand different ramifications, into which the rays of this central light are streaming with brightness and glory. Here we are led to examine why human beings have any rights. It is because they are moral beings; the rights of all men, from the king to the slave, are built upon their moral nature: and as all men have this moral nature, so all men have essentially the same rights. These rights may be plundered from the slave, but they cannot be alienated: his right and title to himself is as perfect now, as is that of Lyman Beecher: they are written in his moral being, and must remain unimpaired as long as that being continues. Now it naturally occurred to me, that if rights were founded in moral being, then the circumstance of sex could not give to man higher rights and responsibilities, than to woman. To suppose that it did, would be to deny the self-evident truth, "that the physical constitution is the mere instrument of the moral

---

The Liberator, Aug. 2, 1837; reprinted later in Angelina E. Grimké, *Letters to Catherine E. Beecher, in Reply to an Essay on Slavery and Abolitionism* (Boston: Knapp, 1838).

nature." To suppose that it did, would be to break up utterly the relations of the two natures, and to reverse their functions, exalting the animal nature into a monarch, and humbling the moral into a slave; "making the former a proprietor, and the latter its property." When I look at human beings as moral beings, all distinction in sex sinks to insignificance and nothingness; for I believe it regulates rights and responsibilities no more than the color of the skin or the eyes. My doctrine then is, that whatever it is morally right for man to do, it is morally right for woman to do. Our duties are governed, not by difference of sex, but by the diversity of our relative connections in life, and the variety of gifts and talents committed to our care, and the different eras in which we live.

This regulation of duty by the mere circumstance of sex, rather than by the fundamental principle of moral being, has led to all that multifarious train of evils flowing out of the anti-christian doctrine of masculine and feminine virtues. By this doctrine, man has been converted into the warrior, and clothed in sternness, and those other kindred qualities, which, in the eyes of many, belong to his character as a man; whilst woman has been taught to lean upon an arm of flesh, to sit as a soul arrayed "in gold and pearls, and costly array," to be admired for her personal charms, and caressed and humored like a spoiled child, or converted into a mere drudge to suit the convenience of her lord and master. This principle has spread desolation over the whole moral world, and brought into all the diversified relations of life, "confusion and every evil work." It has given to man a charter for the exercise of tyranny and selfishness, pride and arrogance, lust and brutal violence. It has robbed woman of essential rights, the right to think and speak and act on all great moral questions, just as men think and speak and act; the right to share their responsibilities, dangers, and toils; the right to fulfill the great end of her being, as a help meet for man, as a moral, intellectual and immortal creature, and of glorifying God in her body and her spirit which are His. Hitherto, instead of being a help meet to man, in the highest, noblest sense of the term, as a companion, a co-worker, an equal; she has been a mere appendage of his being, and instrument of his convenience and pleasure, the pretty toy, with which he wiled away his leisure moments, or the pet animal whom he humored into playfulness and submission. Woman, instead of being regarded as the equal of man, has uniformly been looked down upon as his inferior, a mere gift to fill up the measure of his happiness. . . . This idea of woman's being "the last best gift of God to man," however pretty it may sound to the ears of those who love to discourse upon the poetry of "romantic gallantry, and the generous promptings of chivalry," has nevertheless been the means of sinking her from an end into a mere means—of turning her into an appendage to, instead of recognizing her as part of man—of destroying her individuality, and rights, and responsibilities, and merging her moral being into that of man. Instead of Jehovah being her king, her lawgiver, and her judge, she has been taken out of the exalted scale of existence in which He placed her, and crushed down under the feet of man. . . .

Measure her rights and duties by the sure, unerring standard of moral being, not by the false rights and measures of a mere circumstance of her human existence, and then will it become a self-evident truth, that whatever it is morally right for a man to do, it is morally right for a woman to do. I recognize no rights but human rights—I know nothing of men's rights and women's rights; for in Christ Jesus, there is neither male or female; and it is my solemn conviction, that, until this important principle of equality is recognized and carried out into practice, that vain will be the efforts of the church to do anything effectual for the permanent reformation of the world. Woman was the first transgressor, and the first victim of power. In all the heathen nations, she has been the slave of man, and no Christian nation has ever acknowledged her rights. Nay more, no Christian Society has ever done so either, on the broad and solid basis of humanity. I know that in some few denominations, she is permitted to preach the gospel; but this is not done from a conviction of her equality as a human being, but of her equality in spiritual gifts—for we find that woman, even in these Societies, is not allowed to make the Discipline by which she is to be governed. Now, I believe it is her right to be consulted in all the laws and regulations by which she is to be governed, whether in Church or State, and that the present arrangement of Society, on those points, are a violation of human rights, an usurpation of power over her, which is working mischief, great mischief, in the world. If Ecclesiastical and Civil governments are ordained of God, then I contend that woman has just as much right to sit in solemn counsel in Conventions, Conferences, Associations, and General Assemblies, as man—just as much right to sit upon the throne of England, or in the Presidential chair of the United States, as man. . . .

I believe the discussion of Human Rights at the North has already been of immense advantage to this country. It is producing the happiest influence upon the minds and hearts of those who are engaged in it; . . . Indeed, the very agitation of the question, which it involved, has been highly important. Never was the heart of man so expanded; never were its generous sympathies so generally and so perseveringly excited. These sympathies, thus called into existence, have been useful preservatives of national virtue. I therefore do wish very much to promote the Anti-Slavery excitement at the North, because I believe it will prove a useful preservative of national virtue. . . .

The discussion of the wrongs of slavery has opened the way for the discussion of other rights, and the ultimate result will most certainly be "the breaking of every yoke," the letting the oppressed of every grade and description go free — an emancipation far more glorious than any the world has ever yet seen, an introduction into that liberty wherewith Christ hath made his people free.

THY FRIEND,
ANGELINA E. GRIMKÉ

33

SARAH GRIMKÉ

"Legal Disabilities of Women":
Letter to Mary Parker

September 6, 1837

Addressed to Mary Parker, President of the Boston Female Anti-Slavery Society, Sarah's book of Letters *aimed to provide a scriptural basis for women's equality. This twelfth letter, however, offered an effective critique of secular and ecclesiastical laws that kept women inferior, just as laws kept slaves in bondage. Published individually in* The Liberator, *the* Letters *appeared as a book in 1838.*

MY DEAR SISTER:
There are few things which present greater obstacles to the improvement and elevation of woman to her appropriate sphere of usefulness and duty, than the laws which have been enacted to destroy her independence, and crush her individuality; laws which, although they are

The Liberator, Feb. 2, 1838; reprinted later in Sarah Grimké, *Letters on the Equality of the Sexes and the Condition of Woman* (Boston: Knapp, 1838).

framed for her government, she has had no voice in establishing, and which rob her of some of her essential rights. Woman has no political existence. With the single exception of presenting a petition to the legislative body, she is a cipher in the nation; or, if not actually so in representative governments, she is only counted, like the slaves of the South, to swell the number of law-makers who form decrees for her government, with little reference to her benefit, except so far as her good may promote their own. . . . I shall confine myself to the laws of our country. These laws bear with peculiar rigor on married women. Blackstone, in the chapter entitled "Of husband and wife," says: —

> By marriage, the husband and wife are one person in law; that is, the very being, or legal existence of the woman is suspended during the marriage, or at least is incorporated and consolidated into that of the husband under whose wing, protection and cover she performs everything.[1] . . .

Here now, the very being of a woman, like that of a slave, is absorbed in her master. All contracts made with her, like those made with slaves by their owners, are a mere nullity. Our kind defenders have legislated away almost all our legal rights, and in the true spirit of such injustice and oppression, have kept us in ignorance of those very laws by which we are governed. They have persuaded us, that we have no right to investigate the laws, and that, if we did, we could not comprehend them; they alone are capable of understanding the mysteries of Blackstone, &c. . . .

> The husband is bound to provide his wife with necessaries by law, as much as to himself; and if she contracts debts for them, he is obliged to pay for them; but for anything besides necessaries, he is not chargeable.

Yet a man may spend the property he has acquired by marriage at the ale-house, the gambling table, or in any other way that he pleases. Many instances of this kind have come to my knowledge; and women, who have brought their husbands handsome fortunes, have been left, in consequence of the wasteful and dissolute habits of their husbands; in straitened circumstances, and compelled to toil for the support of their families. . . .

[1]In his *Commentaries on the Laws of England* (1765–69), William Blackstone (1723–1780) interpreted English Common Law traditions, including *feme covert* laws through which the legal identity of married women was absorbed into that of their husbands.

A woman's personal property by marriage becomes absolutely her husband's, which, at his death, he may leave entirely away from her.

And farther, all the avails of her labor are absolutely in the power of her husband. All that she acquires by her industry is his; so that she cannot, with her own honest earnings, become the legal purchaser of any property. If she expends her money for articles of furniture, to contribute to the comfort of her family, they are liable to be seized for her husband's debts: and I know an instance of a woman, who by labor and economy had scraped together a little maintenance for herself and a do-little husband, who was left, at his death, by virtue of his last will and testament, to be supported by charity. . . .

The laws above cited are not very unlike the slave laws of Louisiana. "All that a slave possesses belongs to his master; he possesses nothing of his own, except what his master chooses he should possess." . . .

As these abuses do exist, and women suffer intensely from them, our brethren are called upon in this enlightened age, by every sentiment of honor, religion, and justice, to repeal these unjust and unequal laws, and restore to woman those rights which they have wrested from her. Such laws approximate too nearly to the laws enacted by slaveholders for the government of their slaves, and must tend to debase and depress the mind of that being whom God created as a help meet for man, or helper "like unto himself," and designed to be his equal and his companion. Until such laws are annulled, woman never can occupy that exalted station for which she was intended by her Maker. And just in proportion as they are practically disregarded, which is the case to some extent, just so far is woman assuming that independence and nobility of character which she ought to exhibit. . . .

Hoping that in the various reformations of the day, women may be relieved from some of their legal disabilities, I remain,

THINE IN THE BONDS OF WOMANHOOD,
SARAH M. GRIMKÉ

Some Contexts of the Sisters' Victory, 1837–1838

34

Resolutions Adopted by the Providence, Rhode Island, Ladies' Anti-Slavery Society

October 21, 1837

Published in The Liberator, *these resolutions show how the debates over women's rights were resounding within women's antislavery societies. Opposition to women's rights fueled the resolve of many societies.*

Whereas we believe the cause of the slave to be one of neglected humanity, and the southern portion of the Union to be one of the waste places of Zion, where for justice is oppression, and for righteousness, behold, a cry—therefore,

Resolved, That we act as moral agents and Christians fearlessly in this cause—thinking and acting in view of our accountability to our Maker—remembering that our rights are sacred and immutable, and founded on the liberty of the gospel, that great emancipation act for women. We further resolve, that we will not be turned aside from the object we have espoused, by the intimidations of ridicule, or the intoxicating flatteries of men and women, whose god is their selfishness, nor be cajoled into a selfish conceit of our superiority over the millions of females in our country, whose unuttered and unutterable cries of agony from oppression will, as they rise to heaven, shake terribly our guilty land; but we will turn our eyes, for example and imitation, to those

---

"Voice of Women," *The Liberator,* Nov. 3, 1837.

philanthropists in Europe and America, who, through self-denial and persecution, have become pioneers in the cause of emancipation, some of whom we have seen face to face; and while they command our reverence, they call forth our gratitude as women for the shadowing out they have given of our rights, by means of the full light which their benevolent efforts have shed on the equality of the rights of man.

Whereas strenuous exertions are making at the present day, to counteract the disinterested labors of women in behalf of the oppressed, by representing them as "over-stepping the boundaries of their sex"— therefore,

Resolved, That we will not be influenced by such considerations, to shrink from the performance of the duty we owe to the suffering slave. Believing that woman can plead for the slave, without forsaking her "appropriate sphere of action," we rejoice that there are so many who possess strong minds and vigorous intellects, and are willing to labor in this cause. In accordance with these views, we deem the self-denying labors of the Misses Grimké worthy of all praise, and cordially approve of the course pursued by them in the cause of abolition.

Resolved, That we totally disapprove of the late Clerical Protests, regarding them as injudicious and unchristian; and believing that *The Liberator* has ever proven itself the firm and uncompromising friend of the slave, our confidence in the integrity and ability of its editor remain unshaken: Resolved, That the foregoing resolutions be forwarded to the editor of *The Liberator.*

SARAH PRATT, SECRETARY

35

"Just Treatment of Licentious Men":
Letter to the Friend of Virtue
January 1838

Although nowhere so avidly defended or fully articulated as in the anti-slavery movement, women's rights ideas also appeared in other social movements, including moral reform. In this letter to the Friend of Virtue, *the chief publication of the New England branch of the moral reform movement, the writer condemned predatory male sexuality. Although these women tended to be more conservative than Garrisonian abolitionist women in their views of women's public rights, they were radical in their defense of women's right to control their own bodies and in their call for a single standard of sexual behavior for men and women.*

DEAR SISTERS:

As members with us of the body of the Lord Jesus Christ, we take the liberty of addressing you on a subject near our hearts, and of the deepest interest to our sex. We ask your serious attention, while we press upon your consciences the inquiry, "Is it right to admit to the society of virtuous females, those unprincipled and licentious men, whose conduct is fraught with so much evil to those who stand in the relation to us of sisters?" True, God designed that man should be our protector, the guardian of our peace, our happiness, and our honor; but how often has he proved himself a traitor to his trust, and the worst enemy of our sex? The deepest degradation to which many of our sex have been reduced, the deepest injuries they have suffered, have been in consequence of his perfidy. He has betrayed, and robbed, and forsaken his victim, and left her to endure alone the untold horrors of a life embittered by self-reproach, conscious ignominy, and exclusion from every virtuous circle.

Is there a woman among us, whose heart has not been pained at the fall and fate of some one sister of her sex? Do you say the guilty deserve to suffer and must expect it? Granted. But why not let a part

---

Friend of Virtue, Jan. 1838, 2–4; reprinted by Daniel Wright, "What Was the Appeal of Moral Reform to Antebellum Northern Women?" online in *Women and Social Movements in the United States,* Vol. 3 (1999).

of this suffering fall on the destroyer? Why is he caressed and shielded from scorn by the countenance of the virtuous, and encouraged to commit other acts of perfidy and sin, while his victim, for one offence, is trampled upon, despised and banished from all virtuous society; The victim thus crushed, yields herself to despair, and becomes a practical illustration of the proverb that, "A bad woman is the worst of all God's creatures." Surely, if she is worse, after her fall, than man equally fallen, is there not reason to infer that in her nature there is something more chaste, more pure and refined, and exalted than in his? Is it then not worth while to do something to prevent her from becoming a prey to the perfidy and baseness of unprincipled man, and a disgrace to her sex? Do you ask, what can woman do, and reply as have some others, "We must leave this work for the men?" Can we expect the wolf, ravenous for his prey, to throw up a barrier to protect the defenceless sheep? As well might we expect this, as to expect that men as a body will take measures to redress the wrongs of woman.

Dear sisters, women have commenced this work, and women must see it carried through. . . . Moral Reform is the first of causes to our sex. It involves principles, which if faithfully and perseveringly applied, will preserve the rights and elevate the standing of our sex in society. As times have been, the libertine has found as ready a passport to the society of the virtuous, as any one, and he has as easily obtained a good wife, as the more virtuous man. But a new era has commenced. Woman has erected a standard, and laid down the principle, that man shall not trample her rights, and on the honor of her sex with impunity. She has undertaken to banish licentious men from all virtuous society. And mothers, wives, sisters, and daughters will you lend your influence to this cause? Prompt action in the form of association will accomplish this work. Females in this manner must combine their strength and exert their influence. Will you not join one of these bands of the pious? The cause has need of your interest, your prayers, and your funds. Come then to our help, and let us pray and labor together.

YOURS, AFFECTIONATELY, L.T.Y.

36

ANGELINA GRIMKÉ WELD

Speech at Pennsylvania Hall

Philadelphia, May 16, 1838

In her last public speech Angelina Grimké persisted, despite the siege of the building by an anti-abolitionist mob. This was her only speech to be transcribed — in a shorthand process that was called phonographic. Her oratory shows that she had become adept at improvisation. Bracketed comments about the mob's assault were added by the transcriber.

Men, brethren, and fathers-mothers, daughters and sisters, what came ye to see? A reed shaken with the wind? Is it curiosity merely, or a deep sympathy with the perishing slave, that has brought this large audience together? [A yell from the mob without the building.] Those voices without ought to awaken and call out our warmest sympathies. Deluded Beings! "they know not what they do."[1] They know not that they are undermining their own rights and their own happiness, temporal and eternal. Do you ask, "what has the North to do with slavery?" Hear it — hear it. Those voices without tell us that the spirit of slavery is *here,* and has been roused to wrath by our abolition speeches and conventions: for surely liberty would not foam and tear herself with rage, because her friends are multiplied daily, and meetings are held in quick succession to set forth her virtues and extend her peaceful kingdom. This opposition shows that slavery has done its deadliest work in the hearts of our citizens.

Do you ask, then, "what has the North to do?" I answer, cast out first the spirit of slavery from your own hearts, and then lend your aid to convert the South. Each one present has a work to do, be his or her situation what it may, however limited their means, or insignificant their supposed influence. The great men of this country will not do this work;

[1]Luke 23:34.

Samuel Webb, ed., *History of Pennsylvania Hall, Which Was Destroyed by a Mob, on the 17th of May, 1838* (Philadelphia: Merrihew and Gunn, 1838), 123–26.

the church will never do it. A desire to please the world, to keep the favor of all the parties and of all conditions, makes them dumb on this and every other unpopular subject. They have become worldly-wise, and therefore God, in his wisdom, employs them not to carry on his plans of reformation and salvation. He hath chosen the foolish things of the world to confound the wise, and the weak to overcome the mighty.[2]

As a Southerner I feel that it is my duty to stand up here tonight and bear testimony against slavery. I have seen it—I have seen it. I know it has horrors that can never be described. I was brought up under its wing: I witnessed for many years its demoralizing influences, and its destructiveness to human happiness. It is admitted by some that the slave is not happy under the *worst* forms of slavery. But I have *never* seen a happy slave. . . .

[Just then stones were thrown at the windows,—a great noise without, and commotion within.] What is a mob? What would the levelling of this Hall be? Any evidence that we are wrong or that slavery is a good and wholesome institution? What if the mob should now burst in upon us, break up our meeting and commit violence upon our persons—would this be anything compared with what the slaves endure? No, no: and we do not remember them "as bound with them," if we shrink in time of peril, or feel unwilling to sacrifice ourselves, if need be, for their sake. [Great noise.] . . .

Much will have been done for the destruction of Southern slavery when we have so reformed the North that no one here will be willing to risk his reputation by advocating or even excusing the holding of men as property. The South know it, and acknowledged that as fast as our principles prevail, the hold of the master must be relaxed. [Another outbreak of mobocratic spirit, and some confusion in the house.] . . .

I feel that all this disturbance is but an evidence that our efforts are the best that could have been adopted, or else friends of slavery would not care for what we say and do. The South know what we do. I am thankful that they are reached by our efforts. Many times have I wept in the land of my birth over the system of slavery. I knew none who sympathized in my feelings—I was unaware that any efforts as these were being made to deliver the oppressed—no voice in the wilderness was heard calling on the people to repent and do works meet for repentance[3]—and my heart sickened within me. Oh, how should I have rejoiced to know that such efforts as these were being made.

[2]I Corinthians 1:27–29.
[3]Matthew 3:3.

I only wonder that I had such feelings. I wonder when I reflect under what influence I was brought up, that my heart is not harder than the nether millstone. But in the midst of temptation, I was preserved and my sympathy grew warmer, and my hatred of slavery more inveterate, until at last I have exiled from my native land because I could no longer endure to hear the wailing of the slave. I fled to the land of Penn; for here, thought I, sympathy for the slave will surely be found. But I found it not. The people were kind and hospitable, but the slave had no place in their thoughts. Whenever questions were put to me as to his condition, I felt that they were dictated by an idle curiosity, rather than by that deep feeling which would lead to effort for his rescue. I therefore shut up my grief in my own heart. I remembered that I was a Carolinian, from a state which framed this iniquity by law. I knew that throughout her territory was continued suffering, on the one part, and continual brutality and sin on the other. Every Southern breeze wafted to me the discordant tones of weeping and wailing, shrieks and groans, mingled with prayers and blasphemous curses. I thought there was no hope; that the wicked would go on in his wickedness, until he had destroyed both himself and his country. My heart sunk within me at the abominations in the midst of which I had been born and educated. What will it avail, cried I in bitterness of spirit, to expose to the gaze of strangers the horrors and pollutions of slavery, when there is no ear to hear nor heart to feel and pray for the slave. . . . But how different do I feel now! Animated with hope, Nay, with an assurance of the triumph of liberty and good will to man, I will lift up my voice like a trumpet, and show this people their transgression, their sins of omission towards the slave, and what they can do towards affecting Southern mind[s], and overthrowing Southern oppression. . . . [Shoutings, stones thrown against the windows, &c.]

There is nothing to be feared from those who would stop our mouths, but they themselves should fear and tremble. The current is even now setting fast against them. . . . [Mob again disturbed the meeting.]

We often hear the question asked, "What shall we do?" Here is an opportunity for doing something now. Every man and woman present may do something by showing that we fear not a mob, and, in the midst of threatening and revilings, by opening our mouths for the dumb and pleading the cause of those who are ready to perish.

To work as we should in this cause, we must know what Slavery is. Let me urge you then to buy the books which have been written on this subject and read them, and then lend them to your neighbors. Give your money no longer for things which pander to pride and lust, but aid in scattering "the living coals of truth" upon the naked heart of this nation,—in circulating appeals to the sympathies of Christians in behalf of the outraged and suffering slave. . . .

Women of Philadelphia! allow me as a Southern woman, with much attachment to the land of my birth, to entreat you to come up to this work. Especially let me urge you to petition. Men may settle this and other questions at the ballot-box, but you have no such right; it is only through petitions that you can reach the Legislature. It is therefore peculiarly your duty to petition. Do you say, "It does no good?" The South already turns pale at the number sent. They have read the reports of the proceedings of Congress, and there have seen that among the other petitions were very many from the women of the North on the subject of slavery. This fact has called the attention of the South to the subject. How could we expect to have done more as yet? Men who hold the rod over slaves, rule in the councils of the nation: and they deny our right to petition and to remonstrate against abuses of our sex and of our kind. We have these rights, however, from our God. Only let us exercise them: and though often turned away unanswered, let us remember the influence of importunity upon the unjust judge, and act accordingly. The fact that the South look with jealousy upon our measures shows that they are effectual. There is, therefore, no cause for doubting or despair, but rather for rejoicing.

It was remarked in England that women did much to abolish Slavery in her colonies. . . . When the women of these States send up to Congress such as petition, our legislators will arise as did those of England, and say, "When all the maids and matrons of the land are knocking at our doors we must legislate." Let the zeal and love, the faith and works of our English sisters quicken ours—that while the slaves continue to suffer, and when they shout deliverance, we may feel that satisfaction of *having done what we could.*

37

The Burning of Pennsylvania Hall
May 17, 1838

Constructed in 1837 by donations from Philadelphia's radical reform organizations, the hall was burned to the ground by a mob of about 10,000 anti-abolitionist men.

Courtesy the Quaker Collection, Haverford College Library

The Antislavery Movement Splits Over the Women's Rights Question, 1837–1840

38

ANGELINA GRIMKÉ WELD

Letter to Anne Warren Weston

Fort Lee, New Jersey, July 15, 1838

Angelina's letter to a leading member of the Boston Female Anti-Slavery Society inquired about the split within the movement and described the sisters' "domestic characters."

MY DEAR ANNA:

. . . I thank thee also for thy account of the N E Convention in reference to the Woman Question. Like all other truth, when brought out *practically,* it is causing deep searchings of heart & revealing the secrets of the soul. I believe this can no more be driven back from the field of investigation than the doctrine of Human rights, of which it is a part, & a very important part. And N E will be the battleground, for she is most certainly the moral light house of our nation. Perhaps it was all for the best Abby [Kelley] had to stand alone. I know how strengthening it is to feel that we have no arms of flesh to lean on, & for her sake I rejoice in her loneliness. . . . I cannot help hoping [Abby Kelley] will yet come out as a lecturer in the cause of the poor slave. Such practical advocacy of the rights of woman are worth every thing to *every* reform, at least, so I believe.

Angelina Grimké Weld to Anne Warren Weston, Boston Public Library, MS. A.9.2. v.10, 38.

Has unity of spirit been restored to the Female Society in Boston? I long to hear from your *striving together* in the faith of Abolition as you once did. What plans are you pursuing this year? What are you doing with your friends?

We keep no help & therefore are filling up "the appropriate sphere of woman" to admiration, in the kitchen with baking pans & pots & steamers &c., & in the parlor & chambers with the broom & the duster. Indeed, I think our enemies wld rejoice, could they only look in upon us from day to day & see us toiling in domestic life, instead of lecturing to *promiscuous* audiences. Now I verily believe that we are *thus* doing *as much* for the cause of woman as we did by public speaking. For it is absolutely necessary that we should show that we are *not* ruined as domestic characters, but so far from it, *as soon* as duty calls us home, we can & do rejoice in the release from public service, & are as anxious to make good bread as we ever were to deliver a good lecture. Our ignorance and inexperience often leads to mistakes & failures in the cooking department, but to Theodore's contented and cheerful mind everything is good and home is delightful. We all like doing without a [hired] girl very much indeed for we find that it is very sweet to serve one another in love, each bearing a part of the burden, & so by a division of labor, rendering it comparatively easy to get along. . . .

I REMAIN THINE — ANGELINA G. WELD

LYDIA MARIA CHILD

Letter to Angelina Grimké

Boston, September 2, 1839

Child's published letter reviewed the causes of the split within the antislavery movement and asserted her own moderate but firm position on women's rights.

DEAR FRIEND.

You ask me what I am thinking about the anti-slavery controversy, and whether I am not disheartened by recent divisions. . . .

With regard to the Woman Question, as it is termed . . . the Massachusetts Society have simply refused to take action upon it when the minority have urged them to do it. In the beginning, we were brought together by strong sympathy for the slave, without stopping to inquire about each other's religious opinions, or appropriate spheres. Then, women were hailed by acclamation as helpers in the great work. They joined societies, they labored diligently, and they stood against a scoffing world bravely.

When the two Grimkés came among us, impediments in the way of their lecturing straight-way arose, particularly among the clergy. The old theological argument from St. Paul was urged, and the Grimkés replied in their own defense. A strong feeling of hostility to woman's speaking in public had always been latent in the clergy, and this incident aroused it all over the country. The sisters found obstacles so multiplied in their path, that they considered the establishment of woman's free-dom of vital importance to the anti-slavery cause. "Little can be done for the slave," said they, "while this prejudice blocks up the way." They urged me to say and do more about woman's rights, nay, at times they gently rebuked me for my want of zeal.

I replied, "It is best not to talk about our rights, but simply go for-ward and do whatsoever we deem a duty. In toiling for the freedom of others, we shall find our own." On this ground I have ever stood; and

---

"On the Present State of the Anti-Slavery Cause," *The Liberator*, Sept. 6, 1839.

so have my anti-slavery sisters. Instead of forcing this "foreign topic" into antislavery meetings or papers, we have sedulously avoided it. *The Liberator* has not meddled with the discussion, except when attacks upon the Grimkés seemed to render replies on their part absolutely necessary.

From that day to this, the clergy, as a body, have been extremely sensitive on the subject. Different minds assign different causes for this sensitiveness. Some respect it, as occasioned by a conscientious interpretation of Scripture; others consider it an honest but narrow bigotry; while others smiling say, "They are afraid the women will preach better and charge less." Without imputing motives, I simply state an obvious fact.

If there are clergymen, or others, in our ranks, who conscientiously believe it wrong for woman freely to utter her thoughts and impart her knowledge to any body who can derive benefit from the same, I should be the last to put any constraint on his opinions. . . .

From the beginning, women, by paying their money, have become members of Anti-Slavery societies and conventions in various free states. They have behaved with discretion and zeal, and been proverbially lavish of exertion. We claim no authority to prescribe or limit their mode of action, any more than we do that of other members. . . .

For my individual self, I now, as ever, would avoid any discussion of the woman question in Anti-Slavery meetings, or papers. But when a man advises me to withdraw from a society or convention, or not to act there according to the dictates of my own judgment, I am constrained to reply, "Thou canst not touch the freedom of my soul. I deem that I have duties to perform here. I make no onset upon your opinions and prejudices; but my moral responsibility lies between God and my own conscience. No human being can have jurisdiction over that."

But, my dear friend, these questions of Non-Resistants, Woman's Rights, &c. are only urged to effect a secret purpose far more important in the eyes of our opponents; viz. to get Garrison formally disowned by the abolitionists of Massachusetts. The causes which lead to this desire lie deep and spread wide. Many men can talk of the necessity of an Isaiah among the Jewish priests, who are unwilling to acknowledge the need of a prophet among a time-serving priesthood now.

To your second question, I answer that I am not discouraged by these dissensions. Disagreeable they unquestionably are; so much so, that we would be willing to give up anything but principle to avoid them; but, under God's Providence, they will mightily promote the cause of general freedom. . . .

God bless the Massachusetts Anti-Slavery Society! Good men and true women from the beginning until now!

YOURS AFFECTIONATELY,
L. MARIA CHILD

40

THE BOSTON FEMALE ANTI-SLAVERY SOCIETY

Annual Meeting

October 1839

This report offers a window onto the struggles within women's organizations in 1839, as women chose sides in the break between the AASS and the "new organization."

The regular time for the annual meeting, occurred on the second Wednesday of October. A large number of women assembled, and after the usual devotional services, the Annual Report was read and accepted. There was in it no allusion relative to the present aspect of the antislavery cause. . . . [T]he election of officers came on, Miss Parker presiding. Mrs. Child nominated Mrs. Southwick for President, and immediately some one nominated Miss Mary S. Parker. Mrs. Child said, that in the present state of the Society, we needed to have an impartial President. She would say, in all kindness and courtesy to Miss Parker, that this was not the case at present. She had been pained at the last meeting by the great want of impartiality with which the duties of the chair had been discharged. . . .

A number of members attempted to speak, and calls for the vote to be fairly taken were uttered from all parts of the room. Mrs. Southwick in a firm tone said—"I protest against this whole proceeding, and move that Miss Parker leave the chair, and Miss Sullivan take it, that the business of this meeting may be properly transacted." Mrs. Southwick was heard,—though all the time she was speaking, Miss Parker uttered incessant cries of there is no motion before the house. "Sit down, take your seat, Mrs. Southwick. You shall sit down." After Mrs. Southwick had so far succeeded in attracting Miss Parker's notice as to make her comprehend that she was submitting as a motion, that Miss Sullivan should be called to the chair, in the same hurried manner that characterized all she did during the latter portion of the afternoon, Miss Parker submitted the motion, declaring almost at the same instant, "It is not a vote." She then said—"Miss Mary Parker is elected President." . . .

The vote was taken by rising, and Miss Parker declared it to be carried. The vote was doubted, and though a number of ladies had left the house, and though the members seemed nearly equally divided, no counting was permitted. One lady said to Miss Parker, "I doubt the vote." "Take your seat," said she. "But I doubt the vote." "Then you may doubt it to the day of your death," was Miss Parker's rejoinder. . . . The pretended election of the other officers was carried on in an equally unconstitutional manner. . . . An adjournment was moved, and declared by Miss Parker to be carried.

What should be the course of faithful members of the Society at this time? The principles of the Society are inviolate. While they continue so, let us seek to save it from destruction. The ground on which we stand is holy. Let us not leave it, but contend for it, till falsehood and duplicity are fully exposed.

A LIFE-MEMBER OF THE BOSTON F. A. S. SOCIETY.
[ANNE WARREN WESTON]

41

HENRY CLARKE WRIGHT

Letter to The Liberator

New York, May 15, 1840

Wright was biased against the "new organization," but his account of their secession from the American Anti-Slavery Society quoted their leaders accurately.

MY BROTHER:

The deed is done. The spirit of new organization, which is the spirit of slavery in disguise, — has, to the delight of pro-slavery ministers, editors and politicians, effected a division in the American Anti-Slavery Society. The Journal of Commerce, the Courier and Enquirer, the Commercial Advertiser and Herald, well known and staunch advocates of slavery and enemies of human rights, have extended to those who have gone out from among us the right hand of fellowship. A new society is formed, called the American and Foreign Anti-Slavery Society.

What is the basis of this new organization? THE AMERICAN SOCIETY REFUSED TO PRECLUDE WOMEN FROM THE RIGHTS OF MEMBERSHIP. This, and this only, according to the public statement of those who formed it, is the cause. Women have been invited to join the society from the beginning. Women have joined, under the impression that, according to the Constitution, they should be entitled to all the privileges of membership. Last year, urged on to the work by Sarah and Angelina Grimké, women were present at the anniversary, spoke and voted in the meetings, and were appointed on committees by Gerrit Smith. This year, women came forward to join with their brethren in this labor of love to sustain the cause of human rights. A business committee was appointed, consisting of Lewis Tappan, Charles W. Denison, Amos A. Phelps, Abby Kelley and others. Because a woman was on the committee, Lewis Tappan declined serving—giving as his reasons the following —

"The New National Organization," *The Liberator*, May 22, 1840.

1. "To put a woman on a committee with men, is contrary to the Constitution of the Society."
2. "It is throwing a fire brand into the anti-slavery ranks."
3. "It is contrary to the usages of civilized society." A. A. Phelps and C. W. Denison, refused for the same reasons, adding this further reason —
4. "It was contrary to the gospel and to their consciences."

Rev. Messrs. Denison and Dunbar, though they were conscientiously opposed to having women enjoy all the privileges of membership, strenuously urged the women to vote against A. Kelley's being on the committee. When they could not succeed in excluding members from the constitutional rights of membership, Lewis Tappan and C. W. Denison arose in the meeting and gave the following notice: "All who voted against the appointment of women on committees are requested to meet and form an American and Foreign Anti-Slavery Society."

Those who were opposed to women's acting in our Anti-Slavery Society with men, on the principle of equality of rights, went off and formed a new society.

Thus, because the society would not deny to the women their constitutional rights on the anti-slavery platform, Lewis Tappan . . . and others have seceded and set up another organization, from which woman is to be virtually excluded, because she is woman.

With what propriety is this "new organization" called an Anti-Slavery society? Anti-Slavery asserts the equality of human rights. It looks at man as man; it estimates man, not by his accidents and adjuncts — not by sex, color, tribe, nation, country or condition — but as man — and recognizes every human being, without regard to complexion, sex, or condition, as being the image and representative of God on earth — having an equal dominion over this lower world. But here is a society which excludes one half of the human race from its platform because of sex. How can any woman who feels for the virtue, honor and true dignity and glory of her sex, give any countenance to such a pro-slavery organization? The only reason given by Lewis Tappan and C. W. Denison, when they invited us to aid in its formation, was, in substance, to have a society which should exclude women, because they are women, from participating in its business transactions — from speaking, voting, and acting on committees in business meetings — for they invited only those to attend who were opposed to women thus acting. Women may speak, vote and act on committees, but by themselves. They must not presume to speak, vote and act with men in Anti-Slavery meetings.

What spirit is this but the spirit of despotism, which crushes women on three-fourths of the globe? The same spirit that originated the American and Foreign Anti-Slavery Society, has precluded woman from the society of man all over the East—shut her up in harems and seraglios, to keep her from mingling with her brother in the affairs of life—which has ever made woman the slave, the uncomplaining, suffering slave of man. Because her God made her a woman, she is thrust off from that platform where her brother acts. Where are those women, Sarah M. Grimké and Angelina E. Weld, who, for a brief space, so powerfully advocated the cause of human rights with tongue and pen? Has God stricken them with paralysis? Is their light gone out in total darkness? Oh that God would move them to speak once more in this crisis.

That same spirit which excludes the colored man, because of his color, from our schools, colleges, churches, legislatures, travelling conveyances, and from our social sympathies and circles, has originated in this new society. The colored people may go off by themselves to Liberia or elsewhere, and act by themselves; but they must not mingle with the whites. So has this new organization colonized the women. "The women may speak, vote, and act by themselves, but not with us, They are women.". . . And this is the end of Lewis Tappan's regard to the holy principles of human rights! He will no longer work in the American Anti-Slavery Society to sustain and propagate these eternal, immutable principles of liberty, justice, and equality, solely because that society will not deny to woman her right as a human being to speak and act with her brethren on the anti-slavery platform. How art thou fallen, my brother! When thou art interrogated why thou didst lead in this unhappy division, at heaven's tribunal, wilt thou answer—Woman—WOMAN—was the cause? She came forward and joined her brethren to counsel and act with them for crushed humanity, and I would not receive her aid, because it was "contrary to the usages of civilized society, and would throw a firebrand into the Anti-Slavery ranks."

H. C. WRIGHT

An Independent Women's Rights Movement Is Born, 1840–1858

42

ELIZABETH CADY STANTON

Letter to Sarah Grimké and Angelina Grimké Weld

London, June 25, 1840

Stanton's letter to the Grimké sisters depicts her sympathy for the Garrisonian women at the London conference even though her husband had joined the "new organization." She was particularly impressed with Lucretia Mott.

DEAR SISTERS, SARAH & ANGELINA:

Yesterday the convention closed, & I hasten to redeem my promise, to tell you something about it. We send you papers containing a minute account of all the proceedings, therefore I shall be very general in what I write. All things considered the convention has passed off more smoothly than any of us anticipated. The woman's rights question besides monopolizing one whole day has by being often referred to, created some little discord, for on this point we find a difference of opinion among the men & women here as well as with us in America. Garrison arrived on the fourth day of the meeting, but as the female delegates were not received and were not permitted to take their seats as delegates, he refused to take his, consequently his voice was not heard throughout the meeting. . . .

Weld-Grimké Papers, Clements Library, University of Michigan, Ann Arbor.

Lucretia Mott has just given me a long message for you, which condensed is that she thinks you have both been in a state of retiracy long enough, & that it is not right for you to be still, longer, that you should either write for the public or speak out for *oppressed woman.* Sarah in particular she thinks should appear in public again as she has no duties to prevent her. She says a great struggle is at hand & that all the friends of freedom for woman must rally round the *Garrison standard.* I have had much conversation with Lucretia Mott & I think her a peerless woman. She has a clear head & warm heart—her views are many of them so new & strange that my *causality* finds great delight in her society. The quakers here have not all received her cordially, they fear her heretical notions. I am often asked if you have not changed your opinions on woman's rights & I have invariably taken the liberty to say no. . . .

Your names are always mentioned with great enthusiasm. You would laugh I am sure to see the look of surprize when to the list of virtues I add your great skill in discharging all your domestic avocations. Dear friends how much I love you!! What a trio! for me to love. You have no idea what a hold you have on my heart. The two green spots to me in America are the peaceful abodes of cousin Gerrit [Smith] & Theodore Weld, oh! I cannot tell you with what delight I look forward to the many hours I hope to spend in those places of pleasant memories. . . .

Henry wishes me to say that he attributes his freedom from seasickness to *his strict observance of the Graham system.* . . .

YOURS IN LOVE
ELIZABETH C. STANTON

43

ELIZABETH CADY STANTON

Planning the Seneca Falls Convention

1881

A casual social visit turned into a serious planning meeting for the first women's rights convention in the western world. Elizabeth Stanton's later account of that meeting reveals the improvisation that produced the convention's chief document, the "Declaration of Sentiments."

Woman's Rights Convention. — A Convention to discuss the social, civil, and religious condition and rights of woman, will be held in the Wesleyan Chapel, at Seneca Falls, N.Y., on Wednesday and Thursday, the 19th and 20th of July, current; commencing at 10 o'clock A.M. During the first day the meeting will be exclusively for women, who are earnestly invited to attend. The public generally are invited to be present on the second day, when Lucretia Mott, of Philadelphia, and other ladies and gentlemen, will address the convention.

This call, without signature, was issued by Lucretia Mott, Martha C. Wright, Elizabeth Cady Stanton, and Mary Ann McClintock. At this time Mrs. Mott was visiting her sister Mrs. Wright, at Auburn, and attending the Yearly Meeting of Friends in Western New York. Mrs. Stanton, having recently removed from Boston to Seneca Falls, finding the most congenial association of Quaker families, met Mrs. Mott incidentally for the first time since her residence there. They at once returned to the topic they had so often discussed, walking arm in arm in the streets of London, and Boston, "the propriety of holding a woman's convention." These four ladies, sitting round the tea-table of Richard Hunt, a prominent Friend near Waterloo, decided to put their long-talked-of resolution into action, and before the twilight deepened into night, the call was written, and sent to the *Seneca County Courier.* On Sunday morning they met in Mrs. McClintock's parlor to write their declaration, resolutions,

Elizabeth Cady Stanton, Susan B. Anthony, Matilda Gage Joslyn, and Ida Husted Harper, *History of Woman Suffrage* (New York: Fowler & Wells, 1881) 1:67–69.

and to consider subjects for speeches. As the convention was to assemble in three days, the time was short for such productions; but having no experience in the *modus operandi* of getting up conventions, nor in that kind of literature, they were quite innocent of the herculean labors they proposed. On the first attempt to frame a resolution; to crowd a complete thought, clearly and concisely, into three lines; they felt as helpless and hopeless as if they had been suddenly asked to construct a steam engine. And the humiliating fact may as well now be recorded that before taking the initiative step, those ladies resigned themselves to a faithful perusal of masculine productions. The reports of Peace, Temperance, and Anti-Slavery conventions were examined, but all alike seemed too tame and pacific for the inauguration of a rebellion such as the world had never before seen. They knew women had wrongs, but how to state them was the difficulty, and this was increased from the fact that they themselves were fortunately organized and conditioned; they were neither "sour old maids," childless women," nor "divorced wives," as the newspapers declared them to be. While they had felt the insults incident to sex, in many ways, as every proud, thinking woman must, in the laws, religion, and literature of the world, and in the invidious and degrading sentiments and customs of all nations, yet they had not in their own experience endured the coarser forms of tyranny resulting from unjust laws, or association with immoral and unscrupulous men, but they had souls large enough to feel the wrongs of others, without being sacrificed in their own flesh.

After much delay, one of the circle took up the Declaration of 1776, and read it aloud with much spirit and emphasis, and it was at once decided to adopt the historic document, with some slight changes such as substituting "all men" for "King George." Knowing that women must have more to complain of than men under any circumstances possibly could, and seeing the Fathers had eighteen grievances, a protracted search was made through statute books, church usages, and customs of society to find that exact number. Several well-disposed men assisted in collecting the grievances, until, with the announcement of the eighteenth, the women felt they had enough to go before the world with a good case. One youthful lord remarked, "Your grievances must be grievous indeed, when you are obliged to go to books in order to find them out."

44

Report of the Woman's Rights Convention held at Seneca Falls, N.Y.

July 19–20, 1848

The length and complexity of this report reflected the strength of the reform culture that created it. Those who attended the Seneca Falls Convention were experienced conference goers. They knew how to create a community of concerns from diverse individual perspectives, and how to gain a hearing for those concerns within the broader society.

A Convention to discuss the Social, Civil, and Religious Condition of Woman, was called by the Women of Seneca County, N.Y., and held at the village of Seneca Falls, in the Wesleyan Chapel, on the 19th and 20th of July, 1848.

The question was discussed throughout two entire days: the first day by women exclusively, the second day men participated in the deliberations. Lucretia Mott, of Philadelphia, was the moving spirit of the occasion.

On the morning of the 19th, the Convention assembled at 11 o'clock. The meeting was organized by appointing Mary M'Clintock Secretary. The object of the meeting was then stated by Elizabeth C. Stanton; after which, remarks were made by Lucretia Mott, urging the women present to throw aside the trammels of education, and not allow their new position to prevent them from joining in the debates of the meeting. The Declaration of Sentiments, offered for the acceptance of the Convention, was then read by E. C. Stanton. A proposition was made to have it re-read by paragraph, and after much consideration, some changes were suggested and adopted. The propriety of obtaining the signatures of men to the Declaration was discussed in an animated manner: a vote in favor was given; but concluding that the final decision would be the legitimate business of the next day, it was referred.

Adjourned to half-past two.

Report of the Woman's Rights Convention, Held at Seneca Falls, N.Y., July 19th and 20th, 1848 (Rochester, 1848); italicized portion from Stanton et al., *History of Woman Suffrage,* 1:73.

In the afternoon, the meeting assembled according to adjournment, and was opened by reading the minutes of the morning session. E. C. Stanton then addressed the meeting, and was followed by Lucretia Mott. The reading of the Declaration was called for, an addition having been inserted since the morning session. A vote taken upon the amendment was carried, and papers circulated to obtain signatures. The following resolutions were then read:

The following resolutions were discussed by Lucretia Mott, Thomas and Mary Ann McClintock, Amy Post, Catherine A. F. Stebbins, and others, and were adopted.

WHEREAS, The great precept of nature is conceded to be, that "man shall pursue his own true and substantial happiness." Blackstone in his Commentaries remarks, that this law of Nature being coeval with mankind, and dictated by God himself, is of course superior in obligation to any other. It is binding over all the globe, in all countries and at all times; no human laws are of any validity if contrary to this, and such of them as are valid, derive all their force, and all their validity, and all their authority, mediately and immediately, from this original;

Therefore,

Resolved, That such laws as conflict, in any way, with the true and substantial happiness of woman, are contrary to the great precept of nature and of no validity, for this is "superior in obligation to any other."

Resolved, That all laws which prevent woman from occupying such a station in society as her conscience shall dictate, or which place her in a position inferior to that of man, are contrary to the great precept of nature, and therefore of no force or authority.

Resolved, That woman is man's equal — was intended to be so by the Creator, and the highest good of the race demands that she should be recognized as such.

Resolved, That the women of this country ought to be enlightened in regard to the laws under which they live, that they may no longer publish their degradation, by declaring themselves satisfied with their present position, nor their ignorance, by asserting that they have all the rights they want.

Resolved, That inasmuch as man, while claiming for himself intellectual superiority, does accord to woman moral superiority, it is preeminently his duty to encourage her to speak and teach, as she has an opportunity, in all religious assemblies.

Resolved, That the same amount of virtue, delicacy, and refinement of behavior, that is required of woman in the social state, should also be required of man, and the same transgressions should be visited with equal severity on both man and woman.

Resolved, That the objection of indelicacy and impropriety, which is so often brought against woman when she addresses a public audience, comes with a very ill-grace from those who encourage, by their attendance, her appearance on the stage, in the concert, or in feats of the circus.

Resolved, That woman has too long rested satisfied in the circumscribed limits which corrupt customs and a perverted application of the Scriptures have marked out for her, and that it is time she should move in the enlarged sphere which her great Creator has assigned her.

Resolved, That it is the duty of women of this country to secure themselves their sacred right to the elective franchise.

Resolved, That the equality of human rights results necessarily from the fact of the identity of the race in capabilities and responsibilities.

Resolved, therefore, That, being invested by the Creator with the same capabilities, and the same consciousness of responsibility for their exercise, it is demonstrably the right and duty of woman, equally with man, to promote every righteous cause by every righteous means; and especially in regard to the great subjects of morals and religion, it is self-evidently her right to participate with her brother in teaching them, both in the private and public, by writing and by speaking, by any instrumentalities proper to be used, and in any assemblies proper to be held; and this being a self-evident truth growing out of the divinely implanted principles of human nature; any custom or authority adverse to it, whether modern or wearing the hoary sanction of antiquity, is to be regarded as a self-evident falsehood, and at war with the interests of mankind.

Lucretia Mott read a humorous article from a newspaper, written by Martha C. Wright. After an address by E. W. M'Clintock, the meeting adjourned to 10 o'clock the next morning.

In the evening, Lucretia Mott spoke with her usual eloquence and power to a large and intelligent audience on the subject of reforms in general.

THURSDAY MORNING

The Convention assembled at the hour appoint, James Mott, of Philadelphia, in the Chair. The minutes of the previous day having been read, E. C. Stanton again read the Declaration of Sentiments, which was freely discussed by Lucretia Mott, Ansel Bascom, S. E. Woodworth, Thomas and Mary Ann M'Clintock, Frederick Douglass, Amy Post, Catharine Stebbins, and Elizabeth C. Stanton, and was unanimously adopted, as follows:

DECLARATION OF SENTIMENTS

When, in the course of human events, it becomes necessary for one portion of the family of man to assume among the people of the earth a position different from that which they have hitherto occupied, but one to which the laws of nature and of nature's God entitle them, a decent respect to the opinions of mankind requires that they should declare the causes that impel them to such a course.

We hold these truths to be self-evident: that all men and women are created equal: that they are endowed by their Creator with certain inalienable rights; that among these are life, liberty, and the pursuit of happiness; that to secure these rights governments are instituted, deriving their just powers from the consent of the governed. Whenever any form of government becomes destructive of these ends, it is the right of those who suffer from it to refuse allegiance to it, and to insist upon the institution of a new government, laying its foundation on such principles and organizing its powers in such form, as to them shall seem most likely to effect their safety and happiness. Prudence, indeed, will dictate that governments long established should not be changed for light and transient causes; and accordingly all experience hath shown that mankind are more disposed to suffer, while evils are sufferable, than to right themselves by abolishing the forms to which they were accustomed. But when a long train of abuses and usurpations, pursuing invariably the same object evinces a design to reduce them under absolute despotism, it is their duty to throw off such government, and to provide new guards for their future security. Such has been the patient sufferance of the women under this government, and such is now the necessity which constrains them to demand the equal station to which they are now entitled.

The history of mankind is a history of repeated injuries and usurpations on the part of man toward woman, having in direct object the establishment of an absolute tyranny over her. To prove this, let facts be submitted to a candid world.

He has never permitted her to exercise her inalienable right to the elective franchise.

He has compelled her to submit to laws, in the formation of which she had no voice.

He has withheld from her rights which are given to the most ignorant and degraded men—both natives and foreigners.

Having deprived her of this first right of a citizen, the elective franchise, thereby leaving her without representation in the halls of legislation, he has oppressed her on all sides.

He has made her, if married, in the eye of the law, civilly dead.

He has taken from her all right to property, even to the wages she earns.

He has made her, morally, an irresponsible being, as she can commit many crimes with impunity, provided they be done in the presence of her husband. In the covenant of marriage, she is compelled to promise obedience to her husband, he becoming, to all intents and purposes, her master—the law giving him the power to deprive her of her liberty, and to administer chastisement.

He has so framed the laws of divorce, as to what shall be the proper causes, and in case of separation, to whom the guardianship of the children shall be given, as to be wholly regardless of the happiness of women—the law, in all cases, going upon a false supposition of the supremacy of man, and giving all power into his hands.

After depriving her of all rights as a married woman, if single, and the owner of property, he has taxed her to support a government which recognizes her only when her property can be made profitable to it.

He has monopolized nearly all the profitable employments, and from those she is permitted to follow, she receives but a scanty remuneration.

He closes against her all the avenues to wealth and distinction which he considers most honorable to himself. As a teacher of theology, medicine, or law, she is not known.

He has denied her the facilities for obtaining a thorough education—all colleges being closed against her.

He allows her in Church, as well as State, but in a subordinate position, claiming Apostolic authority for her exclusion from the ministry, and with some exceptions, from a public participation in the affairs of the Church.

He has created a false public sentiment by giving to the world a different code of morals for men and women, by which moral delinquencies which exclude women from society, are not only tolerated, but deemed of little account in man.

He has usurped the prerogative of Jehovah himself, claiming it as his right to assign her a sphere of action, when that belongs to her conscience and to her God.

He has endeavored, in every way that he could, to destroy her confidence in her own powers, to lessen her self-respect, and to make her willing to lead a dependent and abject life.

Now in view of this entire disfranchisement of one-half the people of this country, their social and religious degradation—in view of the unjust laws above mentioned, and because women do feel themselves aggrieved, oppressed, and fraudulently deprived of their most sacred rights, we insist that they have immediate admission to all the rights and privileges which belong to them as citizens of the United States.

In entering upon the great work before us, we anticipate no small amount of misconception, misrepresentation, and ridicule; but we shall use every instrumentality within our power to effect our object. We shall employ agents, circulate tracts, petition the State and National legislatures, and endeavor to enlist the pulpit and the press in our behalf. We hope this Convention will be followed by a series of Conventions embracing every part of the country.

Firmly relying upon the final triumph of the Right and the True, we do this day affix our signatures to this declaration, [signatures of 68 women, Lucretia Mott's first].

The following are the names of the gentlemen present in favor of the movement: [signatures of 32 men, including Frederick Douglass].

The meeting adjourned until two o'clock.

AFTERNOON SESSION

At the appointed hour the meeting convened. The minutes having been read, the resolutions of the day before were read and taken up separately. Some, from their self-evident truth, elicited but little remark; others, after some criticism, much debate, and some slight alterations, were finally passed by a large majority. . . .

[The only resolution that was not unanimously adopted was the ninth, urging women of the country to secure themselves the elective franchise. Those who took part in the debate feared a demand for the right to vote would defeat others they deemed more rational, and make the whole movement ridiculous.

But Mrs. Stanton and Frederick Douglass, seeing that the power to choose rulers and make laws was the right by which all others could be secured, persistently advocated the resolution, and at last carried it by a small majority.]

The meeting closed with a forcible speech from Lucretia Mott.

Adjourned to half-past seven o'clock.

EVENING SESSION

The meeting opened by reading the minutes, Thomas M'Clintock in the Chair. As there had been no opposition expressed during the Convention to this movement, and although, after repeated invitations, no objections had presented themselves, E. C. Stanton volunteered an address in defence of the many severe accusations brought against the much-abused "Lords of Creation."

Thomas M'Clintock then read several extracts from Blackstone, in proof of woman's servitude to man; after which Lucretia Mott offered and spoke to the following resolution:

Resolved, That the speedy success of our cause depends upon the zealous and untiring efforts of both men and women, for the overthrow of the monopoly of the pulpit, and for the securing to woman an equal participation with men in the various trades, professions, and commerce. The Resolution was adopted.

M. A. M'Clintock, Jr. delivered a short, but impressive address, calling upon woman to arouse from her lethargy and be true to herself and her God. When she had concluded, Frederick Douglass arose, and in an excellent and appropriate speech, ably supported the cause of woman.

The meeting was closed by one of Lucretia Mott's most beautiful and spiritual appeals. She commanded the earnest attention of that large audience for nearly an hour.

45

Proceedings of the Colored Convention

Cleveland, September 6, 1848

The first women's rights speaker in the National Negro Convention Movement, Mrs. Sanford, was probably a friend of Frederick Douglass from Rochester (Douglass was president of the convention). She mentioned married women's property rights, and the hope "to co-operate

The North Star 1, no. 40 (Sept 29, 1848): 1.

in making the laws we obey." After her speech, Frederick Douglass outmaneuvered the opponents of women's rights, and the convention passed a resolution in favor of women's participation in future meetings.

. . . After an animated discussion upon the indefinite postponement, the Rules were suspended to hear remarks from a lady who wished to say something on the rights of Woman. The President then introduced to the audience, Mrs. Sanford, who made some eloquent remarks of which the following is a specimen:

> From the birthday of Eve, the then prototype of woman's destiny, to the flash of the star of Bethlehem, she had been the slave of power and passion. If raised by courage and ambition to the proud trial of heroism, she was still the marred model of her first innocence; if thrown by beauty into the ordeal of temptation, man lost his own dignity in contemning her intellectual weight, and refusing the right to exercise her moral powers; if led by inclination to the penitential life of a recluse, the celestial effulgence of a virtuous innocence was lost, and she lived out woman's degradation!
>
> But the day of her regeneration dawned. The Son of God had chosen a mother from among the daughters of Eve! A Saviour, who could have come into this a God-man ready to act, to suffer, and be crucified, came in the helplessness of infancy, for woman to cherish and direct. Her *exaltation was consummated!*
>
> True, we ask for the Elective Franchise; for right of property in the marriage covenant, whether earned or bequeathed. True, we pray to co-operate in making the laws we obey; but it is not to domineer, to dictate or assume. We ask it, for it is a right, granted by a higher disposer of human events than man. We pray for it now, for there are duties around us, and we weep at our inability.
>
> And to the delegates, officers, people and spirit of this Convention, I would say, God speed you in your efforts for elevation and freedom; stop not; shrink not, look not back, till you have justly secured an *unqualified citizenship of the United States, and those inalienable rights granted you by an impartial Creator.*

Convention passed a vote of thanks to Mrs. Sanford, and also requested a synopsis of her, from which the above are extracts.

A vote of thanks was here passed to John M. Sterling, Esq., of Cleveland, for the presentation of a bundle of books entitled "Slavery as it is."[1]

Discussion was resumed on the indefinite postponement of the Resolution as to Woman's Right. Objection was made to the resolution, and in favor of its postponement, by Messrs. Langston and Day, on the ground that we had passed one similar, making all colored persons present, delegates to this Convention, and they considered *women persons.*

Frederick Douglass moved to amend the 33d Resolution, by saying that the word persons used in the resolution designating delegates be understood to include *woman.* On the call for the previous question, the Resolution was not indefinitely postponed. Mr. Douglass's amendment was seconded and carried, with three cheers for woman's rights. . . . [Resolutions]

33. Whereas, we fully believe in the equality of the sexes, therefore,

Resolved, That we hereby invite females hereafter to take part in our deliberations. . . .

[1]Published by the AASS and edited primarily by Theodore Weld, *American Slavery as It Is* first appeared in 1839.

46

"Woman's Rights"
October 1, 1849

Many popular periodicals promoted ideas about women's rights in the 1840s. A flourishing popular press provided many links between the emerging women's rights movement and other social movements. Women's rights were especially represented in a women's temperance periodical, The Lily, *founded in 1849 by Amelia Bloomer, a Seneca Falls writer who had attended the 1848 convention. In 1853 the magazine moved to Ohio and claimed a national readership of 6,000, but it ceased publication in 1856.*

The Lily 1, no. 10 (Oct. 1, 1849).

Start not dear reader, as your eye rests upon the above words, nor think that we are going to nominate either you or ourself for the Governorship or the Presidency. No, it is not time to make lady Presidents yet, and for ourself we can say that we have no aspirations of the kind at present;—but according to the belief of some, the day will soon come when woman may claim her "rights," in this respect, and then we may not be backward in taking a seat in the Presidential chair, provided the good people shall so will it.

It is not our right to hold office or to rule our country, that we would not advocate. Much, very much, must be done to elevate and improve the character and minds of our sex, before we are capable of ruling our own households as we ought, to say nothing of holding in our hands the reins of government. But woman has rights which she knows not of, or knowing, disregards. She has rights of which she is deprived—or rather, of which she deprives herself. She is willing to sit down within the narrow sphere assigned her by man, and make no effort to obtain her just rights, or free herself from the oppressions which are crushing her to the earth. She tamely submits to be governed by such laws as man sees fit to make and in making which she has no voice. We know that many of us think we have rights enough, and we are content with what we have; but we forget how many thousand wives and mothers worthy as ourselves, are compelled by the unjust laws of our land, to drag out a weary life and submit to indignities which no man would bear. It is stated that thirty thousand die annually from the effects of intoxicating drinks; an equal number of drunkards must stand ready to fall. Think of the wives and mothers of this great number—of their untold griefs—of their hidden sorrows—of their broken hearts—of their hunger and nakedness—their unwearied toil to procure a bare pittance to save their little ones from starvation—of the wretched life they lead, and the unmourned death they die. Think of all this, and then tell us not that woman has her rights. Many of the number thus destroyed inch by inch, have been reared amid all the luxuries that wealth and power can bestow. Many of them possess accomplishments that might have graced the most refined society, and who, had their lots been differently cast, would have been courted and sought after by those who now spurn them—and for what? Simply because they have been so unfortunate as to wed a drunkard—or rather because they upon whom they bestowed their young affections, and who vowed to love and protect them, have proved false to all their vows, and left them to the rough blasts of an un-pitying world. What rights have the drunkard's wife and children?—Who listens to their tale of woe, or lends a pitying ear to their cry?

A woman is entitled to the same rights as a man, but does she have them? Dare men pretend that she does? What right have they to make laws which deprive her of every comfort, strip her of every friend, and doom her to a wretched existence? And yet they do this, and then if she dare to complain, and ask to be relieved from these tyranical laws, she is thought to be out of her place, and overstepping the bounds of female delicacy! This is why they so tamely submit to martyrdom by the laws. The statute book of this free country bears upon its leaves a foul stain called a license law [a license to sell alcoholic beverages]. By this law men are bidden to go forth and pursue a business which deprives thirty thousand annually of life—worse than murders twenty thousand wives and mothers, and sixty thousand children. For the privilege thus allowed, the law claims in return a few dollars from those who pursue this *moral* and *honorable* business! It is useless for our sex to seek redress at the hands of the law, from the cruel wrongs inflicted upon them, for it will give them none—it does not recognise their right to protection. But should they dare to raise their hand against their destroyers, and return injury for injury, then the law quickly defends its agents and metes out punishment for her who ventures to defend herself.

We ask not for the honors or emoluments of office for our sex, but we claim that they are unjustly deprived of their rights. We do not believe that man has the *right,* if he has the power, to make laws which will deprive us of any of the comforts of life—or if he does make the laws without our consent, we are not bound to obey them. Unless those who claim the power of legislating for us, will do something to ameliorate the condition of the down trodden victims of their cruel enactments, it is not only the right, but the duty of those trampled upon, to assert their claim to protection.

47

ABBY H. PRICE

Address to the "Woman's Rights Convention"

Worcester, Massachusetts, October 1850

Abby Price exemplified the increasingly secular language used to advocate women's rights at the many women's rights conventions in northern states in the 1850s.

The natural rights of woman are co-equal with those of man. So God created man in his own image; in the image of God created he him; male and female, created he them. There is not one particle of difference intimated as existing between them. They were both made in the image of God. Dominion was given to both over every other creature, but not over each other. They were expected to exercise the viceregency given to them by their Maker in harmony and love.

In contending for this co-equality of woman's with man's rights, it is not necessary to argue, either that the sexes are by nature equally and indiscriminately adapted to the same positions and duties, or that they are absolutely equal in physical and intellectual ability; but only that they are absolutely equal in their rights to life, liberty, and the pursuit of happiness—in their rights to do, and to be, individually and socially, all they are capable of, and to attain the highest usefulness and happiness, obediently to the divine moral law.

These are every man's rights, of whatever race or nation, ability or situation, in life. These are equally every woman's rights, whatever her comparative capabilities may be—whatever her relations may be. These are human rights, equally inherent in male and female. To repress them in any degree is in the same degree usurpation, tyranny, and oppression. We hold these to be self-evident truths, and shall not now discuss them. We shall assume that happiness is the chief end of all human beings; that existence is valuable in proportion as happiness

Proceedings of the Woman's Rights Convention Held at Worcester, October 23rd and 24th, 1850 (Boston: Prentiss & Sawyer, 1851).

is promoted and secured; and that, on the whole, each of the sexes is equally necessary to the common happiness, and in one way or another is equally capable, with fair opportunity, of contributing to it. Therefore each has an equal right to pursue and enjoy it. This settled, we contend:

1. That women ought to have equal opportunities with men for suitable and well compensated employment.
2. That women ought to have equal opportunities, privileges, and securities with men for rendering themselves pecuniarily independent.
3. That women ought to have equal legal and political rights, franchises, and advantages with men. . . .

Human beings cannot attain true dignity or happiness except by true usefulness. This is true of women as of men. It is their duty, privilege, honor, and bliss to be useful. Therefore give them the opportunity and encouragement. If there are positions, duties, occupations, really unsuitable to females, as such, let these be left to males. If there are others unsuitable to men, let these be left to women. Let all the rest be equally open to both sexes. And let the compensation be graduated justly, to the real worth of the services rendered, irrespective of sex. . . .

What good reason is there why women should not be educated to mercantile pursuits, to engage in commerce, to invent, to construct, in fine [in sum] to do anything she can do? Why so separate the avocations of the sexes? I believe it impossible for woman to fulfil the design of God in her creation until her brethren mingle with her more as an equal, as a moral being, and lose in the dignity of her immortal nature the idea of her being a female. Until social intercourse is purified by the forgetfulness of sex we can never derive high benefit from each other's society in the active business of life. Man inflicts injury upon woman, unspeakable injury in placing her intellectual and moral nature in the background, and woman injures herself by submitting to be regarded only as a female. She is called upon loudly, by the progressive spirit of the age, to rise from the station where man, not God, has placed her, and to claim her rights as a moral and responsible being, equal with man.

As such, both have the same sphere of action, and the same duties devolve on both, though these may vary according to circumstances. Fathers and mothers have sacred duties and obligations devolving upon them which cannot belong to others. These do not attach to them as man and woman, but as parents, husbands, and wives. In all the majesty of moral power, in all the dignity of immortality let woman plant herself side by side with man on the broad platform of equal human rights. . . .

Our sisters, whose poverty is caused by the oppressions of society, who are driven to sin by want of bread,—then regarded with scorn and turned away from with contempt! I appeal to you in their behalf, my friends. Is it not time to throw open to women, equal resources with men, for obtaining honest employment? If the extremity of human wretchedness—a condition which combines within itself every element of suffering, mental and physical, circumstantial and intrinsic—is a passport to our compassion, every heart should bleed for the position of these poor sufferers. . . .

Let us arise then in all the majesty of renewed womanhood and say, we must be free. We will attend to our previous home duties faithfully, cheerfully, but we must do it voluntarily, in obedience to our Maker, who placed these responsibilities more especially upon us. If the affairs of the nation demand the attention of our fathers, our husbands, and our brothers, allow us to act with them for the right, according to the dictates of our own consciences. Then we will educate our sons and our daughters as equal companions, alike interested in whatever concerns the welfare of the race. Our daughters, equally provided for the serious business of life, shall no longer be dependent upon the chances of marriage; teaching them not to live wholly in their affections, we will provide for them, as for our sons, a refuge from the storms of life, by opening to them the regions of high intellectual culture, of pecuniary independence, and of moral and political responsibilities.

The Problematics of Race within the New Movement, 1850

48

PARKER PILLSBURY

Letter to Jane Swisshelm

November 18, 1850

In a letter to Swisshelm reprinted in The North Star, *Pillsbury represented the well-established view of the Garrisonian movement — and of many within the women's convention movement — that race had to be mentioned at women's rights conventions if those meetings were to encompass the needs of black women. Pillsbury, an editor and former minister, was among the most radical abolitionist leaders, especially in his condemnation of the proslavery sympathies of the northern clergy and in his support of women's rights within the antislavery movement.*

DEAR MRS. SWISSHELM:

In the last Visiter, you say of a resolution relating to people of color, offered by Mr. Wendell Phillips in the late Convention of Women, at Worcester, Mass. —

"We are pretty nearly out of patience with the dogged perseverance with which so many of our Reformers persist in their attempt to do everything at once." And again: "In a Woman's Rights Convention, the question of color had no right to a hearing."

"Woman's Rights Convention and People of Color," *The North Star*, Dec. 5, 1850.

It seemed as though the usually kindly spirit and good judgment of the Visiter were a little wanting in these two utterances. . . .

But by way of explanation, (or if you please, apology), permit me to say that colored persons are held in such estimation in this country, that you must specify them whenever or wherever you mean to include them.

Lyceums, circuses, menageries, ballrooms, billiard-rooms, conventions, everything, "the Public are respectfully invited to attend." But who ever dreamed that "the public" meant anything colored? From church and theatre; from stage-coach, steam-ship and creeping canal-boat; from the infant school, law school and theological seminary; from museum, athenaeum and public garden, the colored race are either excluded altogether, or are admitted only by sufferance, or some very special arrangement, and under disadvantages to which no white person would or should submit for a moment. . . .

We have striven to separate the Ethiopian from all claim to human recognition and human sympathy. Nobody but abolitionists ever mean *colored* people, no matter how often they speak of "the public," or of their "fellow citizens" or "fellow sinners." . . .

And his race know it and feel it, as we cannot. Even the women's Convention demonstrated this, for scarcely a colored person, man or woman, appeared in it.

On the large committees appointed to carry out the plans of the Convention, embracing many persons in all, not a single colored member was placed. It is to be presumed that nobody thought of it, for we are not expected to think of colored people at all.

Under such circumstances, is it strange, is it an unpardonable sin, is it "dogged perseverance," to declare in a Convention called to demand and extend the rights of women, that we mean women of sable as well as sallow complexion? of the carved in ebony as well as the chiseled in ivory? If we did thus mean, the Convention should not have been held, or being held, it would only deserve the scorn and contempt of every friend of God and his children. Color was not discussed there—it need not have been. But it was heeded that the declaration be made in regard to it. That ANY woman have rights, will scarcely be believed; but that colored women have rights, would never have been thought of, without a specific declaration.

MOST TRULY YOURS,
PARKER PILLSBURY
CONCORD, N. H., NOV. 18

49

JANE SWISSHELM

"Woman's Rights and the Color Question"
November 23, 1850

In her reply to Pillsbury, Swisshelm argued in favor of single-issue reform and said the women's rights movement had no obligation to eradicate differences based on race or class.

We give [print] Mr. Pillsbury's article on this subject, and if we failed to prove the bad policy of linking these two questions, Mr. Pillsbury will surely succeed. Every thing he says about the exclusion of colored people from places and positions they have a right to occupy, is so much against uniting their cause to that of woman. The women of this glorious Republic are sufficiently oppressed without linking their cause to that of the slave. The slave is sufficiently oppressed without binding him to the stake which has ever held woman in a state of bondage. . . .

You, sir, show dogged perseverance in insisting that our starving seamstresses shall not strike for higher wages unless they put in a protest in favor of the boot-blacks—that woman shall not strike off her shackles until she can liberate every man that wears one—that she shall take no step forward until she overcomes a prejudice which oppresses another branch of humanity. You, Mr. Pillsbury, and the rest of your male coadjutors, enjoying all the rights for which women contend, have not been able to conquer the American prejudice against color, and now you expect that woman, crippled, helpless, bound, shall do what you have failed to perform with the free use of all your powers and faculties! . . .

As for colored women, all the interest they have in this reform is *as women*. All it can do for them is to raise them to the level of men of their own class. Then as that class rises let them rise with it. We only claim for a white wood-sawyer's wife that she is as good as a white wood-sawyer—a blacksmith's mother is a good as a blacksmith—a lawyer's sister is as good as a lawyer; at least this is our way of understanding this

---

"Woman's Rights and the Color Question," *The Saturday Visiter*, Nov. 23, 1850.

question. . . . The call [to the Convention] was explicit. It was to discuss the rights of Sex. We signed that call . . . and had no thought it was to be converted into an abolition meeting. With quite as much propriety it might have been turned into a Temperance or Law-Reform meeting, or a meeting to express sympathy with the Hungarian refugees. . . . We feel as if our name had been used for a purpose for which we did not give it, and we know of other signers of that call who are in the same predicament. It was a breach of trust, and one we shall remember when our name is asked for to answer another call.

50

SOJOURNER TRUTH

Speech at Akron Women's Rights Convention
Ohio, June 1851

Reprinted in a variety of forms, this notable speech by Sojourner Truth—seer, abolitionist, and women's rights advocate—was most accurately rendered in The Anti-Slavery Bugle *of Salem, Ohio. There it appeared with an introductory paragraph.*

One of the most unique and interesting speeches of the Convention was made by Sojourner Truth, an emancipated slave. It is impossible to transfer it to paper, or convey any adequate idea of the effect it produced upon the audience. Those only can appreciate it who saw her powerful form, her whole-souled, earnest gesture, and listened to her strong and truthful tones. She came forward to the platform and addressing the President said with great simplicity:

May I say a few words? Receiving an affirmative answer, she proceeded; I want to say a few words about this matter. I am a woman's rights [*sic*]. I have as much muscle as any man, and can do as much work as any man. I have plowed and reaped and husked and chopped and mowed, and can any man do more than that? I have heard much about the sexes being equal; I can carry as much as any man, and eat as much too, if I can get it. I am as strong as any man that is now.

As for intellect, all I can say is, if woman have a pint and man a quart—why can't she have her little pint full? You need not be afraid to give us our rights for fear we will take too much—for we won't take more than our pint'll hold.

The poor men seem to be all in confusion and don't know what to do. Why children, if you have woman's rights give it to her and you will feel better. You will have your own rights, and they won't be so much trouble.

I can't read, but I can hear. I have heard the Bible and have learned that Eve caused man to sin. Well if woman upset the world, do give her a chance to set it right side up again. The lady has spoked about Jesus, how he never spurned woman from him, and she was right. When Lazarus died, Mary and Martha came to him with faith and love and besought him to raise their brother. And Jesus wept—and Lazarus came forth. And how came Jesus into the world? Through God who created him and woman who bore him. Man, where is your part?

But the women are coming up bless be God and a few of the men are coming up with them. But man is in a tight place, the poor slave is on him, woman is coming on him, and he is surely between a hawk and a buzzard.

Free Black Women Become Public Speakers against Slavery and Racial Prejudice, 1850–1860

51

LUCY STANTON

A Plea for the Oppressed

December 17, 1850

Lucy Stanton graduated from Oberlin College in 1850, becoming the first African American woman college graduate in the United States. Enrolled in the "Female Department," she was president of the Oberlin Ladies Literary Society. Stanton developed solid speaking and writing skills, yet she did not find a venue for public speaking and became a teacher.

When I forget you, Oh my people, may my tongue cleave to the roof of my mouth, and may my right hand forget her cunning! Dark hover the clouds. The Anti-Slavery pulse beats faintly. The right of suffrage is denied. The colored man is still crushed by the weight of oppression. He may possess talents of the highest order, yet for him is no path of fame or distinction opened. He can never hope to attain those privileges while his brethren remain enslaved. Since, therefore, the freedom of the slave and the gaining of our rights, social and political, are inseparably connected, let all the friends of humanity plead for those who may not plead their own cause.

"A Plea for the Oppressed," *Oberlin Evangelist*, Dec. 17, 1850.

Reformers, ye who have labored long to convince man that happiness is found alone in doing good to others, that humanity is a unit, that he who injures one individual wrongs the race;—that to love one's neighbor as one's self is the sum of human virtue—ye that advocate the great principles of Temperance, Peace, and Moral Reform, will you not raise your voice in behalf of these stricken ones!—will you not plead the cause of the Slave?

Slavery is the combination of all crime. It is War.

Those who rob their fellow-men of home, of liberty, of education, of life, as really war against them as though they cleft them down upon the bloody field. It is intemperance; for there is an intoxication when the fierce passions rage in man's breast, more fearful than the madness of the drunkard, which if let loose upon the moral universe would sweep away every thing pure and holy, leaving but the wreck of man's nobler nature. Such passions does Slavery foster—yea, they are a part of herself. It is full of pollution. Know you not that to a slave, virtue is a sin counted worthy of death? That many, true to the light within, notwithstanding the attempts to shut out the truth, feeling that a consciousness of purity is dearer than life, have nobly died? Their blood crieth to God, a witness against the oppressor.

Statesmen, you who have bent at ambition's shrine, who would leave your names on the page of history, to be venerated by coming generations as among those of the great and good, will you not advocate the cause of the down-trodden, remembering that the spirit of liberty is abroad in the land? The precious seed is sown in the heart of the people, and though the fruit does not appear, the germ is there, and the harvest will yet be gathered. Truly is this an age of reform. The world is going on, not indeed keeping pace with the rapid tread of its leaders, but none the less progressing. As the people take a step in one reform, the way is prepared for another. Now while other evils in man's social and political condition are being remedied, think you that Slavery can stand that searching test—an enlightened people's sense of justice? Then speak the truth boldly; fear not loss of property or station. It is a higher honor to embalm your name in the hearts of a grateful people than to contend for the paltry honors of party preferment.

Woman, I turn to thee. Is it not thy mission to visit the poor? to shed the tear of sympathy? to relieve the wants of the suffering? Where wilt thou find objects more needing sympathy than among the slaves?

Mother, hast thou a precious gem in thy charge, like those that make up the Savior's jewels? Has thy heart, trembling with its unutterable joyousness, bent before the throne of the Giver with the prayer that thy child might be found in his courts? Thou hast seen the dawning of intelligence in its bright eye, and watched with interest the unfolding of its powers. Its gentle, winning ways have doubly endeared it to thee. Death breathes upon the flower, and it is gone. Now thou canst feel for the slave-mother who has bent with the same interest over her child, whose heart is entwined around it even more firmly than thine own around thine, for to her it is the only ray of joy in a dreary world. She returns weary and sick at heart from the labors of the field; the child's beaming smile of welcome half banishes the misery of her lot. Would she not die for it? Ye who know the depths of a mother's love, answer! Hark! Strange footsteps are near her dwelling! The door is thrown rudely open! Her master says—"There is the woman!" She comprehends it all—she is sold! From her trembling lips escape the words—"my child!" She throws herself at the feet of those merciless men, and pleads permission to keep her babe, but in vain. What is she more than any other slave, that she should be permitted this favor? They are separated.

Sister, have you ever had a kind and loving brother? How often would he lay aside his book to relieve you from some difficulty? How have you hung upon the words of wisdom that he has uttered? How earnestly have you studied that you might stand his companion—his equal. You saw him suddenly stricken by the destroyer. Oh! How your heart ached!

There was a slave-girl who had a brother kind and noble as your own. He had scarcely any advantages: yet stealthily would he draw an old volume from his pocket, and through the long night would pore over its contents. His soul thirsted for knowledge. He yearned for freedom, but free-soil was far away. That sister might not go, he staid with her. They say that slaves do not feel for or love each other; I fear that there are few brothers with a pale face who would have stood that test. For her he tamed the fire of his eye, toiled for that which profited him not, and labored so industriously that the overseer had no apology for applying the lash to his back. Time passed on: that brother stood in his manhood's prime as tenderly kind and as dearly beloved as ever. That sister was insulted;—the lash was applied to her quivering back; her brother rushed to save her! He tore away the fastenings which bound her to the whipping post, he held her on his arm—she was safe. She looked up, encountered the ferocious gaze of the overseer, heard the report of a pistol, and felt the heart's blood of a brother gushing over her. But we draw the veil.

Mother, sister, by thy own deep sorrow of heart; by the sympathy of thy woman's nature, plead for the downtrodden of thy own, of every land. Instill the principles of love, of common brotherhood, in the nursery, in the social circle. Let these be the prayer of thy life.

Christians, you whose souls are filled with love for your fellow men, whose prayer to the Lord is, "Oh! that I may see thy salvation among the children of men!" Does the battle wax warm? dost thou faint with the burden and heat of the day? Yet a little longer; the arm of the Lord is mighty to save those who trust in him. Truth and right must prevail. The bondsman shall go free. Look to the future! Hark! the shout of joy gushes from the heart of earth's freed millions! It rushes upward; the angels on heaven's outward battlements en[r]ich the sound on their golden lyres, and send it thrilling through the echoing arches of the upper world. How sweet, how majestic, from those starry isles float those deep inspiring sounds over the ocean of space! Softened and mellowed they reach earth, filling the soul with harmony, and breathing of God—of love—and of universal freedom.

52

FRANCES ELLEN WATKINS

Letters to William Still

1854–1856

Born and raised in Baltimore, Frances Ellen Watkins was educated by her uncle, William Watkins, a Garrisonian abolitionist, clergyman, and educator of free black children. In 1850, at the age of 25, Watkins left Baltimore to become a teacher in schools for free black children in Ohio and Pennsylvania. Her meteoric rise as an antislavery speaker, from 1854 to 1856, was partly due to her ability to speak about the brutality of slavery in Maryland, as well as her substantial literary gifts as a writer and poet. Her first book, Poems on Miscellaneous Subjects, *was published in 1854.*

William Still, *The Underground Rail Road* (Philadelphia: Porter & Coats, 1872), 758–61.

"WELL I AM OUT LECTURING," FRANCES ELLEN WATKINS TO WILLIAM STILL, PROVIDENCE, RHODE ISLAND, AUGUST 1854

"Well, I am out lecturing. I have lectured every night this week; besides addressed a Sunday-school, and I shall speak, if nothing prevent, to-night. My lectures have met with success. Last night I lectured in a white church in Providence. Mr. Gardener was present, and made the estimate of about six hundred persons. Never, perhaps, was a speaker, old or young, favored with a more attentive audience. . . . My voice is not wanting in strength, as I am aware of, to reach pretty well over the house. The church was the Roger Williams; the pastor, a Mr. Furnell, who appeared to be a kind and Christian man. . . . My maiden lecture was Monday night in New Bedford on the Elevation and Education of our People. Perhaps as intellectual a place as any I was ever at of its size."

"THE AGENT OF THE STATE ANTI-SLAVERY SOCIETY OF MAINE TRAVELS WITH ME," FRANCES ELLEN WATKINS TO WILLIAM STILL, BUCKSTOWN CENTRE, MAINE, SEPTEMBER 28, 1854

"The agent of the State Anti-Slavery Society of Maine travels with me, and she is a pleasant, dear, sweet lady. I do like her so. We travel together, eat together, and sleep together. (She is a white woman.) In fact I have not been in one colored person's house since I left Massachusetts; but I have a pleasant time. My life reminds me of a beautiful dream. What a difference between this and York! . . . I have met with some of the kindest treatment up here that I have ever received. . . . I have lectured three times this week. After I went from Limerick, I went to Springvale; there I spoke on Sunday night at an Anti-Slavery meeting. Some of the people are Anti-Slavery, Antirum and Anti-Catholic; and if you could see our Maine ladies, — some of them among the noblest types of womanhood you have ever seen! They are for putting men of Anti-Slavery principles in office, . . . to cleanse the corrupt fountains of our government by sending men to Congress who will plead for our down-trodden and oppressed brethren, our crushed and helpless sisters, whose tears and blood bedew our soil, whose chains are clanking 'neath our proudest banners, whose cries and groans amid our loudest paeans rise."

"ON FREE PRODUCE," FRANCES ELLEN WATKINS TO WILLIAM STILL, TEMPLE, MAINE, OCTOBER 20, 1854

"I spoke on Free Produce, and now by the way I believe in that kind of Abolition. Oh, it does seem to strike at one of the principal roots of the matter. I have commenced since I read Solomon Northrup. Oh, if Mrs. Stowe has clothed American slavery in the graceful garb of fiction, Solomon Northrup comes up from the dark habitation of Southern cruelty where slavery fattens and feasts on human blood with such mournful revelations that one might almost wish for the sake of humanity that the tales of horror which he reveals were not so. Oh, how can we pamper our appetites upon luxuries drawn from reluctant fingers? Oh, could slavery exist long if it did not sit on a commercial throne? I have read somewhere, if I remember aright, of a Hindoo being loth to cut a tree because cause being a believer in the transmigration of souls, he thought the soul of his father had passed into it. . . . Oh, friend, beneath the most delicate preparations of the cane can you not see the stinging lash and clotted whip? I have reason to be thankful that I am able to give a little more for a Free Labor dress, if it is coarser. I can thank God that upon its warp and woof I see no stain of blood and tears; that to procure a little finer muslin for my limbs no crushed and broken heart went out in sighs, and that from the field where it was raised went up no wild and startling cry unto the throne of God to witness there in language deep and strong, that in demanding that cotton I was nerving oppression's hand for deeds of guilt and crime. If the liberation of the slave demanded it, I could consent to part with a portion of the blood from my own veins if that would do him any good."

"I HAVE GAZED FOR THE FIRST TIME ON FREE LAND," FRANCES ELLEN WATKINS TO WILLIAM STILL, NIAGARA FALLS, SEPTEMBER 12, 1856

"Well, I have gazed for the first time upon Free Land, and, would you believe it, tears sprang to my eyes, and I wept. Oh, it was a glorious sight to gaze for the first time on a land where a poor slave flying from our glorious land of liberty would in a moment find his fetters broken, his shackles loosed, and whatever he was in the land of Washington, beneath the shadow of Bunker Hill Monument or even Plymouth Rock, here he becomes a man and a brother. I have gazed on Harper's Ferry, or rather the rock at the Ferry; I have seen it towering up in simple grandeur, with the gentle Potomac gliding peacefully at its feet, and felt that that was God's masonry, and my soul had expanded in gazing on its sublimity. I have seen the ocean singing its wild chorus of sounding waves, and ecstacy has thrilled upon the living chords of my heart. I have since then seen the rainbow-crowned Niagara chanting the choral hymn of Omnipotence, girdled with grandeur, and robed with glory; but none of these things have melted me as the first sight of Free Land. Towering mountains lifting their hoary summits to catch the first faint flush of day when the sunbeams kiss the shadows from morning's drowsy face may expand and exalt your soul. The first view of the ocean may fill you with strange delight. Niagara—the great, the glorious Niagara—may hush your spirit with its ceaseless thunder; it may charm you with its robe of crested spray and rainbow crown; but the land of Freedom was a lesson of deeper significance than foaming waves or towering mounts."

53

FRANCES ELLEN WATKINS

"Bury Me in a Free Land"

1858

First published in The Anti-Slavery Bugle, *Watkins's poem was inspired by her vision of the free land of Canada, described in her 1856 letter to William Still. Watkins supported herself and contributed to William Still's underground railroad work by selling volumes of her poetry at her lectures.*

You may make my grave wherever you will,
   In a lowly vale or a lofty hill;
You may make it among earth's humblest graves,
   But not in a land where men are slaves.

"Bury Me in a Free Land," *The Anti-Slavery Bugle*, New-Lisbon, Ohio, Nov. 20, 1858.

I could not sleep if around my grave
    I heard the steps of a trembling slave;
His shadow above my silent tomb
    Would make it a place of fearful gloom.

I could not rest if I heard the tread
    Of a coffle-gang to the shambles led,
And the mother's shriek of wild despair
    Rise like a curse on the trembling air.

I could not rest if I heard the lash
    Drinking her blood at each fearful gash,
And I saw her babes torn from her breast,
    Like trembling doves from their parent nest.

I'd shudder and start, if I heard the bay
    Of the bloodhounds seizing their human prey;
And I heard the captive plead in vain
    As they bound afresh his galling chain.

If I saw young girls, from their mothers' arms
    Bartered and sold for their youthful charms
My eye would flash with a mournful flame,
    My death-paled cheek grow red with shame.

I would sleep, dear friends, where bloated might
    Can rob no man of his dearest right;
My rest shall be calm in any grave
    Where none calls his brother a slave.

I ask no monument proud and high
    To arrest the gaze of passers-by;
All that my spirit yearning craves,
    Is bury me not in the land of slaves.

54

T. R. DAVIS

Lectures by Miss Watkins

Margaretta, Ohio, February 9, 1860

*Frances Ellen Watkins's success as an antislavery lecturer inspired north-
ern audiences. After her lectures in and around Sandusky, Ohio, a local
antislavery group sent stirring ant-slavery resolutions to* The Liberator.

Dear Sir—About ten days since, Miss Frances Ellen Watkins—believed
here to be one of the most worthy and efficient anti-slavery lecturers
who have visited the western country—made her appearance in our
township, greatly to the satisfaction of all acquainted with her by reputation or otherwise.

Miss Watkins first lecture here was given one week ago last Tuesday
evening, greatly to the edification and entertainment of all the friends
of freedom. Our worthy and truly philanthropic citizen, R. H. Rogers,
being called to the chair, in a few appropriate and timely remarks, introduced her to the audience.

Miss Watkins spoke in the house the following evening, and at several other places during that week. She spoke in Sandusky City, last
Monday evening, to an immense audience, with the best effect. She is
to speak there again next Monday evening. At all the places where Miss
Watkins has spoken, save one, where whiskey and contemptible ignorance are the ruling elements, there have been thronged audiences, and
the most respectful order.

The effect of these lectures upon this part of the country cannot but
be most favorable, not only politically, but in dispelling this unreasoning
and unreasonable prejudice against the colored people of the country.

At the close of her last lecture in this township, the following preamble and resolutions were unanimously adopted, and by the request of
your readers here, I send them to *The Liberator* for publication: —

Whereas, it is our settled and unalterable opinion, that American
Slavery is the complete representative and full embodiment of every

---

"Lectures by Miss Watkins," *The Liberator,* Feb 24, 1860.

crime known to humanity; that it is truly what John Wesley called it, "the sum of all villanies"; and,

Whereas, we are bound, by every consideration of justice, to deny that there can be any law, in the proper sense of the term, for slavery, or of its constituent crimes; and,

Whereas, we acknowledge it to be our duty, as good citizens, as friends of truth and virtue, to act decidedly and efficiently against crime, whether found increasingly as in the numerous abuses of the day, or collectively as in slavery; therefore,

Resolved, That, from the nature of slavery, it is the duty of every friend of morality, virtue, good citizenship and education, to act determinedly and constantly, by every means within the range of conscientious action, against it, as an impious and barefaced outrage upon human rights.

Resolved, That all human laws which are valid derive their validity, mediately or immediately, from the laws of nature, or the Divine Law.

Resolved, That these laws are coeval with mankind, and being dictated by God himself, are, of course, superior in obligation to any others. They are binding over all the globe, in all countries, and at all times; and those human enactments which conflict with these divine enactments, we affirm are not our rules of action.

Resolved, That, as citizens of Ohio, obedience to Divine injunction, we shall never allow ourselves to be the passive and menial instruments for the support and perpetuation of an institution which is the hydra curse of the civilized world.

Resolved, That the Fugitive Slave Law, and all slave laws, are monuments of despotism; and we firmly resolve, with heart, and hand, and sleepless vigilance, to work for their eradication.

Resolved, that any institution, or any men or sot of men, that in any way favor slavery, show themselves to be unworthy of the support, respect or confidence of any friend of freedom.

Resolved, That, in the light of the foregoing principles, it is with feelings of deep regret and utter disgust that we thing of our Governor, Ex-Governor, and Legislature, welcoming to our noble State House, and to the free soil of Ohio, the Governors and Legislators of two of the States of this Union, which, in the most loathsome manner, are continually practicing all the abuses of slavery, and striving for its extension.

Resolved, That it is our sincere wish that the great Republican party, instead of following and seconding this unwise movement of some of its leaders, may repudiate and denounce this not only unwise, but presumptuous effort to identify the freemen of Ohio in reciprocal sympathy with the minions and myrmidons of slavery—men that live by selling babies, and revel in their debauchery at the expense of innocence and virtue.

Resolved, That it is with feeling of the deepest respect and gratitude, that we regard this timely visit of Miss Watkins to our township, to tell us of the wrongs of the slave, and to increase our zeal and determination to act vigorously and decidedly our part in the truly "irrepressible conflict" between Freedom and Slavery.

T. R. DAVIS. *SECRETARY.*

The New Movement Debates Questions of Race and Sex, 1866–1869

55

FRANCES ELLEN WATKINS HARPER

Speech at the Eleventh Woman's Rights Convention: "We Are All Bound Up Together"

New York, May 1866

In 1860 Frances Ellen Watkins married and retired from public speaking, but after her husband died in 1864, she renewed and expanded her career as a lecturer. At the first women's rights convention after the Civil War, she explained the origins of her support of women's rights. Telling truth to the power of the assembled white women, she also spoke about the cruel effects of racism. Her words were recorded in a way that helps us glimpse the audience's reactions.

MRS. HARPER, OF OHIO, SAID:
I feel I am something of a novice upon this platform. Born of a race whose inheritance has been of outrage and wrong, most of my life had been spent in battling against those wrongs. But I did not feel as keenly as others, that I had these rights, in common with other women, which are now demanded. About two years ago, I stood within the shadows of my home. A great sorrow had fallen upon my life. My husband had died suddenly, leaving me a widow, with four children, one my own, and

Proceedings of the Eleventh Woman's Rights Convention, May, 1866 (New York: Robert Johnston, 1866), 45–48.

the others step-children. I tried to keep my children together. But my husband died in debt; and before he had been in his grave three months, the administrator had swept the very milk-crocks and wash tubs from my hands. I was a farmer's wife and made butter for the Columbus market; but what could I do, when they had swept all away? They left me one thing—and that was a looking-glass! Had I died instead of my husband, how different would have been the result! By this time he would have had another wife, it is likely; and no administrator would have gone into his house, broken up his home, and sold his bed, and taken away his means of support.

. . . And I went back to Ohio with my orphan children in my arms, without a single feather bed in this wide world, that was not the custody of the law. I say, then, that justice is not fulfilled so long as woman is unequal before the law.

We are all bound up together in one great bundle of humanity, and society cannot trample on the weakest and feeblest of its members without receiving the curse in its own soul. You tried that in the case of the negro. You pressed him down for two centuries; and in so doing you crippled the moral strength and paralyzed the spiritual energies of the white men of the country. When the hands of the black were fettered, white men were deprived of the liberty of speech and the freedom of the press. Society cannot afford to neglect the enlightenment of any class of its members. At the South, the legislation of the country was in behalf of the rich slaveholders, while the poor white man was neglected. What is the consequence to-day? From that very class of neglected poor white men, comes the man who stands to-day with his hand upon the helm of the nation. He fails to catch the watchword of the hour, and throws himself, the incarnation of meanness, across the pathway of a nation. My objection to [President] Andrew Johnson is not that he has been a poor white man; my objection is that he keeps "poor whites" all the way through. (Applause.) That is the trouble with him.

This grand and glorious revolution which has commenced, will fail to reach its climax of success, until throughout the length and breadth of the American Republic, the nation shall be so color-blind, as to know no man by the color of his skin or the curl of his hair. It will then have no privileged class, trampling upon and outraging the unprivileged classes, but will be then one great privileged nation, whose privilege will be to produce the loftiest manhood and womanhood that humanity can attain.

I do not believe that giving the woman the ballot is immediately going to cure all the ills of life. I do not believe that white women are dew-drops just exhaled from the skies. I think that like men they may be divided into three classes, the good, the bad, and the indifferent. The good would vote according to their convictions and principles; the bad, as dictated by prejudice or malice; and the indifferent will vote on the strongest side of the question, with the winning party.

You white women speak here of rights. I speak of wrongs. I, as a colored woman, have had in this country an education which has made me feel as if I were in the situation of Ishmael, my hand against every man, and every man's hand against me.[1] Let me go to-morrow morning and take my seat in one of your street cars—I do not know that they will do it in New York, but they will in Philadelphia—and the conductor will put up his hand and stop the car rather than let me ride.

A lady: They will not do that here.

Mrs. Harper: They do in Philadelphia. Going from Washington to Baltimore this Spring, they put me in the smoking car. (Loud voices— "Shame.") Aye, in the capital of the nation, where that black man consecrated himself to the nation's defence, faithful when the white man was faithless, they put me in the smoking car! They did it once; but the next time they tried it, they failed; for I would not go in. I felt the fight in me; but I don't want to have to fight all the time. To-day I am puzzled where to make my home. I would like to make it in Philadelphia, near my own friends and relations. But if I want to ride in the streets of Philadelphia, they send me to ride on the platform with the driver. (Cries of "Shame.") Have women nothing to do with this? Not long since, a colored woman took her seat in an Eleventh street car in Philadelphia, and the conductor stopped the car, and told the rest of the passengers to get out, and left the car with her in it alone, when they took it back to the station. One day I took my seat in a car, and the conductor came to me and told me to take another seat, I just screamed "murder." The man said if I was black I ought to behave myself. I knew that if he was white he was not behaving himself. Are there not wrongs to be righted?

In advocating the cause of the colored man, since the Dred Scott decision, I have sometimes said that I thought the nation had touched bottom. But let me tell you there is a depth of infamy lower than that. It is when the nation, standing upon the threshold of a great peril, reached out its hands to a feebler race, and asked that race to help it and when the peril was over, said, You are good enough for soldiers, but not good enough for citizens. When Judge Taney said that the men of my race had

[1]Genesis 16:12.

no rights which the white man was bound to respect, he had not seen the bones of the black man bleaching outside of Richmond.[2] He had not seen the thinned ranks and the thickened graves of the Louisiana Second, a regiment which went into battle nine hundred strong, and came out with three hundred. He had not stood at Olustee and seen defeat and disaster crushing down the pride of our banner, until word was brought to Col. Hallowell, "The day is lost; go in and save it;" and black men stood in the gap, beat back the enemy, and saved your army. (Applause.)

We have a woman in our country who has received the name of "Moses," not by lying about it, but by acting it out (applause) — a woman who has gone down into the Egypt of slavery and brought out hundreds of our people into liberty.[3] The last time I saw that woman, her hands were swollen. That woman who had led one of Montgomery's most successful expeditions, who was brave enough and secretive enough to act as a scout for the American army, had her hands all swollen from a conflict with a brutal conductor, who undertook to eject her from her place. That woman, whose courage and bravery won a recognition from our army and from every thoroughfare of travel. Talk of giving women the ballot-box? Go on. It is a normal school, and the white women of the country need it. While there exists this brutal element in society which tramples upon the feeble and treads down the weak, I tell you that if there is any class of people who need to be lifted out of their airy nothings and selfishness, it is the white women of America. (Applause.)

[2]In the 1857 Dred Scott case, Roger B. Taney (1777–1864), fifth chief justice of the U.S. Supreme Court, writing for the majority, held that free blacks were not citizens and could not sue in federal courts; that Congress had no power to exclude slavery from the territories, as provided for in the Missouri Compromise; and that slaves who escaped to the North could be legally recaptured and returned to their owners in the South.

[3]Refers to Harriet Tubman (c. 1820–1913), a fugitive slave who in the 1850s returned to Maryland around nineteen times and guided to freedom between sixty and three hundred enslaved people. See Catherine Clinton, *Harriet Tubman: The Road to Freedom* (New York: Little, Brown, 2004).

56

EQUAL RIGHTS ASSOCIATION

Proceedings

New York City, May 1869

Created at the 1866 Woman's Rights Convention in New York to support both black suffrage and woman suffrage, the American Equal Rights Association offered a timely forum for a renewal of the cross-race coalition of the 1830s. However, debate at the 1869 convention reflected the formidable obstacles that such a coalition faced.

Mr. [Frederick] Douglass: I must say that I do not see how any one can pretend that there is the same urgency in giving the ballot to woman as to the negro. With us, the matter is a question of life and death, at least, in fifteen States of the Union. When women, because they are women, are hunted down through the cities of New York and New Orleans, when they are dragged from their houses and hung upon lampposts; when their children are torn from their arms, and their brains dashed out upon the pavement; when they are objects of insult and outrage at every turn; when their children are not allowed to enter schools; then they will have an urgency to obtain the ballot equal to our own. (Great applause.)

A Voice: Is that not all true about black women?

Mr. Douglass: Yes, yes, yes; it is true of the black woman, but not because she is a woman, but because she is black. (Applause.) Julia Ward Howe at the conclusion of her great speech delivered at the convention in Boston last year, said: "I am willing that the negro shall get the ballot before me." (Applause.) Woman! why, she has 10,000 modes of grappling with her difficulties. I believe that all the virtue of the world can take care of all the evil. I believe that all the intelligence can take care of all the ignorance. (Applause.) I am in favor of woman's suffrage in order that we shall have all the virtue and vice confronted. Let me tell you that when there were few houses in which the black man could have put his head, this woolly head of mine found a refuge in the house of Mrs. Elizabeth Cady Stanton, and if I had been blacker than sixteen midnights, without a single star, it would have been the same. (Applause.)

Elizabeth Cady Stanton, Susan B. Anthony, and Matilda Joslyn Gage, eds., *History of Woman Suffrage* (New York: Fowler & Wells, 1882), 2:382–84, 391–92, 397.

Miss [Susan B.] Anthony: The old anti-slavery school says women must stand back and wait until the negroes shall be recognized. But we say, if you will not give the whole loaf of suffrage to the entire people, give it to the most intelligent first. (Applause.) If intelligence, justice, and morality are to have precedence in the Government, let the question of woman be brought up first and that of the negro last. (Applause.) While I was canvassing the State with petitions and had them filled with names for our cause to the Legislature, a man dared to say to me that the freedom of women was all a theory and not a practical thing. (Applause.) When Mr. Douglass mentioned the black man first and the woman last, if he had noticed he would have seen that it was the men that clapped and not the women. There is not the woman born who desires to eat the bread of dependence, no matter whether it be from the hand of father, husband, or brother; for any one who does so eat her bread places herself in the power of the person from whom she takes it. (Applause.) Mr. Douglass talks about the wrongs of the negro; but with all the outrages that he to-day suffers, he would not exchange his sex and take the place of Elizabeth Cady Stanton. (Laughter and applause.) . . .

Mrs. Lucy Stone: Mrs. Stanton will, of course, advocate the precedence for her sex, and Mr. Douglass will strive for the first position for his, and both are perhaps right. If it be true that the government derives its authority from the consent of the governed, we are safe in trusting that principle to the uttermost. If one has a right to say that you can not read and therefore can not vote, then it may be said that you are a woman and therefore can not vote. We are lost if we turn away from the middle principle and argue for one class. . . . Over in New Jersey they have a law which says that *any* father—he might be the most brutal man that ever existed—*any* father, it says, whether he be under age or not, may by his last will and testament dispose of the custody of his child, born or to be born, and that such disposition shall be good against all persons, and that the mother may not recover her child; and that law modified in form exists over every State in the Union except Kansas. Woman has an ocean of wrongs too deep for any plummet, and the negro, too, has an ocean of wrongs that can not be fathomed. There are two great oceans; in one is the black man, and in the other is the woman. But I thank God for that XV Amendment, and hope that it will be adopted in every State. I will be thankful in my soul if *any* body can get out of the terrible pit. But I believe that the safety of the government would be more promoted by the admission of woman as an element of restoration and harmony than the negro. I believe that the influence of woman will save the country before every other power. (Applause.) I see the signs of the times pointing to this consummation, and I believe that in some parts of the country women will vote for the President of these United States in 1872. (Applause.) ...

Mrs. Paulina W. Davis said that she would not be altogether satisfied to have the XVth Amendment passed without the XVIth, for woman have a race of tyrants raised above her in the South, and the black women of that country would also receive worse treatment than if the Amendment was not passed. ...

Mr. Douglass said that all the disinterested spectators would concede that this Equal Rights meeting had been pre-eminently a Woman's Rights meeting. (Applause.) They had just heard an argument with which he could not agree—that the suffrage to the black men should be postponed to that of the women. ...

The President, Mrs. Stanton, argued that not another man should be enfranchised until enough women are admitted to the polls to outweigh those already there. (Applause.) She did not believe in allowing ignorant negroes and foreigners to make laws for her to obey (Applause.)

Mrs. Harper (colored) asked Mr. Blackwell to read the fifth resolution of the series he submitted, and contended that that covered the whole ground of the resolutions of Mr. Douglass. When it was a question of race, she let the lesser question of sex go. But the white women all go for sex, letting race occupy a minor position. She liked the idea of working women, but she would like to know if it was broad enough to take colored women?

[Blackwell's fifth proposed resolution: "Resolved, That any party professing to be democratic in spirit or republican in principle, which opposes or ignores the political rights of woman, is false to its professions, short sighted in its policy, and unworthy of the confidence of the friends of impartial liberty."]

Miss Anthony and several others: Yes, yes.

Mrs. Harper said that when she was at Boston there were sixty women who left work because one colored woman went to gain a livelihood in their midst. (Applause.) If the nation could only handle one question, she would not have the black women put a single straw in the way, if only the men of the race would obtain what they wanted. (Great applause.) ...

Miss Anthony protested against the XVth Amendment because it wasn't Equal Rights. It put two million more men in position of tyrants over two million women who had until now been the equals of the men at their side.

57

Founding of the National Woman Suffrage Association

New York, 1869

Two days after the Equal Rights Association adjourned, Elizabeth Cady Stanton and Susan B. Anthony held a reception that became the founding meeting of the National Woman Suffrage Association. The association's goal was the passage of a sixteenth amendment to guarantee woman suffrage. That year Lucy Stone and other supporters of the Fifteenth Amendment organized the American Woman Suffrage Association in Boston. The two groups finally merged in 1890. Another thirty years of campaigning were required to achieve the ratification of the Nineteenth Amendment, which guaranteed women's right to vote in every state in 1920.

Out of these broad differences of opinion on the amendments, as shown in the debates, divisions grew up between Republicans and Abolitionists on the one side, and the leaders of the Woman Suffrage movement on the other. The constant conflict on the Equal Rights platform proved the futility of any attempt to discuss the wrongs of different classes in one association. A general dissatisfaction had been expressed by the delegates from the West at the latitude of debate involved in an Equal Rights Association. Hence, a change of name and more restricted discussions were strenuously urged by them. Accordingly . . . a meeting was called . . . which resulted in reorganization under the name of "The National Woman Suffrage Association.". . .

Delegates from nineteen States, including California and Washington Territory, were present on the occasion, and all felt the importance of an organization distinctively for Woman's Suffrage, in view of the fact that a Sixteenth Amendment to the Federal Constitution to secure this is now before the people. The Association has held several meetings to plan the work for the coming year. Committees are in correspondence with friends in the several States to complete the list of officers.

Elizabeth Cady Stanton, Susan B. Anthony, and Matilda Joslyn Gage, eds., *History of Woman Suffrage* (New York: Fowler & Wells, 1882), 2:400.

A Chronology of the Antislavery and Women's Rights Movements (1830–1870)

1800– **1860**	Second Great Awakening.
1816	Founding of the American Colonization Society.
1821	Sarah Grimké leaves Charleston to live with Quakers in Philadelphia.
1828	Angelina Grimké joins Sarah Grimké in Philadelphia.
1829	Publication of David Walker's *Appeal to the Colored Citizens of the World.*
1831	William Lloyd Garrison founds *The Liberator.*
1831	Founding of the Female Literary Association of Philadelphia.
1832	Black women in Salem, Massachusetts, found the first women's antislavery society.
1832	Maria W. Stewart becomes one of the first women to speak publicly to an audience of women and men in Boston.
1833	Stewart lacks supporters and leaves Boston for New York City.
1833	Founding of the American Anti-Slavery Society by Garrison and others.
1833	Parliament abolishes slavery in the British West Indies.
1834	Angelina Grimké leaves her Quaker community, joins the American Anti-Slavery Society (AASS), writes *Appeal to the Christian Women of the South*, and promotes the antislavery petition movement.
1836	"Gag rule" passed in Congress.
1836	Sarah Grimké and Angelina Grimké begin to speak for the AASS.
1837	Angelina Grimké presents her book, *Appeal to the Women of the Nominally Free States.*
1837, **1838,** **1839**	National conventions of antislavery women.

1837   Grimké sisters speaking tour of Massachusetts.

1838   Sarah Grimké presents her book, *Letters on the Equality of the Sexes and the Condition of Woman*; Angelina Grimké presents her book, *Letters to Catherine E. Beecher.*

1839   The antislavery movement splits on the question of women's rights; American and Foreign Antislavery Society formed; Liberty Party founded.

1840   World's Antislavery Convention, London: U.S. women delegates are not seated; Elizabeth Cady Stanton meets Lucretia Mott.

1848   Women's Rights Convention, Seneca Falls, New York, followed by about twenty other women's rights conventions, 1848–1866.

1850   Compromise of 1850: California admitted as free state; popular sovereignty allows slavery north of 36 degrees 30 minutes in Kansas and Nebraska territories, nullifying the Compromise of 1820.

1850   Fugitive Slave Act allows persons to be claimed as slaves before a commission rather than a jury trial.

1852   Publication of *Uncle Tom's Cabin* by Harriet Beecher Stowe.

1854–
1860   Frances Ellen Watkins lectures for the American Anti-Slavery Society to great acclaim.

1858   Publication of Henry Clarke Wright's *Marriage and Parentage; or the Reproductive Element in Man, as a Means to His Elevation and Happiness.*

1861–
1865   Civil War.

1867   American Equal Rights Association meets in Brooklyn Heights.

1869   The American Woman Suffrage Association formed (Boston); the National Woman Suffrage Association formed (New York).

Questions for Consideration

1. What kinds of public activities did Garrisonian antislavery women pursue?
2. What was the goal of the petition movement?
3. How did the antislavery movement challenge established notions of manhood and womanhood?
4. Why was the issue of racial prejudice linked to the goal of immediate abolition?
5. How did the Grimké sisters campaign against racial prejudice?
6. Why did Angelina and Sarah Grimké defy convention and advocate for women's rights?
7. Which men facilitated women's antislavery activism? How did they help?
8. How did women's organizations support women's antislavery activism?
9. Why did Massachusetts clergy oppose the public speaking of the Grimké sisters?
10. Why did the antislavery movement split into two groups in 1839?
11. Why was Lucretia Mott not seated as a delegate to the 1840 antislavery convention in London?
12. Who organized the 1848 Seneca Falls Women's Rights Convention, and why?
13. How did the 1848 convention differ from the 1837 women's antislavery convention?
14. Was the women's rights convention movement of the 1840s and 1850s successful? Why or why not?
15. Why was Frances Ellen Watkins a successful antislavery speaker?
16. What similarities and differences do you see between Frances Ellen Watkins and Maria Stewart?
17. Why did the emerging women's suffrage movement split on the issue of race?

Selected Bibliography

PRIMARY SOURCES

Blight, David W., ed. *Frederick Douglas: My Bondage* and *My Freedom*. New Haven: Yale University Press, 2014.

Greene, Dana, ed. *Lucretia Mott: Her Complete Speeches and Sermons*. New York: Mellen, 1980.

Meltzer, Milton, and Patricia G. Holland, eds. *Lydia Maria Child: Selected Letters, 1817–1880*. Amherst: University of Massachusetts Press, 1982.

Pelaez, Monica. *Lyrical Liberators: The American Antislavery Movement in Verse, 1831–1865*. Athens: Ohio University Press, 2018.

Wilbanks, Charles, ed. *Walking by Faith: The Diary of Angelina Grimké, 1828–1835*. Columbia: University of South Carolina Press, 2003.

SECONDARY SOURCES

The Anti-Slavery Movement and the Women's Rights Movement, 1820–1870

Abzug, Robert H. *Passionate Liberator: Theodore Dwight Weld and the Dilemma of Reform*. New York: Oxford University Press, 1980.

Anderson, Bonnie S. *The Rabbi's Atheist Daughter: Ernestine Rose, International Feminist Pioneer*. Oxford: Oxford University Press, 2017.

Clinton, Catherine. *Harriet Tubman: The Road to Freedom*. New York: Little, Brown and Company, 2004.

Dunbar, Erica Armstrong. *A Fragile History: African American Women and Emancipation in the Antebellum City*. New Haven: Yale University Press, 1996.

Faulkner, Carol. *Women's Radical Reconstruction: The Freedmen's Aid Movement*. Philadelphia: University of Pennsylvania Press, 2004.

Goodman, Paul. *Of One Blood: Abolitionism and the Origins of Racial Equality*. Berkeley: University of California Press, 1998.

Jones, Martha S. *Birthright Citizens: A History of Race and Rights in Antebellum America*. Cambridge: Cambridge University Press, 2018.

Mandel, Bernard. *Labor, Free and Slave: Workingmen and the Anti-Slavery Movement in the United States*. Urbana: University of Illinois Press, 2007.

McFadden, Margaret H. *Golden Cables of Sympathy: The Transatlantic Sources of Nineteenth-Century Feminism.* Lexington: University of Kentucky Press, 1999.

McKivigan, John R., and Mitchell Snay, eds. *Religion and the Antebellum Debate over Slavery.* Athens: University of Georgia Press, 1998.

Melder, Keith E. *Beginnings of Sisterhood: The American Woman's Rights Movement, 1800–1850.* New York: Schocken, 1977.

Moody, Joycelyn. *Sentimental Confessions: Spiritual Narratives of Nineteenth-Century African American Women.* Athens: University of Georgia Press, 2001.

Penny, Sherry H., and James D. Livingston. *A Very Dangerous Woman: Martha Wright and Women's Rights.* Amherst: University of Massachusetts Press, 2004.

Perry, Mark. *Lift Up Thy Voice: The Grimké Family's Journey from Slaveholders to Civil Rights Leaders.* New York: Penguin Books, 2001.

Porter, Dorothy Burnett. *The Remonds of Salem Massachusetts: A Nineteenth Century Family Revisited.* Worcester: American Antiquarian Society, 1985.

Pryor, Elizabeth Stordeur. *Colored Travelers: Mobility and the Fight for Citizenship before the Civil War.* Durham: University of North Carolina Press, 2016.

Ridarsky, Christine L., and Mary M. Huth, eds. *Susan B. Anthony and the Struggle for Equal Rights.* Rochester: Rochester University Press, 2012.

Ryan, Mary P. *Women in Public: Between Banners and Ballots, 1825–1880.* Baltimore: Johns Hopkins University Press, 1990.

Stewart, James Brewer. *Abolitionist Politics and the Coming of the Civil War.* Amherst: University of Massachusetts Press, 2008.

Temple, Brian. *Philadelphia Quakers and the Antislavery Movement.* Jefferson: McFarland & Company, Inc., Publishers, 2014.

Winch, Julie. *Philadelphia's Black Elite: Activism, Accommodation, and the Struggle for Autonomy, 1787–1848.* Philadelphia: Temple University Press, 1993.

Slavery

Bailey, Anne C. *The Weeping Time: Memory and the Largest Slave Auction in American History.* New York: Cambridge University Press, 2017.

Beckert, Sven. *Empire of Cotton: A Global History.* New York: Alfred A. Knopf, 2014.

Berlin, Ira. *The Long Emancipation: The Demise of Slavery in the United States.* Cambridge, MA: Harvard University Press, 2015.

Bynum, Victoria E. *The Long Shadow of the Civil War: Southern Dissent and its Legacies.* Chapel Hill: University of North Carolina Press, 2010.

Camp, Stephanie M. H. *Closer to Freedom: Enslaved Women & Everyday Resistance in the Plantation South.* Chapel Hill: University of North Carolina Press, 2004.

Jay, Bethany, and Cynthia Lynn Lyerly, eds. *Understanding and Teaching American Slavery*. Madison: University of Wisconsin Press, 2016.

Johnson, Walter. *Soul by Soul: Life Inside the Antebellum Slave Market*. Cambridge, MA: Harvard University Press, 1999.

Krauthamer, Barbara. *Black Slaves, Indian Masters: Slavery, Emancipation, and Citizenship in the Native American South*. Chapel Hill: University of North Carolina Press, 2013.

Melish, Joanne Pope. *Disowning Slavery: Gradual Emancipation and Race in New England, 1780–1860*. Ithaca, NY: Cornell University Press, 2000.

Morgan, Jennifer L. *Laboring Women: Reproduction and Gender in New World Slavery*. Philadelphia: University of Pennsylvania Press, 2004.

Oaks, James. *Freedom National: The Destruction of Slavery in the United States, 1860–1865*. New York: Norton, 2014.

O'Toole, Marjory Gomez. *If Jane Should Want to be Sold: Stories of Enslavement, Indenture and Freedom in Little Compton, Rhode Island*. Little Compton: Little Compton Historical Society, 2016.

Scully, Pamela, and Diana Paton, eds. *Gender and Slave Emancipation in the Atlantic World*. Durham, NC: Duke University Press, 2005.

White, Deborah Gray. *Ar'n't I a Woman? Female Slaves in the Plantation South*. New York: Norton, 1985.

Index

common law, 2
Confederate States of America, 17
Congregational Church, 27
  *Pastoral Letter: The General
    Association of Massachusetts
    to Churches under Their Care,*
    119–20
Congregationalists, 5
contraceptives, 50. *See also* birth
    control
cotton gin, 5

Davis, Jefferson, 17
Davis, Paulina Wright, 37, 41, 197
Davis, T. R., 54
  Lectures by Miss Watkins, 188–90
Declaration of Independence, 30
Declaration of Sentiments
  *Declaration of Sentiments at the
    Founding of the American
    Anti-Slavery Society,* 80–81
  description at Seneca Falls
    Convention, 42–44
  *Report of the Women's Rights
    Convention Held at Seneca Falls,
    N.Y.,* 164–66
Douglass, Frederick, 43, 46, 48, 167, 195
Douglass, Sarah Mapps
  background on, 13
  description of, 12, 21–22
  "Ladies Department, Mental Feast,"
    12–13, 74–77
  Letter to Sarah Douglass, April 3,
    1837 (Grimké), 97–98
  Letter to Sarah Douglass, February
    22, 1837 (Grimké), 94–95
  Philadelphia Female Anti-Slavery
    Society, 82
  Preamble to the Constitution
    (Female Literary Association of
    Philadelphia), 70–71
Dred Scott decision, 11, 56, 194

education
  social movements in, 10
  women's right to, 46, 173
elective franchise
  for black women, 49
  for women, 43

enslaved people
  cruelty against, 4
  economic power of, 5
  house servants, children of, 4
  punishment and torture of, 4
  revolts by, 4
Episcopalianism, 5–6
equality of men and women,
    30–31
*Essay on Slavery and Abolitionism,
    with Reference to the Duty of
    American Females* (Beecher),
    23, 108–11

family life
  social movements in, 10
  women's power in, 108
*Farewell Address to Her Friends in
    the City of Boston* (Stewart),
    79–80
female anti-slavery societies, 12
Female Anti-Slavery Society
  Boston, 22, 25, 32, 36, 152–53
  description of, 16
  New York, 21
  Philadelphia, 22, 29
Female Literary Association of
    Philadelphia, 12
  Preamble to Constitution,
    70–71
Female Literary Society, 15
Female Moral Reform Society, 3, 24,
    36, 41, 50
Fifteenth Amendment, 57, 198
Finney, Charles Grandison, 49
First Amendment, 18
Forten, Sarah, 22
  biography of, 99
  Letter to Angelina Grimké, April 15,
    1837, 22, 99–101
Foster, Stephen, 37
Fourteenth Amendment, 56
Freedom's Journal, 11
Friend of Virtue
  *"Just Treatment of Licentious Men":
    Letter to the Friend of Virtue,*
    141–42
Fugitive Slave Act, 49, 52,
    54, 189